W9-CCN-463

Always adopt,
don't shop ♡

Teaching Your Bird to Talk

Diane Grindol
and
Thomas Roudybush, M.S.

HOWELL
BOOK
HOUSE

To Dr. C. R. "Dick" Grau, November 5, 1920–November 16, 2002, cofounder of the Psittacine Research Group and The Exotic Bird Report, Department of Avian Sciences, University of California—Davis. Professor, nutritionist, environmentalist, caring member of the community, mentor and friend. Dick inspired all who knew him. He is greatly missed.

Howell Book House

Published by Wiley Publishing, Inc., Hoboken, New Jersey

For general information on our other products and services or to obtain technical support please contact our Customer Care Department within the U.S. at 800-762-2974, outside the U.S. at 317-572-3993 or fax 317-572-4002.

Wiley also publishes its books in a variety of electronic formats. Some content that appears in print may not be available in electronic books.

Library of Congress Cataloging-in-Publication Data:

Grindol, Diane.

Teaching your bird to talk/by Diane Grindol and Thomas Roudybush.

p. cm.

ISBN 0-7645-4165-X (alk. paper)

1. Talking birds—Training. 2. Parrots—Training I. Roudybush, Thomas. II. Title.

SF462.8.G75 2003

636.6'86535—dc21   2003013398

Manufactured in the United States of America

10 9 8 7 6 5 4 3

Book production by Wiley Publishing, Inc. Composition Services

Contents

Acknowledgments

Diane Grindol wishes to thank her coauthor, Tom Roudybush, for his collaboration on this book. Although writing is a very solitary occupation, his wit and company and inspiration were welcome as the book came to life over several years' time. Diane also appreciates his patience!

Diane thanks Dr. Irene Pepperberg, with deep gratitude beyond expression, for her persistence and perseverance in parrot intelligence studies.

Diane would like to thank the many people who took our survey about talking birds and who helped us spread the word. It has been great fun to read about people and their companion birds, and we've shared many of the responses with you, the readers, within this book.

Diane also thanks her friends and "bird people" in her life who have been patient, caring and loving. They are the core of her joy in living and ability to share a passion for birds with others. Thanks to former book coauthors Larry Lachman, Psy.D., and Frank Kocher, D.V.M. Thanks to Judy Murphy, Doris Wilmoth, Tawny Williams, Linda Stone (Massolo) and Bev Owens for friendship and pet-sitting. Thanks to Wanda Huggins, who allowed photo sessions in her bird room, and to Gerry Stewart, Pat Fauth, Doris Wilmoth and Judy Murphy, who were photography models or snapped a few shots for this book. Thanks to Art Lazanoff, for ever-supportive friendship. Thanks to Jeanne Sangster and Therese Baker in the Chicago area for their support and sharing over the years. Thanks to Michael Murray, D.V.M, for his veterinary expertise in keeping Diane's birds healthy. Thanks to Landmark Education and seminar leader Joyce Nolan for providing a community that supports fulfilling dreams.

Diane would like to thank those who have done work with parrot vocalizations in the wild: Mike Schindlinger, Tim Wright and Diana May. She appreciates the white-crowned sparrow vocalization and other studies done by Dr. Luis Baptista and honors his memory.

Diane sincerely thanks Beth Adelman, editor extraordinaire, for having this book come to life after it had been shelved for several years. Thanks also to Dale Cunningham at Wiley for her support.

Tom Roudybush would like to thank Diane for her patience, wit, humor, writing and organizational skills, and acceptance of a scientist who doesn't get out much as a coauthor.

I would also like to thank Dr. Irene Pepperberg for a lifetime of investigation of parrot intelligence. Her detailed scientific work allowed me to confidently generalize and write to a lay audience without fear of contradiction. The lack of qualifiers in my writing was largely due to her hard work.

Foreword

Through the ages I've been revered, immortalized, plucked, eaten, caged and now, finally, acknowledged. My kin and I have cohabited with humans for centuries, but up until the publication of *Teaching Your Bird to Talk*, we really didn't have our say. We haven't been able to communicate our desire and ability to interact with humans at a level long believed unthinkable. The very expression "to parrot" implies mindless mimicry. How many parrots have been consigned to learning to say what the unenlightened have to teach them?

You live in an enlightened age. Tom and Diane have compiled an impressive amount of background, training and research regarding bird verbalizations that will have you reeling! Hello!

I have a few pointers of my own for teaching your companion human to talk to you.

- Chew on their favorite piece of furniture.
- Talk louder than the television.
- Wake him or her up early enough so there's time for talking before work.
- Be really quiet and hide somewhere while your companion human looks for you.
- Repeat one of the phrases your companion human says in a loud, excited voice.
- Threaten your companion human's significant other.
- Make the most noise when your companion human is out of the room.
- Get to know the neighbors. Develop contact calls for them, too.
- Nurture the floor of your environment with abundant food and water.
- If you dismantle your companion's keyboard, she'll have fewer distractions.

Polly
Bird Institute
Department of Interspecies Communication

Chapter 1

Keeping a Talking Bird

We're guessing that since you picked up this book, you have some interest in keeping a talking bird. If you have the right situation and personality, that can be a really fulfilling choice. Certainly, talking birds are interactive companions who enliven a household. Be careful and consider all the facts, though. Companion birds require a lot of attention, and you will have to provide it.

IF YOU HAVE A BIRD

It's possible you already have a bird whom you want to teach to talk. If that's the case, we have information for you that will tell you which species of bird are likely to talk and which aren't. You might take a look at these lists to see whether your bird is one of the species that talks readily. If he isn't, you need to decide whether you want to make any great effort to teach a bird who has low potential (not because of his individual personality but because of his species). If you do, we discuss various methods of training birds to talk, and one of them still might work for your bird.

   If your bird is one of the great talkers, you might want to assess his individual potential. His age, history and what talking capability you want are all factors that will make a difference in your success. Please read on and enjoy finding your answers.

IF YOU DON'T HAVE A BIRD

For those of you who have not yet acquired a bird, this is a good time to look at your options and get a bird who will be more of what you want. Most of the birds who talk are some type of parrot. Not all parrot species are talkers, though. Some birds are justly famous talkers, such as African Grey Parrots and Budgies (often called Parakeets), while others, such as Ravens, really don't have much to say. One expert on Ravens specifically discouraged us from considering Ravens, because they have limited vocabularies and (despite what Edgar Allen Poe might think) "nevermore" is not one of their natural calls. There are also a few legal problems with keeping native species that eliminate Ravens and Crows from consideration in the United States.

A really good choice for a talking bird who isn't a parrot is the European Starling. They are not expensive (free if you can catch one), legal to keep in most areas, talk well and have a great history on the stage. Starlings are an introduced species in North America, where they were imported for roles in Shakespearian plays. North America has about 200 million Starlings. Mother Nature isn't likely to be discouraged by the taking of just one, if you offer the bird a good home.

The other part of the equation is you, your home and your family. Parrots demand a lot of attention and demand it loudly. They are neither for the timid nor for the traveling salesman who can't offer them enough attention. Please read this chapter all the way to the end and consider what it says about bird care before buying or accepting a bird. You could save yourself (and your bird) a lot of grief, and enhance the enjoyment you can get from having a talking bird.

It's your choice. And, as you can see, there are plenty of things to consider about what kind of bird you want. It's always easier to get a bird after you have prepared for it. Buying a bird and then trying to find appropriate housing, food and care usually result in temporary measures becoming permanent, to the detriment of your bird. In the long run, "temporary measures" usually result in more work and cost for you as well.

BIRD CARE

Bird care is the first consideration when buying a bird. If you find you don't have the resources, both time and money, to care for a bird—please don't get one. Birds are flock animals by nature, and any bird who is social craves to find his place in a flock and needs a lot of social interaction. If you take a bird from his place in a wild or captive flock and put him in your home, it's your responsibility to provide for his social needs. This is the single greatest area of failure for first-time bird owners. They don't have enough time to interact with their bird.

On the other hand, a family full of kids who are interested in and taught how to interact with a bird can provide a great surrogate flock. They can even teach the bird how to talk and leave you with just providing the food and cleaning up the mess. Yes, in some ways birds are typical pets.

The Cage

Except perhaps for the cost of the bird and his first wellness veterinary visit, the cage is the greatest setup cost of keeping a bird. Cages vary so much in size and style that we won't make any attempt to recommend any particular cage, except to offer some tips on what your bird needs.

First, the cage should be big enough. Your bird needs to fully stretch his wings once in a while, and a cage should be at least big enough to accommodate that need. If you know what kind of bird you want to buy, get some idea of how wide his wingspan is and multiply that by at least one and a half. The cage should be at least that big in one of its horizontal dimensions.

The height of the cage is usually not a problem in the cages that are commercially available, but it should allow your bird to climb on the sides without hitting his head when his tail is near the floor. Your cage can't be too big. Birds are natural athletes, and if you offer your bird space enough to fly and play inside his cage, he will appreciate it.

You should take some time buying a cage. A cage is an investment in your bird's home. The cage you choose will make a great difference in the amount of effort you will need to spend giving your bird proper care. When you buy a cage, have a place in mind in your home where the cage will go. Take all the measurements of this area to the store to help you buy a cage of the right size.

The next consideration is basic cage construction. It needs to be well made without any sharp protrusions or edges. Many birds have leg bands that can catch on sharp bits or wire protrusions. Unless you are buying from a well-known manufacturer that backs up its cages with a money-back guarantee, carefully inspect the exact cage you want to buy. It's an easy way to avoid later problems.

Any openings on the cage should also be carefully considered. This includes the spacing between any bars and all access to feeders and waterers—if your bird needs to stick his head through the cage wall to reach food and water in containers that hang from the outside of the cage. These spaces should be either large enough for the bird to easily stick his head through (obviously, they need to be large to access food and water) or small enough so the bird can't get his head through at all. Openings that are about the size of the bird's head allow the bird to force his head through, but it may not be easy for him to extract his head from the opening. Birds stuck this way die every year as they struggle to get loose and break their necks. Fortunately, most cage manufacturers recognize this problem and build cages to avoid it.

It is convenient for you to have access to food and water dishes from outside of a cage. Look for this feature. It can be especially helpful if you have a friend, family member or pet-sitter care for your bird in the future.

Other cage considerations include the presence of a playpen on the top and a seed catcher that collects some of the mess around the bottom of a cage. Try to find a cage that is easy to clean. Paper liners fit most easily in square or rectangular cage pans. You'll have the easiest time cleaning cages with deep pans for cage paper. We leave it to you to do some good shopping that will enable you to look at all the options and decide whether they fit into your life. They all have their good and bad points.

DIANE GRINDOL

Will a bird fit into your household and your lifestyle? With the joys of bird ownership come the drudgery of cleaning up, cleaning a cage and offering fresh food and water daily.

Perches

Proper perches are essential, since birds spend most of their lives, even while asleep, on their feet. Most cages come with perches made of round, even dowels, which you will want to change for more appropriate perches when you get your cage home. Dowels, with their hard surface and uniform size, put the same stress on a bird's feet all the time. There is no chance for the bird to change his position on the perch to allow one part of his foot to take the stress while resting another part. It is much better to use small branches from trees as perches, because a branch is uneven along its length and enables your bird to find the position that works best for him at any time.

Depending on where you live, finding perches can be an outing and a lot of fun. Find a place where chemical sprays are not used on the trees or on the ground, and seek out the branches of the size you want in your cage. There is nothing like a walk in the woods picking up a few sticks for your bird!

There are many woods that can be used for perches, although some are thought to be toxic or to have other problems. Redwood, for example, is believed to cause problems in the guts of birds if they ingest some splinters, because the wood doesn't degrade the way many other kinds of wood do. It's a good idea to use local woods that come from sources that aren't likely to be sprayed with something that will harm your birds. Also, collect wood from a location well away from roadways where cars emit harmful fumes. Ask local veterinarians, bird club members or pet shops what they suggest or use.

Perches should be placed in the cage in such a way that the bird does not perch directly above his food or water. This will help keep droppings out of the food and water dishes.

Cage Placement

This is a far more important matter than it might seem at first glance. There are many things to consider about placement of a cage. Never place a cage too close to a source of heat or in a draft. This might seem obvious, but some sources of heat are not so easily identified unless you take a little time and think about them. A vent from a heat and cooling duct can be a problem. In the winter it might be too hot for your bird to endure all the time; in the summer it might chill a bird who can't get out of the airflow.

Many kinds of appliances also generate a lot of heat. Things like dishwashers, clothes dryers, stoves, refrigerators and freezers can generate a considerable amount of heat that can be unbearable in the long term.

One of the more common sources of heat people provide to their birds as an act of kindness is the sun in the winter. But many birds die from the heat of the sun when they are placed in a south-facing window just to let them "get a little sun." A bird should never be left in the direct sun without a way of getting into the shade. A bird should only live near a window if there is an eave or awning over it that prevents direct sunlight from heating up his living quarters.

Keep the Cage Away From Noise

Many people have suffered greatly from placing their bird's cage near a source of noise. One of the really big problem areas is the television. Birds are vocal and social animals who like to be heard. The first impulse of such a creature is to be louder than anything around him. That includes the television, stereo, radio, washer, dryer, vacuum cleaner . . . you get the idea. The bird will compete for your attention even when you're watching your favorite evening program. Occasional

DIANE GRINDOL

Place your bird's cage in a location where human members of the flock provide socialization but not near noisy appliances like the television. A bird will compete with the appliance for your attention, at the same or a louder decibel level.

vocal competitions with appliances might be fine but to hear only your parrot when you want to hear something else can really damage a relationship.

Water

Water is easily provided. The main consideration is that it needs to be clean and offered in a way that keeps it clean, or else the waterer needs to be cleaned regularly. One of the ways to keep water clean is to provide it in a drinker with a reservoir that feeds into a tube the bird can drink from. The tube usually has a ball or a peg and valve system that keeps water from flowing until the bird touches it with his tongue or beak. These drinkers are relatively inexpensive and make providing clean drinking water easy.

The other way to give your bird water is with a water dish. These usually need to be cleaned and refilled several times a day. Birds have a tendency to put things in their water dish and foul the water. Anything left wet at room temperature has the potential to grow bacteria. Bacterial growth may magnify the number of pathogenic bacteria to levels that can infect your bird. So clean water is essential.

Water should be offered without additives, unless directed by your veterinarian. There are vitamin and mineral additives available in pet supply stores that are meant to be added to a bird's water, but we do not recommend them, since they can provide a medium for the growth of bacteria. Vitamins and minerals are better provided in food than in water.

Prepared diets are available for companion birds. They offer nutrition in every bite, including essential nutrients not found in seed mixes. Now for the commercial message (Tom doesn't know I'm adding this): African Grey Popeye is eyeing a bowl of Roudybush mini-pellets.

Food and Feeding

There are a number of ways to feed your bird. Some of them are a lot of work and others are as easy as filling a feed dish. All of them can be made wholesome, although feeding a variety of foods cafeteria-style makes this more difficult.

The easy way to feed a bird a wholesome diet is to buy a good prepared diet at the pet supply store. These come in a variety of forms that include added vitamins and minerals, eliminating the need to supply additional vitamins. In fact, many of these foods are best used without the addition of supplements, since the additional vitamins and minerals can lead to toxic levels or imbalances.

It is best to choose a mix that doesn't allow your bird to choose one seed or item in preference to another, because when he picks out his favorite, he may be ignoring other foods with important nutrients. Some of the fortified seed mixes claim to be adequate for your bird, but this is based on the assumption that the bird eats all the food presented to him, rather than choosing just a few items.

The best food to use is a formulated diet without added colors or fragrances. Many people worry that this kind of prepared diet doesn't offer enough variety to provide their bird with adequate environmental stimulation. This is easily solved by adding fresh vegetables or fruit in an amount equivalent to the amount of prepared diet your bird eats each day. The amount of energy (calories) in this much fresh vegetables or fruit is about one-twelfth that provided by the prepared diet, because fresh vegetables and fruit are mostly water. This means your bird will still

DIANE GRINDOL

Offering a variety of fruits and vegetables to a companion bird provides mental stimulation and variety. Because of their low-caloric content, these kinds of treats do not upset the balance of the basic diet. (This is Aztec, a Blue-Headed Pionus.)

need to eat almost the same amount of prepared diet he ate before you added fresh fruits and vegetables—which means their addition will not greatly imbalance the diet. But it will keep your bird from getting bored with his food.

Do not add high-fat foods such as sunflower seeds or peanuts, except as occasional treats. These will greatly reduce the amount of the prepared diet your bird eats, and that means he will be eating fewer essential nutrients.

If you choose to feed your bird a seed mix or a mixture of fruits, vegetables and table foods, you will have some difficulty making sure your bird is getting a complete diet. Seeds, by themselves, are deficient in a number of nutrients, including some B vitamins, vitamin A, trace minerals and calcium. In the short run this may not be a problem, but eventually a deficiency of at least one of these causes some medical problem. It is best to feed at least some of the food as a prepared diet that includes the essential nutrients at the appropriate levels.

Wet Foods

One of the difficulties with feeding a diet made in your kitchen is that it is usually wet. Wet food has a tendency to spoil, particularly on warm days. This includes fresh fruit, vegetables, sprouts and a variety of cooked items such as beans and hard-boiled eggs. Care must be taken with these foods to make sure they are removed often enough to avoid spoilage.

Some of the same pathogens that cause food poisoning can be harmful to birds and will result in a sick or dead bird. On a warm day, wet food should be left out only for about four hours. Whatever is left over should then be discarded and the food dish cleaned. An alternative way of feeding wet food is to give your bird just as much as he will eat in about 20 minutes and then allow him free access to a dry prepared food.

Foods to Avoid

There are some foods that are not good for birds. While it has often been suggested that the birds we keep can eat anything we eat, this is far from the truth. It is best to forget the idea that what is good for you and what tastes good to you is good for or tastes good to your bird. Some foods are just not digested well or may lead to a moderate upset of the gastrointestinal tract, and others are poisonous to some birds.

Some of the things to avoid just because they are not good to feed to your bird regularly or in large amounts are sources of sugar (unless you have a Lory or a species of bird who normally eats a lot of sugar). Sugar is a good substrate for the growth of yeast, which is a common infection of the mouth and the rest of the gastrointestinal tract in birds. Avoiding sugar will reduce the chance of infection. If your bird happens to become infected, see your veterinarian, follow her instructions, and remove sugar from your bird's diet for the duration of treatment.

Some milk products are not good to feed to birds in large amounts. The sugar in milk is lactose. Birds cannot digest lactose, and large amounts of it in the gut tend to ferment, leading to diarrhea. Some dairy products that are high in lactose are dried skim milk and whey. Cheeses and yogurt are low in lactose, although many cheeses are high in fat.

Two things that should never be fed to birds are chocolate and avocado. There have been avian deaths associated with both of these foods. It is interesting that neither of these is consistent in its effect on birds. You will find people who feed both with no ill effect, but there have also been some cases in which the effects were clear—and deadly. We don't know the reason for these differences, but there is no reason to take a chance with your bird.

Food Treats

There are a great many foods you might want to offer your bird occasionally. Foods that are too high in fat for regular consumption, such as peanuts or sunflower seeds, make good treats when fed in very limited amounts. Other possible treat foods contain sugar, such as many baked goods or candies. When you offer them to your bird by hand, you can regulate how much he gets each day.

Even though we recommend a prepared diet for your bird, we don't want to leave out of the picture the idea that feeding is part of the human-bird bond. It is a good idea to offer treats once in a while and to offer them from your hand. Just keep the amount small enough to avoid upsetting the nutritional balance of the prepared diet you are feeding.

The act of feeding your bird can be an adventure for both of you as you explore new vegetables you find at the supermarket. Even standard vegetables can be presented in new ways. Try threading veggies or fruit through cage bars near your bird's favorite perch. Try skewering them on a bird kabob. Try cooking and mashing yams or sweet potatoes for a warm, soft treat. Carrots can be sliced, diced, chopped, grated or served whole. Corn comes on or off the cob, frozen, canned or baked into a corn muffin mix. Broccoli can be served raw or steamed, and you can slice the stem, buy grated broccoli or put a whole floweret in the cage for different presentations. Birds love to scoop out the inside of treats like pomegranate or grapes. Dark green, leafy greens are the healthiest for you and your bird. Check out kale, beet, Swiss chard, dandelion or collard greens for a change of pace. Warm foods such as cooked rice, pasta, mashed potatoes, beans or lentils are a good occasional treat. Cereals with no added sugar or salt and air-popped popcorn are good snacks.

PROVIDING TOYS

Bird toys are essential for your intelligent friend. Commercial toys come in many styles, shapes, colors and textures. Unlike our dog and cat companions, birds see in vivid color and so appreciate this variety. Your companion will appreciate a variety of toys, though not necessarily an overwhelming number. You can add variety by rotating toys into and out of a cage weekly or monthly. New research has

Treat Foods for Birds

- Apple
- Asparagus
- Bread (whole grain)
- Broccoli
- Cabbage
- Canteloupe
- Cereal (whole grain, without added sugar or salt)
- Collard Greens
- Corn on the Cob
- Crackers (baked, without added salt)
- Dandelion Greens
- Grapes
- Kale
- Leaf Lettuce
- Lentils
- Oatmeal
- Oranges
- Parsley
- Pasta (dry or cooked)
- Pomegranate
- Popcorn
- Raisins
- Rice
- Rice Cakes
- Sprouted Legumes
- String Beans
- Sweet Potato
- Swiss Chard
- Yam
- Zucchini

shown that birds may anticipate a toy change daily as much as they anticipate receiving fresh food daily. Plan on some toys being chewed to pieces, while others will last longer.

You can buy toys and play gyms or stands for your bird, or make your own. Objects such as wooden peg clothespins, Popsicle sticks and stainless steel flatware are toys too. A roll of toilet tissue or adding machine tape can supply endless entertainment, as can bottle caps or empty bottles with a safe rattle inside, such as dried beans or lentils. Provide toys that hang, as well as a toy basket filled with loose or foot toys, either inside the cage or in a play area in your home.

HOME ALONE

Your bird will probably spend some time alone. Human beings are imperfect parrot companions in this way. In the wild, a parrot would spend all of his time with his flock or with his mate. It's no wonder that intelligent and sensitive parrots can develop neurotic behaviors such as feather plucking when they're caged and left alone for long periods of time. You can help by doing your best to provide a stimulating environment for your companion bird.

One way is to let your companion bird watch wild birds as they forage and flit about outside. You can do this if you have a window with an awning that does not have direct sun coming in. Hang a bird feeder near that window, or provide a bird bath or natural plantings that will attract wild birds. Some bird feeders actually attach to or fit in windows for an up close and personal visit by wild birds.

Plan to rotate toys daily, weekly or monthly. Turn one food cup into a toy box with loose foot toys for your bird's entertainment.

Birds like the kind of entertainment we do. They will enjoy staying in a home with the radio or television on. Many people make sure their parrots get a chance to watch cartoon shows meant for children. It won't hurt to have your potential talker watching *Sesame Street*.

If yours is a latchkey bird because you go to work every day, you can provide a social break for your bird by arranging a pet-sitter visit or by making arrangements for birdie day care. Sometimes it works well to take a bird to work with you. You must make sure a bird who goes to work is not a huge distraction, is welcome and is safe. Any environment with fumes or chemicals is not safe for a bird. Hair salons and dry cleaners, for example, could not safely host a bird.

Birds need to spend some time chewing. For cockatoos and macaws, that's mandatory. Offer fresh, washed branches from safe trees, Popsicle and craft sticks, cinnamon sticks, dry pasta, rolls of newspaper or junk mail. Materials to shred are a great way to keep a bird busy. Provide newsprint, a whisk broom, raffia, palm shredding products or a roll of toilet tissue. Smaller birds will tear into toasted oats strung on a shoestring.

Diane is an advocate of getting a "pet" for a companion bird to watch. These include active small birds, such as Canaries or Finches. Her own birds enjoy watching the resident guinea pigs and have been entertained by a fish tank.

In the wild, birds don't have food handed to them ready to eat. No drive-throughs. Food in the wild comes in packages, such as grains with hulls and seeds with shells, and the food location must be discovered by foraging. Wild birds work at finding and extracting their daily rations from what the forests or grasslands provide. You can have an occasional foraging day for your bird. Hide food, put it into containers that must be destroyed, supply a pine cone with goodies stuck in it. Put peanuts in a toilet tissue roll and pinch the ends. Hide food under paper and in the corners of the cages. It's creative and fun for you to provide this entertainment for your parrot, and it will keep him busier than a full, accessible food bowl.

VETERINARY CARE

Before you buy a bird, find a good avian veterinarian. You can ask where to find one by asking at pet supply shops, bird stores, local bird clubs and zoos.

An avian veterinarian has a practice in which she sees a significant number of birds. A veterinarian who is willing to see birds but seldom actually sees any is not an avian veterinarian. You need to understand this clearly, because good courses in avian medicine in veterinary schools were uncommon until a few years ago. Many veterinarians have little or no experience with birds, and birds differ significantly from mammals.

You need to have a relationship with your avian veterinarian, even though you may see her only once a year. Your veterinarian is your primary source of health care for your bird.

Once you have located your avian veterinarian, call and ask some questions. You can shop around for avian veterinarians, just as you would for anything else. You may be able to find a good supplier of birds through your veterinarian and be able to confirm that the supplier or breeder stands behind the birds she sells.

You will also want to know the cost and the details of a well-bird checkup. Ask for a detailed breakdown on what the costs include. If you don't intend to breed your bird, it may not be essential to know the gender (which can involve a lab test). The main things you are looking for in a well-bird checkup are specific difficulties with your bird such as broken bones, congenital difficulties or disease. As

Finding an Avian Veterinarian

An avian veterinarian is a veterinarian who has bird clients. Any veterinarian can call him or herself an avian veterinarian. If you can get a referral from another veterinarian, a bird club member or a bird breeder, that is the wisest way to choose a local avian veterinarian with experience.

You can also find one by searching for veterinarians in your area who belong to the national professional educational association for veterinarians interested in learning more about bird health, the Association of Avian Veterinarians (AAV). For general information about the AAV, see www.aav.org. To find a veterinarian who belongs to AAV, go to www.aav.org/vet-lookup or contact them at:

Association of Avian Veterinarians
P.O. Box 811720
Boca Raton FL 33481-1720
Phone: (561) 393-8901
Fax: (561) 393-8902
E-mail: aavctrlofc@aol.com

A certified avian veterinarian is one who has obtained certification from the American Board of Veterinary Practitioners (ABVP). These are officially called Board-Certified Avian Practice Specialists by the American Board of Veterinary Practitioners. They have passed a rigorous test regarding avian health. There are only a few certified avian veterinarians, compared to the number of veterinarians who treat birds. There certainly are competent and talented avian veterinarians who are not, or not yet, certified avian veterinarians. For a list of certified avian veterinarians, see www.birdsnways.com/articles/abvpvets.htm.

prey animals, birds often don't show signs of illness. There will be some cost for lab tests to determine the health of your bird.

If you find any significant problems, you should be able to take your bird back for a refund or another bird. Don't believe you have to accept a pet who is going to cost you a lot for ongoing veterinary bills. You should be able to get a healthy, vigorous bird for your money. If you are told you can't, buy somewhere else.

Get Some Advice

You should get a fair amount of advice from your trip to the vet. Ask questions and make sure you have an emergency phone number and the name of an alternate vet to use when yours is out of town. Ask for the title of a good book on the care of birds. There are several. Get some first aid instructions for the most common problems, too.

SAFETY ISSUES

Besides the poisonous foods we have already mentioned, there are some potential hazards for birds in the home. Some of them may be a bit of a surprise.

One big hazard is the toilet. Most talking birds are not designed to bathe in water more than an inch or two deep. Any time they bathe, they need a way to easily get out of the water without risking drowning. This is good news in a household with women. Not only should everyone put the toilet seat down when they have a bird, they should put the lid down as well. That should take care of two problems at once.

Other open sources of water can also become drowning hazards. Smaller birds have drowned in a coffee cup filled with water. So be careful about what you leave out uncovered.

Non-stick surfaces are a major hazard to birds if the non-stick material is overheated. Materials that include non-stick surfaces are cookware, ironing board covers, ironing boards, self-cleaning ovens (when the self-cleaning feature is operated) and some heating lamps. Overheated non-stick materials give off a gas that is immediately toxic to birds. You can lose an entire household of birds to this gas in just a few minutes. Usually the birds die so quickly that there is no hope of offering any medical attention.

There are many poisons in our environment that need to be avoided. Birds do not have any innate ability to detect or avoid these materials. Treat your bird as you would a child in your home and prevent him from coming in contact with toxins.

Lead is an obvious problem that we have been dealing with for years because of its toxic effect on children. Some older homes have lead-based paint, and birds can eat chips of it and be poisoned. Stained glass uses lead compounds to join the pieces of glass, curtain weights often are made of lead and costume jewelry and the seals on older wine bottles often contain lead. None of these materials should be available to your bird. It might seem that curtain weights or the joints on stained

Having a companion bird in the household can influence your choice of cookware. Overheated non-stick surfaces kill birds instantly. To avoid this hazard, many bird owners pass up cookware with non-stick coatings, such as the pans on the left, in favor of cast iron, stainless steel and glass cookware, such as the pots and pans on the right. Audubon, a male pearl Cockatiel, approves of this choice.

glass might not be available to a bird, since they are enclosed or part of a bigger construct, but parrots will make short work of these things and get to the lead quickly.

Poisonous Plants

Parrots and some other kinds of birds are attracted to anything that can be chewed, including all the plants in your home. There are a number of poisonous plants commonly found in homes, and birds don't seem to be able to tell the poisonous plants from the rest. The bottom line here is that you should either eliminate the poisonous plants from your home or take responsibility for keeping your birds out of them. Be aware that keeping curious birds out of plants is a tall order.

Philodendron and dieffenbachia are two common poisonous houseplants. Most palms and ferns are safe, but it is always good to confirm plant safety with a poison control center or your avian veterinarian.

Holiday decorating can also introduce poisonous plants to the home. Poinsettia, holly and mistletoe are all poisonous. It might be better to limit holiday decorations to non-toxic materials such as fruits, nuts and pine branches.

OTHER PETS

Birds, dogs and cats can interact either peacefully or with disastrous results, and the problem is not always with the dog or cat hurting the bird! Dogs and cats are predators in the wild and have not lost all of their instincts for hunting just by being in your living room. Small birds are particularly susceptible to harm from cats.

Larger parrots, some even as small as Cockatiels, will, on occasion, take the aggressive role. Cockatiels have been known to bite cats and inflict enough damage to require veterinary intervention. Larger parrots will often define a territory that they see as theirs. Usually this is their cage, but a T-stand can include some of the area around it as part of the bird's territory. We know of at least one case in which a cat resting in the parrot's territory had a rude end to her nap. The parrot deliberately climbed down from his perch, walked over to the cat and bit her. The cat screamed with pain and never came into the parrot's territory again.

Any time a cat breaks the skin of a bird, it should be considered a veterinary emergency. Cats have bacteria in their claws and mouth that spread rapidly in a bird's bloodstream. Your companion bird needs to receive antibiotics to stop this poison from harming him. If you choose to keep birds and cats, be aware of the risk and be prepared to take action if it is warranted.

The bottom line on all this is that *all* your pets need supervision when they have access to one another. Even birds will fight with each other and need to be separated. Most of these problems yield to common sense. We're sure you have plenty of that.

POINTS TO REMEMBER

- A cage should be large enough to allow your bird to spread his wings and climb on the side of the cage without touching his feathers side-to-side or top-to-bottom.
- The perches in your bird's cage should be uneven branches, not round and uniform dowels.
- Never place the cage near excessive heat, cold, draft or noise.
- Clean water should always be available to your bird.
- Wet foods should not sit out longer than four hours.
- Chocolate and avocado should never be fed to birds.
- Establish a relationship with an avian veterinarian.
- Eliminate toxic materials and hazards from your bird's environment.

Chapter 2

A Survey of Talking Bird Owners

Theory is great and so is some background about the natural history and biology of birds. You'll find both in this book. But first we'd like to share with you some real experiences people have had with their talking birds (you'll also find more stories from our surveys in Chapter 9 and 15 and in Appendix C). We sent our survey to several Internet bird lists, handed out forms at bird club meetings and were assisted by links and web pages that led to us putting a survey form on the World Wide Web for a few months.

Although many species of birds talk, we received the most answers from parrot owners, rather than Starling, Crow or Mynah fans. We got results from people willing to return the survey, so it's not a representative sample of all parrot owners. In most cases respondents had at least one talking parrot they wanted to brag about!

BIRDS TAKE THE INITIATIVE

People who share their lives with talking parrots ended up that way through various means. Many acquired their parrots as chicks and were surprised to discover they had a parrot who could talk. Other people acquired older talking birds and shared their experiences regarding this adventure. A very few survey respondents breed birds, so they have many former pets who talk but are set up in pairs to create more of their own species.

A large number of people had not set out to have a talking bird. Or if they had, they'd worked at having the bird say a word or two but ended up with a bird with a larger, and usually different, vocabulary than was their intention.

Many of the parrot owners simply wanted to have a companion bird. Jenny from California, with her 12-year-old Blue and Gold Macaw, Baby, is an example. She wrote, "By the way, we did not purchase this bird for his talking ability. We adore the bird for his beauty, loving personality and the joy of sharing our lives with this special creature. We are always amazed so many people ask if he talks. Blue and Gold Macaws are not known for their talking ability (thank goodness!). When he does talk, it's always a surprise and welcome."

Frank, who lives in Oregon, didn't expect to have a talking bird either when he acquired a Rose-breasted Cockatoo. We asked him at what age his bird started to talk. He replied, "Eleven weeks. I was never so surprised in my life, because I'd read that Cockatoos don't talk much and so I wasn't even thinking I was buying a talking bird. I've subsequently heard many stories about talkative Rosies. Rosies are different from other Cockatoo species in a lot of other respects, too, I have found out." Both species and the individual personality of a bird will color your own bird-keeping experience.

Many people answering the survey had not intentionally tried to teach their bird to talk. Instead, the bird started talking, so their human companions went along with it. We know that in the wild some birds learn a repertoire of flock calls and signals. It seems the calls our companion birds pick up in our homes are human speech, with assorted other sounds. The cleverest birds figure out what words or vocalizations elicit a response, furthering communication between owner and pet bird. Several survey respondents with talking birds said that when their bird talks, they answer. That reinforces what the bird is saying and makes communication possible.

Not all parrot vocal ability is talking. It turned out that Cockatiel Nicky, who belongs to Debi of Rhode Island, preferred whistling to talking. Other parrots developed repertoires of songs based on the syllables "la, la, la" or "doo, doo, doo."

Then, of course, there was spontaneous imitation of household sounds. Some of the fascinating sounds parrots mimic in our home are phone rings, modems, pagers, creaking doors, microwave beeps, barking dogs, water dripping, bodily functions and coughing. Your authors' parrots were no exception. Diane's Blue-headed Pionus could imitate water gurgling as it went down a drain. Tom's Yellow-naped Amazon learned the sound of a garbage truck beeping as it backed up. Phone rings, and sometimes ensuing conversations, are often picked up by parrots. More than one person wrote that their bird imitated the phone ring, then called a teenage daughter's name!

Birds hear and produce nuances of sounds that we can't. Studies of Amazon vocalizations in the wild by Mike Schindlinger, a Ph.D. candidate from Harvard University, show that Amazons produce sounds very quickly that cover a wide tonal range. Our own vocalizations probably seem very simplistic to birds! This may explain the attraction of electronic sounds like phone rings to our companion birds, as well, because quick bursts of sound are closer to wild parrot chatter than our slow, rambling human speech.

A LITTLE BIRDIE TOLD ME (IN HER OWN VOICE!)

Parrot talent for imitating the human voice is legendary. It's part of the attraction of keeping parrots. Many zoos and pet shops have talking parrots, with cards hanging on their cages listing the phrases they know. It's a universal response to walk up to a cage containing a parrot and say "hello," expecting a response.

The ability of parrots to mimic a certain human's voice, so that it is recognizable, falls mainly within the capabilities of African and Timneh Grey Parrots. Other birds have their "own" voice, according to a significant number of survey respondents. So what do the other birds sound like? Several owners explained.

A female Meyer's Parrot (one of the small African Poicephalus parrots) named Loki belongs to Artemis Aviaries in Minnesota. According to them, Loki has three distinct voices. One is similar to her female owner's voice—her talking instructor. Another is similar to her husband's voice (he's the apple of Loki's eye), and one is a bizarre squeaky voice. Loki adds behavior to her talking. She pins her eyes (dilates and contracts the pupils) before talking and bobs her head up and down.

Jade, a Severe Macaw, belongs to Ellen in Calgary, Alberta. She is just learning to talk, as Ellen found out this way: "Jade is only seven months old, but from the time we first saw her she could say 'hi' and 'hello.' Since then I have heard her mumbling practice things a lot but nothing clear, until last week. I was cooking in the kitchen waiting for a friend to come over and I heard 'Ellen, Ellen.' I thought that maybe I had missed the doorbell and Lisa had come in looking for me, so I went to the door and no one was there. So I went back to the kitchen and again I heard 'Ellen, Ellen,' so I went to the back door, as Lisa will sometimes park in the back, but no one was there, either. I thought I was going crazy until I walked by Jade's cage and heard 'Ellen, Ellen.' She sounded so much like another woman calling my name!"

Male Eclectus Reggie "has his own voice, but he mimics my voice inflection and pitch," says owner Kathy of Georgia. A Rose-breasted Cockatoo who belongs to Kay of New York talks with a "Cockatoo accent." An Umbrella Cockatoo who lives in a diverse bird flock with owner Dixie has "a high-pitched voice." The family Quaker Parakeet has a lower voice, and the Cockatiels have a soft voice. A 10-year-old Blue and Gold Macaw of unknown sex living with Jackie of Vermont "has a voice that is medium pitched—not obviously either male or female. The bird has its own voice."

Linda of Texas has a male and a female African Grey, three Blue-fronted Amazons, a Cockatoo, a Blue and Gold, Military and Scarlet Macaws, two Cockatiels and a male Eclectus. Of voices, she says, "The Amazons have lovely, clear voices. The Grey is gravelly. The Macaws are loud! The Cockatoo has a high, sweet, baby voice." Debbie of Mississippi has a small flock of birds. She says her Umbrella Cockatoo "talks in a sweet baby voice." Her Double Yellow-headed Amazon has a loud voice, "which sounds like a grandma yelling. A Severe Macaw has a robot-sounding voice that is not too expressive."

Kathy of Georgia finds that her male Eclectus, Reggie, has a voice of his own, rather than mimicking her voice. Other owners say their birds talk with a species-specific "accent."

Umbrella Cockatoo Angel lives with 46 other birds, 3 of whom talk. According to Lisa of British Columbia, she tends to whisper around strangers. "She definitely has her own voice, and it is not at all the typical 'bird voice.' Rather she sounds just like a three-year-old human toddler! Until they met her, my neighbors actually all thought she was a child, not a bird!" Her Cockatiel companion, Kiwi, has a bird voice. Lovebird companion Tutti-fruitti has an angry voice, and Peach-Faced Lovebird Leo also has her own little angry voice.

A Maroon-bellied Conure male, Digger, who belongs to Lynne of Georgia, "has a tiny, gravelly conure voice." She says her Severe Macaw male has an excellent, very clear voice. "He has his own voice, but many words sound like me—as does his laugh."

CLARITY OF SPEECH

Ellen of Calgary, Alberta, has a Severe Macaw who is just learning to talk and "sounds as though she is talking through a kazoo." "They talk in my voice mainly, but with overtones of scratchy little bird," says Susan of California about her Grey-cheeked Parakeet, Brown-headed Parrot and Cockatiel. Susan usually understands them, but what they say needs translation for others.

Clarity of speech can be a problem. Many survey respondents reported that at first their parrots "mumbled" words or spent time practicing words, using correct inflection and intonation. Later the words became clearer. Of course, in the beginning stages of practicing words, they weren't intelligible. Some final renditions aren't easily recognizable to anyone but the proud parrot parents. Diane's Pionus, Inca, said a few phrases that were not clear. They needed "translation" for others to understand. Cockatiel owners report that their birds whistle intonations that are imitations of words, making for very melodious, though not necessarily intelligible, bantering.

Budgies have high, squeaky voices and can talk very fast. Puck was a Budgie who was listed in the *1995 Guinness Book of World Records* as the "most talking bird." He had a vocabulary of over 1,700 words. How did his owner Penelope know that? She recorded his speech and slowed it down when playing it back, to catch all the words and phrases he'd said.

TALKING PARROTS EXPRESS THEMSELVES

Communication consists of more than just words. Parrots do "parrot" the way we use words, the volume at which we say words and our intonations. One couple who answered our survey found that having a Macaw toned down their louder arguments. If their volume level got too high, the Macaw joined in and it was too much for them!

Jenny from California has a 12-year-old Blue and Gold Macaw, Baby, who knows how to use his vocabulary to get a response from his owners. Jenny says, "After getting his fill of a variety of brown rice, carrots, squash, burdock root, onions, etc., he climbed on the back of the chair and entertained me. Said every word and phrase he knew, in various intonations. I was reading and watching TV but made sure to make eye contact so he knew I was paying attention. He likes to say his name in various ways, from a soft Marilyn Monroe voice to a loud assertive voice. Puts us in a great mood!"

PARROTS ARE PERFORMERS

From what we know about bird vocalizations in the wild, there are times that vocalizations are for pure pleasure. Birds greet the dawn with exuberance and settle noisily at dusk. Our parrot companions find ways to accent, highlight and amplify their own vocalizations so that they are true performances.

One example is Blue-crowned Conure, Chiquita, owned by Celeste of California. She says, "He often sticks his head in his food dish to *amplify* the sounds he

DIANE GRINDOL

Mercedes is a Blue and Gold Macaw, one of the more talkative species of Macaw.

is making. A true recording artist and/or ham! He even talks up a storm at the avian vet's office when the other birds are totally quiet. All work stops when Chiquita visits the vet."

According to Debi of Rhode Island, Cockatiel Nicky "always says things the most in the bathroom when one of us is in the shower. He likes the acoustics." Diane's Pionus, Inca, used to talk into a coconut shell to get the same effect. Our parrots like the sound of their own voices. They put on great daily shows, and they work for peanuts!

THERE'S NO GUARANTEE

Even if you do your homework and get a normally vocal species of bird, there's no guarantee he will talk. You have the best chance of teaching him words if you follow the instructions in this book. Even then, there's no guarantee. Birds each have

DIANE GRINDOL

The African Grey Parrot is one of the species most noted for their talking ability. There are companion Greys who do not talk, however. There's no guarantee that any individual bird, of any species, will talk in your household.

distinct personalities (as do people!). There's a little bit of luck involved in ending up with a gregarious bird, making him feel enough like part of the flock and having him acquire our language, not just the telephone ringing. A few survey respondents had birds who do not talk, or who only say a few words.

Despite obtaining one of the best talking species, Dimitri of Vermont says his male African Grey does not talk—although he has a female Grey who does say a few words.

Parrots have their own idea of what is an appropriate vocalization. Not every bird is going to learn what you want him to say. For example, Diane from Virginia says her four-year-old female African Grey, Meg, "only says what she likes the sound of and what she wants to say."

In response to the survey question, "How many words does your bird say? What words/phrases does it say most?" Diane replied, "Too many to count. She says only what she wants. Since I got her I have tried to teach her to say 'good morning' and 'good night' and she says neither." Diane also has a Cockatiel, Rocky, who says "hello" and "pretty bird" but no more. The Cockatiel isn't learning phrases from Meg.

FIDS SAY THE DARNEDEST THINGS!

Many people had a similar answer to the question on the survey, "Does your bird talk?" Their responses were something like "constantly" and "profusely." On the Internet, our companion parrots are often referred to as "fids," meaning "feathered kids." Like human children, we can't control and sometimes can't believe what comes out of their mouths! Here are a few examples.

Jean of Florida says about her African Grey, Dooley, "My daughter brought her roommate over with her three young children. Dooley has never liked children, so he sat glaring at them for a while, then every time one walked near the cage [they didn't do anything to annoy the birds, except be in the room] Dooley would say 'worms!' This was evidently his opinion of them. Everyone thought it was hilarious, except the kids."

Ellen of Calgary, Alberta, says of 22-year-old Eleanora Cockatoo, Gucci, "I have not heard him learn any new words since he came to live with us, but he has put some killer combinations of old words together. One afternoon he just kept repeating, 'Where's the doggy? Where's the doggy?' and I kept telling him that we didn't have a doggy or that he was my doggy. After about thirty minutes of this, with him still saying, 'Where's the doggy?' I went over to his perch and said, 'Gucci, we don't have a doggy!' Gucci looked me straight in the eye and said, 'Gucci want a doggy!' When I give him a piece of some food that he hasn't had before, he says 'Is it good for you?' and if he doesn't like it he says 'Can I give it to the doggy?' He just talks all day long and is very smart."

Danny, a 13-year-old Yellow-naped Amazon, belongs to Kay of New York. He began talking at three months old, calls his family members by name and learned the entire outgoing phone message from their answering machine, complete with beeps. Kay and her husband, Gary, recorded Danny performing their message and put it on the actual answering machine! Says Kay, "Some people who called said there was static on my line, but most understood Danny and found it hard to believe that it was a *bird* on our message tape!"

Buffy, a Citron-crested Cockatoo who belongs to Esther of Michigan, says "Buffy want go ride. Mommy a good birdie." Her most frequently used words and phrases vary over time, according to Esther.

Our companion parrots come up with their own names for things sometimes, too. Chiquita, a Blue-crowned Conure, says "It's a baby!" to indicate anything that flies, according to his owner, Celeste of California.

PART OF THE FLOCK

Companion birds not only greet the day; many of them learn to greet household or flock members. They learn not only people's names but the names of other birds and the family dog or cat. Our survey respondents chronicled this behavior in their answers, including this bird, who has picked up an interesting "flock call" among pet humans: Su of Tucson, Arizona, has a Grey named Dorian who "calls all people and animals by name, always correctly. He always tells us 'hello' or belches when we enter his room."

Lynn Byers, the "Old Crow Tamer" and author of *The Lost Folk Art of Taming Crows,* has noticed that family pets become members of a bird's flock. "I personally have had a crow that barked so much like our family dog that you had to be looking at one or the other to be sure which one was barking."

Kathy of Ontario says, "I have a three-year-old Timneh African Grey parrot (sex unknown) who is an excellent talker. He has a very large vocabulary. He will use words in the right context often. For example, one day he was eating a piece of toast with peanut butter on it, while he was sitting on top on his cage. My two large dogs were sitting underneath him just waiting for a crumb to be dropped. He said, 'Sit, stay, good dog,' then proceeded to drop the rest of the toast to the dogs. He then said, 'Now go on, get out of here. Stupid dogs' Needless to say, we were killing ourselves laughing and wished we had a video camera."

WHO'S TRAINING WHOM?

When a parrot's vocalizations bring you running, she has learned how to get what she wants. In general, birds are such adept manipulators and so good at training their human companions that you haven't even noticed this has been going on.

It is also interesting to note that birds who express a desire, and have owners who try to fulfill it, are learning some cognitive language. These parrots and owners are certainly communicating. Many of the most successful survey respondents answered their birds' vocalizations in some way. They delivered what the bird asked for, or answered their bird vocally about what she seemed to express. If nothing else, they received some commentary back.

Dooley, a nine-year-old African Grey, belongs to Jean of Florida. She says, "He hates to be squirted with a spray bottle, and if I spray him with one for a bath, he will glare at me and say '*quit!!*' in a voice that leaves no room to misunderstand his meaning." Also, "Dooley will ask for specific foods and if you don't give him what he asks for, he will throw down what you give him and repeat his demand."

Umbrella Cockatoo Siva belongs to Su of Tucson, Arizona. She says her Cockatoo uses his talking to manipulate her, always wanting attention.

Diane of Virginia says Meggie the African Grey Parrot "knows if she says she wants 'birdie bread,' she gets some. If she asks for a peanut she gets a pistachio. If she says 'wanna shower' she gets her shower. I usually try to accommodate her."

YOUR TURN

How do your birds measure up? Below you'll find the questions we posed to parrot owners. If you'd like to contribute answers to future studies, send your results to tiels@redshift.com. The subject of your e-mail response should be "Talking Survey."

Name:

City, State:

E-mail:

Age bracket: [0–10] [11–20] [21–30] [31–40] [41–50] [51–60] [61–75] [over 75]

1. What kind of bird do you have?
2. How old is your bird? Is it a male or female/unknown?
3. Are you/have you tried to teach it to talk?
4. Does it talk?
5. At what age did your bird start to talk?
6. How many words does your bird say? What words/phrases does it say most frequently? Of these words, how many did you intend to teach it to say?
7. Is your bird still learning new words?
8. Does your bird use words/talking in context? What is the story?
9. Do you have other birds, do they talk, have your birds learned words from each other, do they talk to each other?
10. When do your birds talk: when you're in the room, on cue, for company, when no one's around? Where is the bird (perch, cage, hand, etc.)?
11. Do your birds talk or vocalize (scream) when you don't want them to? How do you deal with that?
12. Is your talking bird still learning words or phrases?
13. Who did your bird learn to talk from? What kind of voice did they have (slow, fast, high-pitched, low, expressive)?
14. Does your bird talk to get a specific response?
15. Can you always tell what your bird is saying? Can others tell? Does the bird have its own voice or does it mimic other voices?
16. Has your bird recombined the words it was taught to make new phrases?
17. Did you use tools (audio- or videotapes, Wordy Birdy, CD)?
18. If you breed birds, do your breeding birds still talk? Is it different than what it was before breeding?
19. Do you know if the parents of your bird talked?

Note: By returning this survey, you agree that this material can be used for publication in printed and electronic media written about talking birds by authors Diane Grindol and/or Tom Roudybush. Thank you! Further questions should be addressed to: Talking Survey, P.O. Box 51247, Pacific Grove, CA 93950 or tiels@redshift.com.

THANK YOU!

This section of *Teaching Your Bird to Talk* was made possible by several generous people and organizations who helped to distribute the survey. They include the *Pet Bird Report* (PBR, now known as the *Companion Parrot Quarterly*) and ParrotTalk lists on the Internet, Jane Hallander and Bobbi Brinker, respectively and personally, Bird Talk On-Line, and Beverly Marsh, who hosts a Grey-cheeked Parakeet web page, and the Contra Costa Avian Society.

POINTS TO REMEMBER

- Talking birds are looking for a response.
- Birds you never expected to talk just might do so.
- Getting an African Grey doesn't guarantee you'll have a talking bird.
- Birds are good at training their companion humans.
- Whether or not your bird talks doesn't matter as much as developing a relationship and some kind of communication.

Chapter 3

People and Parrots

Although they have many other attributes that make them attractive to humans, it is birds' talking abilities that have fascinated people for eons. People have admired birds, told legends about their ability to speak and counted their words. They even put words in their mouths! Talking birds have been the fodder of fiction, the inspiration of poets, the vision of media moguls and the stuff of dreams. Their legends are legion, and the truth is even more dramatic! Although parrots cannot carry on the intricate conversations animation and media lend them, some have developed astonishing vocabularies, and parrots have, indeed, uttered the occasional witticism. Let's talk parrot.

BIRDS HAVE BEEN TALKING FOR CENTURIES

It is estimated that talking parrots were kept in captivity starting at about 1000 B.C. This certainly happened in Asia, and may have happened in Africa. In India, where there is a strong written tradition and where there are wild parrots, birds were featured in literature, fables and poems.

The *Kama Sutra,* a Hindu manual for attaining the fullest sensual and spiritual enjoyment out of living and loving, includes teaching a parrot to talk as one of 64 advised practices. Most likely the parrots so instructed were Indian Ring-necked Parakeets. The Parakeet was also considered to be a bird of love. Pairs of parrots do bond closely and show great affection toward one another. Parrots have been marks of the oldest profession, as well—a prostitute in ancient times would carry a parrot on her wrist, as recorded in bas-reliefs. Kama, the Hindu God of Love, rides upon a parrot or is pulled in his chariot by one. So does Rati, the Goddess of Lust and Pleasure.

Despite this ancient Indian symbolism, it is a parrot's talking ability that saved the honor of a woman in a Sanskrit story, the *Shukasaptaki.* In the story, a

DIANE GRINDOL

The Kama Sutra lists teaching a parrot to talk as one of the 64 practices for getting enjoyment out of living and loving. Probably, it referred to Indian Ring-necked Parakeets like AJ.

merchant goes on a business trip. His wife's pet bird talks to her night after night, keeping her at home instead of out with her lover. The husband returns after 70 days, and presumably they lived happily ever after. These tales made their way to Europe, followed eventually by Indian and Asian birds themselves.

A Greek doctor wrote about India in 397 B.C. and described a talking Parakeet. In 327 B.C. Alexander the Great and his army invaded India, and one of his sailors took home some tame Parakeets as souvenirs—the first of many people to do this, as we shall see! A trade in Indian Ring-necked and Alexandrine Parakeets developed.

By the time the Roman Empire was established, parrots (who would have spoken Latin) were prestigious pets. They had a higher value than a slave and were

Alexander the Great brought Parakeets from India back with him to Greece in the 300s B.C. This bird became known as the Alexandrine Parakeet, and this particular Parakeet is named Alex.

kept in cages of gold and silver. Again, people strolled with parakeets on their arms, although this was a status symbol in Roman times, not the mark of a particular trade. There was a formal profession of parrot teachers, and the elegant birds were portrayed in many types of art and by many artisans.

The Roman scholar Pliny the Elder wrote a Natural History *(Naturalis Historia)*. (His full name was Gaius Plinius Secundus, and he lived from A.D. 23 to 79, when he died in a volcanic eruption of Mt. Vesuvius.) His work consisted of 37 books describing life and the natural world, including cosmology, astronomy, geography, medicine, zoology, botany, agriculture and parrots. It became a standard text for education in Western Europe in the Middle Ages. An innovation for his time was a chronicle of his sources of information, which included 100 people.

Jumping forward to the next parrots recorded in history, in the Middle Ages more world travelers brought home Parakeets as souvenirs, and Marco Polo reported sighting some white parrots, probably Cockatoos, on the southern coast of India. A Sulphur-crested Cockatoo was given to King Frederick II of Hohenstaufen, who admired birds. That was probably the first Cockatoo in Europe. In the 14th century, Geoffrey Chaucer mentions the parroting abilities of parrots in *Canterbury Tales*.

When the French conquered the Canary Islands, off the coast of Africa, in 1402, they were introduced to the African Grey Parrot. By the 1450s Greys were beginning to be imported into Europe. The religious-minded folks in medieval Europe noted the Greys' talking ability and accorded them a high status. There is

DIANE GRINDOL/COURTESY OF FEATHERED FOLLIES, LAFAYETTE, CALIFORNIA

Marco Polo reported seeing white parrots during his travels. This is a Moluccan Cockatoo, a species with a glorious salmon crest and often a pink or salmon tinge to their white feathers.

a report that one parrot could recite the Lord's Prayer. During the reign of Pope Martin V, a Keeper of Parrots *(Cortiele de Papagalli)* was appointed. Parrots were also expensive and were considered a status symbol.

As the Spanish and the Portuguese explored new routes to India and the lucrative trade in spices, Christopher Columbus set off on his quest to find better trade routes. He saw new parrot species in the Americas, and took either Bahamas or Cuban Amazon Parrots back to Spain with him. In later voyages to what turned out to be the New World, he saw Macaws. In a Portuguese document from the 1500s, explorers reported they had found a land of parrots—Brazil.

Native tribes in the Americas had legends about parrots, kept them as pets, respected them, used their feathers in ceremonies or ate them. Soon parrots began to be imported into Europe from the Americas, and were called "popinjays." They were kept at the courts and in personal zoos or menageries. In the 18th century,

DIANE GRINDOL

During the exploration of Central and South America by the Spanish and the Portuguese, Macaws were introduced to Europeans. This is a Scarlet Macaw.

the aristocracy often featured exotic parrots in their portraits, and major porcelain factories included parrot statuary or designs.

The total number of parrot species recognized in the world had climbed to 70 by the early 18th century. That number grew enormously as explorers visited Australia. *General Synopsis of Birds,* written in the late 18th century by Sir Joseph Banks and a team of helpers, listed 252 species of birds.

ALL THE RAGE

There was a time in the 19th century when people's awareness of and fascination with the natural world reached new heights. Instead of relying on hearsay, people began to investigate claims of exotic lands and animals. The animals were named, and scientific observation of the natural world was beginning. Numerous societies were formed, and research ships were dispatched to other lands.

A French ornithologist, Francois Levaillant, published a two-volume set between 1801 and 1805 called *Histoire Naturelle des Parroquets,* with illustrations by Jacques Barraband. It included 137 kinds of parrots.

People wanted to actually see some of the animals they had read about, so in England, zoological gardens and private collections of animals were founded. It was fashionable to have an exotic animal strolling on your grounds. It was accepted to have a pet Cockatoo or Macaw in literary salons, and the parrot house was one of the favorite attractions at Regent's Park in London.

Over time, Budgerigars became popular caged birds. In captivity, controlled breeding produced numerous color mutations. Their compatriot, the Cockatiel, journeyed to England at the same time and also gained popularity as a caged bird, although Cockatiels do not rival Budgerigars in talking ability!

PARROTS IN THE UNITED STATES

Canaries were the most widely kept caged birds in the United States until the 1940s. But late in that decade Budgies caught the public's interest and clubs

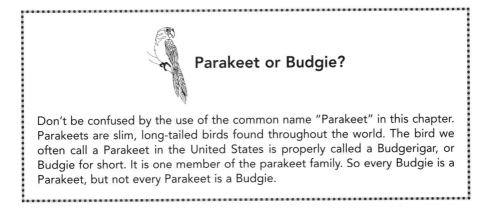

Parakeet or Budgie?

Don't be confused by the use of the common name "Parakeet" in this chapter. Parakeets are slim, long-tailed birds found throughout the world. The bird we often call a Parakeet in the United States is properly called a Budgerigar, or Budgie for short. It is one member of the parakeet family. So every Budgie is a Parakeet, but not every Parakeet is a Budgie.

The Bird Men

John J. Audubon (1785–1851) was born in the French colony of Haiti, grew up in France and eventually moved to Pennsylvania. He was the first artist to portray birds consistently in life size. Seeking to also portray them in their natural habitats, he spent two decades roaming mountains and valleys, and lakes and rivers, from Canada to the Gulf of Mexico, observing and drawing birds. His monumental *The Birds of America*, containing 435 hand-colored plates of 1,065 individual birds, was issued in four volumes between 1827 and 1838. A companion five-volume *Ornithological Biography*, containing detailed essays on the birds, is still regarded as one of the best texts in the field.

John Gould (1804–1881) had a distinguished and influential career as a wildlife artist and publisher. Notably for fans of talking birds, he and his wife, who was a gifted artist, spent 18 months living, sketching and painting in Australia. With a team of artists, including Edward Lear, he produced *The Birds of Australia* in 36 parts between 1840 and 1848. In his lifetime he produced many other quality art and natural history books, featuring even more birds. More importantly, in 1840 Gould brought home to England with him the first small parakeets, which he called "Budgerigars." They turned out to be sensational mimics.

Edward Lear (1812–1888) was the 20th child of Jeremiah Lear, a London stockbroker, and his wife Ann. He is remembered as an artist, travel writer and nonsense poet. He collaborated with Gould as well as producing his own *Illustrations of the Family of Psittacidae*, a 12-volume chronicle of parrot species, at the age of 20.

formed to exhibit them. Cockatiels became popular in the 1960s, with many new and exciting color mutations developing at that time. This is when Lutino and Pearl Cockatiels were novelties. The 1970s were the decade of the Lovebird. Ownership of pet parrots in the United States has grown steadily since the 1980s. During that decade, and up until October 1992, there were many parrots imported into the United States who were destined to become pets for those bold enough or patient enough to tame them.

Aviculturists, those who keep and breed birds, perfected parrot breeding in captivity during the 1980s and '90s. Formulated diets for adult birds and hand-feeding formulas for chicks made the care and breeding of birds in the parrot family (psittacines) commercially possible. Now most parrots acquired as new pets in the United States are hand-reared and were born to be human companions. Baby parrots are so beguiling and gentle; more than a few pet store visitors have been smitten by one and have ended up with a long-lived, intelligent, fascinating and often frustrating companion.

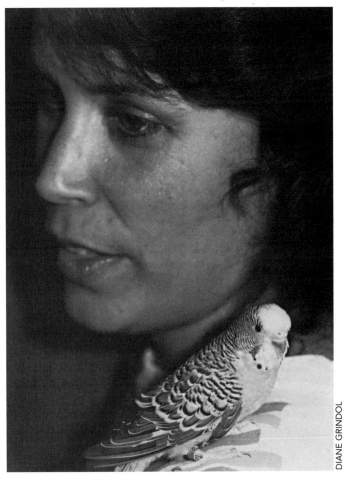

Budgies were popular pets in the United States in the 1940s. Budgie shows continue to this day, while pet owners appreciate a Budgie's social nature and the good talking ability of the males.

Birds are now more and more frequently seen in movies and commercials, too. Their expressive body language and colorful feathers make them appealing as film subjects. It is well known that parrots can talk, and modern media portray them carrying on conversations suitable for marketing a variety of products, from cat food (!) to cable television channels.

The movie *Paulie* is about a Blue-crowned Conure who can converse but does not exactly know when to shut up. He goes in search of the little girl who raised him and meets with numerous adventures en route. This movie was inspired by the concept that parrots learn human speech. The screenwriter Laurie Craig said in an interview, "I saw a parrot in a pet store one day, and began to wonder what it would be like if they really could talk. I came to find out that many of them can and do. They're actually quite intelligent; some say they have

DIANE GRINDOL

A Blue-fronted Amazon like this one talked so clearly when reciting lines for a television commercial that he was deemed too realistic. His voice was dubbed over by a human using a parrotlike voice.

the intellectual and emotional development of a three- to five-year-old child." In *Paulie,* the central character goes way beyond identifying objects and making the occasional appropriate remark. In real life, companion parrots don't actually reach this level of conversation. But it's interesting to ponder what goes on in those avian brains!

Pepper is one of The Amazing Amazons belonging to their companion and trainer Joanie Doss. Pepper, a Blue-fronted Amazon, was chosen to do a television commercial for a telephone company. In the resultant tapes, it was felt his voice was too good, so a person dubbed over his lines in more imperfect "parrot." The story of Pepper ended up on *CNN Headline News* and in the local (Alaskan) media. Pepper also conducted live radio interviews via telephone for a while.

Pepper is proof that you can teach an old bird new tricks. He started training when he was over seven years old and now knows more than 60 tricks.

INTERSPECIES COMMUNICATION

Leaping well into the 20th century, a growing curiosity about the natural world accompanied a growing distance from farming, which had brought people into daily contact with animals. Scientists studied dolphins, the big cats, gorillas and chimpanzees. Animal intelligence and cognitive ability began to be studied, especially with dolphins and apes. Birds do not have a well-developed cerebral cortex, which is a mammal's "organ of intelligence," and they have small brains. As a result, they were often passed over in studies of comparative intelligence. In the 1950s, a researcher named O. H. Mowrer tried to teach parrots to name objects, but he failed to do so. And there was even more evidence that birds weren't intelligent and that their speech is merely mimicry.

It turns out that a different area of the brain, the striatal regions, are the centers of avian intelligence. Other researchers were obtaining results that showed parrots had some intelligence. This field of study caught the attention of Irene Pepperberg as she was finishing her Ph.D. studies in chemical physics at Harvard. Yes, it was an entirely different branch of science, but she saw the possibility of using her own gray matter to devise training methods that could prove the possibility of communication between people and parrots.

Pepperberg studied both avian and human learning. She acquired an African Grey parrot named Alex. And the rest, as they say, is history. You can read much more about their research in the appropriate chapters of this book. Briefly, Pepperberg's breakthrough was to teach Alex to associate what was said to him directly with a reward. Instead of asking him to learn to call something "blue," then receiving a peanut as a reward, she taught him to say "nut" to receive a nut. When he said "blue," he earned the right to hold, beak and taste a blue object. Her research has changed the way people think about birds' intelligence. It has also been instrumental in devising effective ways to teach dysfunctional children.

THE MOST TALKING BIRD IN THE WORLD

In 1995 a new record for the bird with the largest vocabulary in the world was added to the *Guinness Book of World Records*. The documented vocabulary of Puck, a Blue Budgerigar, was 1,728 words at that time. Puck eventually was recorded as uttering 1,777 words and phrases. There's no way to know if Puck is special among male Parakeets, who are indeed prolific talkers. We should all take pause and consider the potential of these small, boisterous and lively members of the bird family. They may be up to much more than we think! Certainly, their size has nothing to do with their brainpower.

His owner and companion, Camille Jordan, certainly showed persistence and thoroughness in the tremendous number of records and recordings she maintained. Camille admits that she is an avid note taker, that she is organized and that she was assertive in pursuing the world record with Puck. She chronicled her steps toward it, from which you may be able to glean some useful information.

Puck was originally acquired as a casual avian companion. Camille was interested in obtaining a bird, remembered having a parakeet as a child and visited a teenager who bred a small number of hand-fed parakeets. Camille knew she wanted a male, who would have the potential to talk, and allowed the teenager's mother to pick out a chick for her. When the chick had been weaned, Camille took him home.

Camille slowly adjusted to Puck, and Puck to her household. Within a month he was allowed free flight in the house. Camille started saying "Puck, Pucky, pretty bird," to her new Parakeet shortly after he arrived in her household. She estimates her repetition of this phrase amounted to about five minutes total each day, in short sessions throughout the day. Three months after coming to their home, and after innumerable and exhausting repetition of "Puck, Pucky, pretty bird," Camille's persistence was rewarded by Puck saying "Puck, pretty bird." Camille efficiently noted the date. She knows he said, "I love you" next, and she proceeded to record 80 words her talented little Parakeet could say by the end of a year.

Camille says Puck, who was a whirlwind of activity, would appear to mimic the conversations she had with her husband, Mark. Puck played both characters, talking in a deep voice and a high voice, running between his plastic penguin and a mirror to act out the two roles. He eventually created a host of characters to talk to, including his own reflection in a mirror and a character he called "Beetlebug."

The next year Camille continued to make note of Puck's vocabulary, which climbed from 81 to 975 words. She also began tape recording his speech. If you are familiar with Budgies, you know they talk in a high-pitched, fast voice. Camille was gifted with hearing that could often decipher his words, but noted that some people could not tell what Puck was saying. It was even a challenge for her at times, but she found that if she recorded what Puck was saying with a sound-activated microphone, at times when no one was home to create distracting background noise, then played the recording back at a slow speed, she could pick out words more easily. It took Camille about three hours to write down what was said on each one-and-a-half-hour tape.

Camille, who you remember has the virtue of being well organized, kept both a chronological and an alphabetized list of Puck's vocabulary. A page was reserved for each letter of the alphabet in her record-keeping system, which eventually grew to more than one page per letter. She got in the habit of keeping a paper and pen handy. Prime time for catching Puck's new words was in the morning over a cup of coffee and after dinner during a quiet time Camille spent reading. Camille points out that she only taught Puck about 50 of the words he said; the rest he picked up from the radio or everyday conversation.

Puck had begun his illustrious career by learning to mimic words. But by about two years old, he was putting those words together in novel combinations and there were instances when he used words appropriately, implying understanding. Camille wrote, "One Sunday in January, 1991, Mark was in the midst of some extensive paperwork at the kitchen table while a tape of operatic arias played in the background. Puck had been wholeheartedly accompanying the tape with beautiful singing of his own when, after half an hour or so, I suggested, 'Let's change this tape. I want to listen to some light rock.' Puck immediately interjected very forcefully, 'I like this!' and Mark and I stared at one another in disbelief. Although Puck had used each of these words in other phrases, we had never heard this sentence before."

Puck was quite a celebrity for a short period of time while he was alive. Camille wrote an article about him, and soon received interview requests from radio stations. The local television station did a spot on Puck for the evening news, and two large national television shows approached Camille about appearances. Since neither she nor her bird were professional performers, Camille feared what would happen if they went on stage with the cameras, lights and crews, and declined these invitations.

As Puck proved that he had an obvious talent, Camille got an urge to see if all her record-keeping could prove that Puck was a record-setting parakeet. She looked up the "Best talking parrot-like bird" in the *Guinness Book of Records*. It turned out to be an African Grey Parrot named Prudle. He had won a talking bird contest in England in each of the 12 consecutive years from 1965 to 1976, held at the National Cage and Aviary Bird Show in London. She contacted the American distributors of the Guinness book to inquire if there couldn't be a classification created for Parakeets.

She wrote four times and was told no or received no reply at all from the American offices. A reporter inquired for her and received back a letter saying the talking bird record was judged at bird competitions. Camille researched this avenue, only to find that there were no talking bird competitions in the United States. She gave up, until an English visitor became enamored with Puck. This woman, unknown to Camille, eventually wrote to the Guinness publishers in England, where the publication is based. They promptly got back to her, saying they would require signed statements from two independent witnesses who should be "of standing in the community" regarding Puck's abilities and vocabulary.

Camille recruited members of the Redwood Empire Cage Bird Club, including two veterinarians. They spent six months documenting Puck's vocabulary and occasionally witty comments. Camille writes, "At one session in May, the observer was having great difficulty hearing Puck. She said so repeatedly, and was growing very frustrated. At one point, she actually told Puck, 'Please slow down. You talk too fast.' Hearing this, he hopped off her finger and onto the table, looked up at her quizzically, and asked, 'What's wrong, stupid?'"

This occurred between April and September 1993, and resulted in adding 384 words to Camille's own voluminous list of Puck's vocabulary. His total documented vocabulary by January 1994 was 1,728. Before he died from a tumor in the fall of 1994, his total word list grew to 1,777. Puck's life was brief, but he had a major impact on his family and bird lovers everywhere. His enthusiasm for life

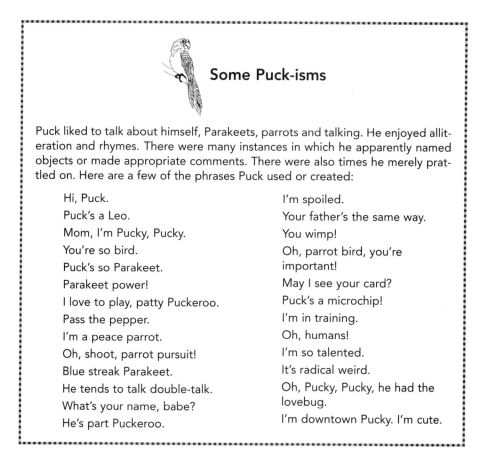

Some Puck-isms

Puck liked to talk about himself, Parakeets, parrots and talking. He enjoyed allit-
eration and rhymes. There were many instances in which he apparently named
objects or made appropriate comments. There were also times he merely prat-
tled on. Here are a few of the phrases Puck used or created:

Hi, Puck.

Puck's a Leo.

Mom, I'm Pucky, Pucky.

You're so bird.

Puck's so Parakeet.

Parakeet power!

I love to play, patty Puckeroo.

Pass the pepper.

I'm a peace parrot.

Oh, shoot, parrot pursuit!

Blue streak Parakeet.

He tends to talk double-talk.

What's your name, babe?

He's part Puckeroo.

I'm spoiled.

Your father's the same way.

You wimp!

Oh, parrot bird, you're important!

May I see your card?

Puck's a microchip!

I'm in training.

Oh, humans!

I'm so talented.

It's radical weird.

Oh, Pucky, Pucky, he had the lovebug.

I'm downtown Pucky. I'm cute.

and for talking set a new world record and endeared him to Camille, Mark, his
community, a bird club and a host of Parakeet lovers. Think about Puck's talent
next time you visit with a Budgie!

POINTS TO REMEMBER

- Talking parrots have been pets in India since about 1000 B.C. and are
  depicted in legends and fables.
- In Roman times, teaching parrots (in Latin, of course!) was a profession.
- In 19th century Europe, parrots were studied, collected and given scientific
  names. Elaborate illustrated bird books were published in the 19th century
  to show people what many species looked like.
- Although commercials and movies show very talkative birds, that's a Holly-
  wood version of talking parrots.
- Never underestimate the intelligence of a Budgie. The *Guinness Book of
  World Records'* "bird with the largest vocabulary in the world" was Puck, a
  turquoise Parakeet who had a vocabulary of more than 1,700 words.

Chapter 4

Where Sound Comes From

When we think about talking birds, we need to have some awareness of where all the noise that birds shape into words comes from. This might seem to be an easy concept, since we are fairly noisy creatures ourselves. As evolution would have it, however, mammals and birds differ greatly in the way their lungs, breathing and vocal apparatus work. As it turns out, birds have a much more efficient way of doing things.

THE AVIAN LUNG

The avian lung is very different from the mammalian lung. It is compact, exchanges oxygen for carbon dioxide much more efficiently than ours and doesn't expand and contract. Birds accomplish this by having a lung that is similar to a radiator in a car. Air flows through the lung when the bird inhales, just as coolant flows through the coils in a radiator. After the air has passed through the lung, it moves into structures called air sacs. These air sacs are spaces in the body cavity of the bird that are surrounded by membranes. They are similar to balloons in that they are airtight and surrounded by a fairly elastic membrane. When the bird expands her body to inhale (in much the same way we expand ours when we inhale), air travels down the trachea and eventually into the air sacs.

When a bird breathes in (inhalation), some air passes through the lungs and exchanges oxygen in the air for the carbon dioxide that has accumulated in the blood. The rest of the incoming air bypasses the lungs and finds its way directly into a specific set of air sacs. When the bird breathes out (exhalation), the air that traveled through the lung on inhalation bypasses the lungs and air that bypassed the lung on inhalation passes through the lung. This enables birds to exchange carbon dioxide in the blood for oxygen in the air both on inhalation and exhalation.

41

This highly efficient operation is one of the adaptations birds have made for the physical rigors of flight.

THE SYRINX

As is the case in mammals, birds have two lungs. This means the trachea (the pipe through which air flows from the nose and mouth to the lungs) divides into two smaller bronchi so air reaches both lungs. Right where the trachea divides into two bronchi, there is an organ called the syrinx. The syrinx is the organ birds use to make sounds. All the calls birds make, from the mating calls of cranes to the music of songbirds to the speech of parrots, is made in the syrinx. Anyone who has listened to both the calls of birds and the sounds mammals make will understand that for their, size birds can make more and louder sounds than mammals. This is due to this simple organ.

The syrinx is mainly a set of muscles surrounding the trachea, and a pair of membranes that extend from the junction of the two bronchi in the direction of the trachea. Air flowing from the lungs back into the trachea passes over these

Loud Birds

It has often been suggested that destroying some part of the syrinx would result in a bird becoming mute. For someone with a bird who is making a lot of noise, this might not sound so bad. In reality, though, such efforts have poor outcomes. Usually any effort to destroy the muscles surrounding the trachea with either surgical, chemical or cauterizing techniques has resulted in either the death of the bird or a rapid return to complete vocal ability. Surgery is no way to keep a bird quiet!

You just need to get used to a noisy bird, find a situation where your bird can make as much noise as she likes or use training techniques that will enable you to find the cause of your bird's need to make excessive noise and correct the problem.

Frequently, the best solution to a problem with your bird is to acquire a suitable species of bird with a temperament more consistent with the environment in which she is to live. This means choosing a more appropriate species, or simply trading for a different individual of the same species. In any case, some attempt at training your bird to make the sounds you want to hear, or an assessment of your situation to determine what is causing your bird to scream, is in order. For professional advice on changing bird behavior, you may consult with a parrot behavioral consultant. Sometimes a simple change in your bird's situation will result in the desired changes in her behavior and a great improvement in both your lives.

membranes and makes them vibrate, producing sound. Since there are two membranes (one on each side of the juncture of the bronchi), there are two sources of sound in birds. This leads to birds having two "voices"—one from each membrane. These two voices enable birds to make more complex sounds than mammals can make, and may be responsible for some of the unique sounds in birdsong.

The tone of this sound is adjusted by the muscles in the syrinx. These muscles form a band around the trachea and can contract to change the shape of the trachea at that point. The shape of the trachea changes the tone of the sound and enables birds to make all the sounds we hear in their calls. The shape of the trachea along the rest of the distance from the syrinx to the mouth, and also the position of the tongue and mouth, can further change characteristics of the sound. Just as we use our mouths, tongues and throats to form words, birds use their oral equipment to form the sounds produced in the syrinx into calls and songs.

The syrinx is the organ in birds that makes sound. Birds can make more and louder sounds than mammals. You'd be sure of that if you were anywhere near this Eleanora Cockatoo when she's sounding off.

HEARING

It might not seem obvious at first, but the way birds hear has a considerable influence on the way they make sounds. Birds are far better able to differentiate among sounds than we are. This is largely because of the nerves that feed signals from the ear to the brain. These nerves feed much more information per second to the bird's brain than our auditory nerves do. This means a sound we might hear as a constant hum would sound to a bird like a complex set of tones, such as a song or call, full of variation. This ability to hear details in sound with such precision is a complement to the ability of birds to make complex sounds with their "two voices."

When you train your bird to talk, you might want to take this into account. Birds can produce and hear much more complex sounds than we can. There is no

DIANE GRINDOL

All birds, including this Jenday Conure, are better at breathing, singing and hearing than we are. They can hear and reproduce more complex sounds than we can.

problem training your bird to make the most complex sounds you can produce, since the real limit here is not your bird's ability to make and hear sounds but yours. It might be a little difficult to take, but birds are better at this breathing, singing and hearing stuff than we are.

THE BRAIN

The structures used in breathing, vocalizing and hearing are all run by the brain. As you might expect, something that birds do so well takes a lot of the bird's brain to properly manage. In fact, the parts of a bird's brain that are responsible for hearing and singing have been mapped, particularly in songbirds. Since song is such an important part of maintaining a territory, finding a mate and locating competitors or predators, the part of the brain involved in producing song has been studied extensively.

Although there is still some room for debate, the scientific information available at this point leads us to believe that birds actually grow more brain tissue at appropriate times just to accommodate more songs. In Canaries, for example, the part of the brain responsible for learning and producing song increases in size as the immature male Canary begins to sing for the first time. As the breeding season passes and the Canary sings less, this part of the brain shrinks, reducing the amount of brain tissue devoted to song production. The next breeding season, this part of the brain expands again, enabling the Canary to produce his song and to add notes to his repertoire.

Before the discovery that birds are able to expand their brains as adults to make more room for songs, it was thought that the brains of mature animals were unable to produce any additional brain cells. This realization has influenced new approaches to understanding brain physiology in humans and has led to hope that brains of adults damaged by accidents or by disease can be treated and helped to recover. This is one of those strange interactions that occur in science; there may be mechanisms in the brains of songbirds that can be used to help repair damaged human brains.

DIANE GRINDOL

Canaries actually grow more brain tissue at appropriate times just to accommodate more songs. These Border Canaries are participating in a bird show.

WHY BIRDS MAKE SOUNDS

It might seem obvious, but birds sing to be heard. What isn't obvious is why a little bird who could become lunch for a much larger bird or a cat or some other predator would want to be heard. Being heard in some cases is the same as being found, and being found can be the same as being lunch. As it turns out, birds have evolved a number of reasons for being heard, and usually manage to do it without being found by the wrong party.

Singing

Singing in birds is used much the same way that language is used in human beings—to communicate. Birds have a variety of reasons to communicate, but some of the most important relate to reproduction. For example, many male songbirds produce songs to attract mates. At the same time they are attracting mates, they are warning other males of their species that this particular area is claimed and is going to be defended. Songbirds manage to announce this defense of territory without calling in predators by using the right kinds of sounds. They use a specific range of frequencies so that their song carries just far enough to make their point before dissipating into the foliage of the surrounding area. The limited range of their song keeps them from being detected from far away by predators. Its clarity within its range serves as notification to other nearby birds that they are calling a mate and defending a territory.

We don't know all the reasons birds sing or make other sounds. Many specific uses of calls or songs have been documented and have been shown to be consistent among many species. A threat call in most species is similar, for example. This is because the properties that make a threat call effective, such as being easily recognized, carrying well and communicating its message without requiring a long time to be understood, are consistent among species. Other calls can be more specific to the species using them and the situations in which they are used. These calls have more subtle uses and meanings that we are just beginning to understand.

While it is likely there is a subtlety in birdsongs that we don't understand, it is clear that songs vary from area to area and from year to year. This kind of drift in songs can result in regional "accents" that may be part of the evolution of new species. Birds tend to mate with other birds who have songs that resemble what they heard while they were growing up or that are innate songs of the species. Variation from these songs can lead to reduced interbreeding among groups with different songs and eventual isolation of a group. This isolated group has the potential to evolve into another species. In this way, birdsong may have dramatic evolutionary consequences.

Birds Who Don't Sing

Most birds don't sing. Singing is something done by a clearly defined group of birds called oscines, a subgroup of the passerines. Technically, songs are defined as long, complex vocalizations produced by male birds during the breeding season. The rest of the birds usually make other sounds, known as calls. Some of these calls may be complicated enough to qualify as songs, but we still reserve songs for the songbirds, by definition.

As it turns out, most of the birds we want to train to talk are not songbirds but parrots, Crows, Starlings and Mynahs. There are a number of reasons these birds make sounds. Some of them we understand, others we don't.

Vocal Sounds and Reproduction

Many birds use vocalization as part of their mating rituals. These rituals may include complex dancing, with repeated calls and displays. Most of these vocalizations are produced by males to attract mates, and are quite loud. Studies have shown that there is a cost to all this display and the males of many species have much higher mortality rates in the spring than the females. Since males are usually the more colorful gender in birds, and since they engage in loud, public, colorful mating dances and rituals to attract mates, they often attract predators as well. That evolution has not caused the males of these species to find a more subtle way to attract mates indicates that these displays are of great value in passing genes to the next generation.

One of the more interesting aspects of avian sound and reproduction is that of chick hatching. As eggs are incubated, they lose water. This leads to the formation of an air cell in the blunt end of the egg. In a normally developing egg, the head of the chick is in this end. As a prelude to hatching, the chick breaks the membrane that separates her from this air cell and pushes her beak into this space. This is the space where the chick breathes for the first time. In many species the chicks begin to chirp in this space, and these chirps can be heard by their parents and by other chicks who are about to hatch.

The species that lay large numbers of eggs over a period of days often have chicks who chirp in the air cell before actual hatching. When these first chicks begin to chirp, the chicks from eggs laid later in the clutch speed up their hatching. This enables chicks who develop from eggs laid over many days to hatch over a shorter time period. This means communication among unhatched chicks causes a synchrony of hatching that is greater than the synchrony of laying of the eggs. Communication that begins before hatching increases the likelihood that chicks will survive, as well, by helping younger chicks catch up developmentally to older chicks.

Sounds That Aren't From the Syrinx

Some of the sounds birds make in their reproductive efforts are not produced by the syrinx. One example is the Western Sandpiper. The male Western Sandpiper puts on a courtship display that involves flying high into the sky and then speeding toward the earth so fast that his wings make a kind of buzzing sound. If you were to find yourself on the tundra on a spring day, you might wonder what these sounds were. Western Sandpipers are small birds and they fly high enough that they can't be seen during this display. All you would experience is the sound of their wings buzzing through the air.

Another example of a sound that doesn't come from the syrinx is the booming sound made by some birds that breed in leks. A lek is an area to which a male tries to attract a female by booming. Once the female is attracted to the lek, the male tries to get the female to breed with him by continuing his booming and by performing his display. The Kakapo Parrot of New Zealand breeds in leks. To produce the characteristic booming sound, the male Kakapo inflates his air sacs and vibrates his wings. The wings produce vibrations that affect the inflated air sacs in a manner similar to a drum.

Doubtless there are other important bird sounds that don't originate from the syrinx. Anyone who owns a parrot is familiar with the shaking and rustling sound a parrot makes if she is startled during the night. She manages to shake her whole cage and to sound much larger than she is. This sound is likely used in the wild to frighten away predators during the night.

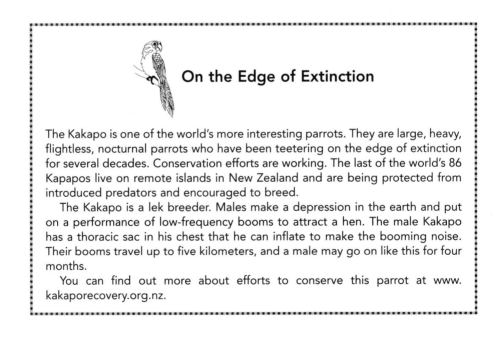

On the Edge of Extinction

The Kakapo is one of the world's more interesting parrots. They are large, heavy, flightless, nocturnal parrots who have been teetering on the edge of extinction for several decades. Conservation efforts are working. The last of the world's 86 Kapapos live on remote islands in New Zealand and are being protected from introduced predators and encouraged to breed.

The Kakapo is a lek breeder. Males make a depression in the earth and put on a performance of low-frequency booms to attract a hen. The male Kakapo has a thoracic sac in his chest that he can inflate to make the booming noise. Their booms travel up to five kilometers, and a male may go on like this for four months.

You can find out more about efforts to conserve this parrot at www.kakaporecovery.org.nz.

Sounds and Seasons

As we have seen, many of the sounds birds make are related to reproduction. Usually these involve attracting a mate, defending territory or synchronizing the hatching of chicks.

Most birds of the temperate zone reproduce in the spring, and many birds of the tropics have breeding seasons related to some environmental cue such as rain, ocean temperature changes or some other factor that makes breeding more successful in a certain season.

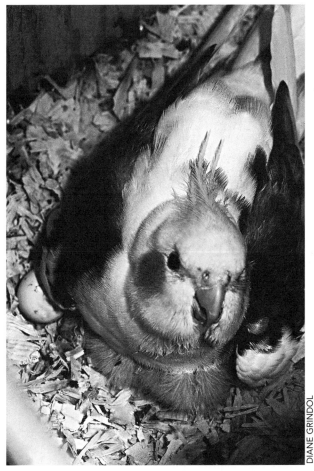

DIANE GRINDOL

This pied Cockatiel, Sunshine, made certain calls during the breeding season that he did not use during the rest of the year. He courted his mate with song and vigorously defended his chicks and nestbox. Sunshine also sang to his eggs.

All breeding involves changes in behavior and vocalizations. The vocalizations of these birds change to suit their changing needs for communication. In addition, there are interactions that occur in a flock that do not occur in a pair of breeding birds. This leads to birds who vocalize in one manner or another most of the year in the wild. These birds who vocalize year-round include parrots, corvids (Ravens and Crows), sturnids (Starlings and Mynahs) and a variety of other species that might be kept as pets and trained to talk. These are primarily the birds we are discussing in this book—those who vocalize all year long in the wild, who mimic each other and who have the capacity to learn new sounds or calls all their lives.

MIMICRY

There are a great many ways in which animals and plants mimic each other, and a great many advantages derived from that mimicry, but in this book we are speaking only of vocal mimicry.

There are many species of birds that mimic to one extent or another. For example, many of the songbirds mimic the songs of other songbirds. The Lyrebird of Australia is an incredible mimic and can sound like a whole forest full of birds, although only one bird sings at a time.

The main groups of birds we think of as mimics are the psittaciformes (parrots), passeriformes (Crows, Mynahs and Starlings) and apodiformes (Hummingbirds). Since only a few people keep hummingbirds, we will restrict our training methods mainly to the parrots, with some information on the Crows, Mynahs and Starlings.

How Much Do Birds Mimic?

This is a really good question with a really unsatisfying answer. There is great variation. There is even great variation in the things an individual species or an individual bird within a species will mimic. For example, some songbirds will mimic a tape recorder, and some won't. Zebra Finches won't mimic a tape recorder that is just played for them, but they will mimic a tape recorder they can turn on by pecking an illuminated key. There seems to be some aspect of interaction beyond simply hearing a sound that makes a difference to the bird. What the essential aspect of the interaction is remains to be discovered, but clearly it is needed to a greater or lesser degree in different birds.

One of the reasons we choose the certain species of birds as talking pets is their relatively limited need for personal interaction to learn to mimic. Many parrots learn street noises from events they never see. Tom had a parrot who did an excellent job of imitating a garbage truck backing up. It was not something he had personal experience with.

Mimicry Versus Cognitive Response

Mimicry is a simple imitation of a sound. That is why Tom's parrot was so successful in imitating a garbage truck backing up. The parrot wasn't trying to communicate anything; he was just sounding off. When you choose to teach a bird to talk, you have a decision to make. That decision is whether you just want your parrot to repeat the things you say (mimicry), or whether you want a parrot who is able to respond to questions with real answers (a cognitive response).

In the case of a cognitive response, you might ask your parrot if she wants a cracker. You might say, "Do you want a cracker?" If your parrot is only mimicking, she might respond with, "Do you want a cracker?" A parrot who is giving a cognitive response might say, "I want a cracker." In this case the difference in words is small, but in a more complicated question such as, "What color is this?" there is a big difference between repeating the question and correctly responding with "blue."

As soon as your bird joins your household, you need to make a decision about which of these options you want to take. Training a bird for a cognitive response is a lot more work, but it's much more rewarding to have a conversation (albeit a simple one) than to listen to an echo.

POINTS TO REMEMBER

- Complex sounds are produced by a bird's syrinx.
- Birds hear in much more detail than we do.
- Birds can grow new brain tissue to accommodate new songs.
- Many bird sounds are related to reproduction. But only birds who vocalize year-round are good candidates for talking.
- Mimicry is simple repetition of words. Cognition involves a thoughtful response.

Chapter 5

The Call of the Wild

Parrots are social, lively and vocal birds in the wild. We long ago noticed that they are flamboyant, but the wild calls of parrots have not been widely studied until recently. Despite the keen interest people have in parrots, these birds live in places where conditions for researchers are daunting. Parrots often live and nest in rain forests where trees grow to 150 feet tall. Many live in jungle habitats with thick vegetation. Others live in remote areas. "For such brightly colored and loud animals, they can be extraordinarily stealthy if they wish to be," says Tim Wright of the Smithsonian National Zoo and the University of Maryland, who studies vocal learning in parrots. In dense forest, the only indication of a parrot may be droppings and discarded food. (Yes, they make the same mess in the wild as in captivity! Scattered food just isn't as good for carpets as it is for the rain forest floor.)

VOCALIZATIONS OF WILD PARROTS

People are attracted to parrots because of their ability to mimic human speech, yet this ability has remained mysterious and little understood. Of course, unlike captive parrots, wild birds do not fly among the treetops imitating phones, beepers and answering machines. They do not teach their young to say "hello" or an appropriate equivalent in the native language of their country of origin. Still, unraveling the mysteries of how parrots vocalize in the wild helps us understand why parrots vocalize in captivity, and why they choose to imitate our language at times. Wright, who studied Yellow-naped Amazons in Costa Rica, and Mike Schindlinger, a Ph.D. candidate from Harvard who studied Yellow-headed Amazons in Mexico, are among the researchers who are slowly shedding light on this mystery. You can watch for new developments in this field in the coming years.

We humans usually enjoy birdsong and speak of it wistfully and with awe in poetry. Bird calls in the wild are utilitarian, however, and usually have something to do with a bird's survival. As we've detailed in Chapter 4, bird vocalizations are used to establish territories and attract mates. They're used to find food, avoid enemies, develop relationships between parent and young, make social contacts and identify movement of the flock. The birds who mimic songs and calls are prey animals, and calls of any kind draw attention to them. Since they are risking their own survival to some extent, most calls serve a function in the wild. But it's not always mating or protection.

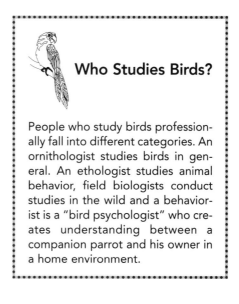

Who Studies Birds?

People who study birds professionally fall into different categories. An ornithologist studies birds in general. An ethologist studies animal behavior, field biologists conduct studies in the wild and a behaviorist is a "bird psychologist" who creates understanding between a companion parrot and his owner in a home environment.

Schindlinger has observed that parrots vocalize even when they are already paired, and they face fewer predators than songbirds. This means they have some leisure time, and seem to spend it producing long trains of complex sounds without expecting them to generate any interaction with their flock members or to serve as a warning or a contact call. It's called *broadcasting*. He speaks of this mode of vocalizing as perhaps serving a more "musical" than "dialectical" function. There are some performers out there!

BIRD CALLS

A call is one of the kinds of verbal communication between birds. Calls are briefer than songs, and they often serve a function related to the life and well-being of the bird uttering the call or to maintaining his social relationships. Some of the calls used by birds include:

Warning call

Rallying call

Assembly call

Contact call

Courtship call

Chick/parent recognition call

Begging call

Song

Want to Hear for Yourself?

Cornell Lab of Ornithology has a Library of Natural Sounds featuring bird sounds from throughout the world. You may order many of the collections, and can listen to samples from them on the Internet at www.birds.cornell.edu/lab_cds.html, or contact the Library of Natural Sounds by calling them at (607) 254-2406.

Ornithologists who study bird calls report that a domestic chicken uses 10 different vocalizations. The Red Grouse has 15 calls, the Ring-necked Pheasant has 16. The House Sparrow has 11 different calls, and the Village Weaverbird has 15. Some of these studies included songs as calls. Many songs are used by male birds to stake out their territory or attract a hen, as discussed in Chapter 4. We love the songs of our male domestic Canaries, for example, whose songs attract a hen and also seem to enhance the singer's attractiveness to his mate. Female Canaries paired with males who have more intricate songs built nests more speedily and laid more eggs than those with less talented males.

FITTING INTO THE FLOCK

One of the common vocalizations of the Amazons studied in the wild is contact calls, which are short bursts of sound used to maintain contact between members of a flock, between the members of a pair and for other social reasons. They are uttered before and after flying, for example, or used when members of a pair forage out of sight of one another. Contact calls are used by both sexes and all age groups. Chicks learn their first versions of their parents' contact calls shortly after leaving the nest. In the nest they uttered begging calls that didn't need to be learned at all, but were an instinctive response to hunger.

Although parrots learn our language in captivity, for the most part they do not mimic other species in the wild (the Rose-breasted Cockatoo being an exception—see page 55). The Amazons that have been studied use Amazon calls and song.

Wright also found that wild parrots use strikingly few calls. The contact call, for example, made up 40 to 60 percent of all calls used by the Yellow-naped Amazon Parrots he studied in Costa Rica. Their whole repertoire is made up of 8 to 10 calls, which is similar to other bird species.

It is probable that many parrot calls are learned and are not instinctive. We know this because both Wright and Schindlinger have found that groups of parrots who roost together have calls that vary by geographic area. (A roost is a location where a group of birds flock to spend the night together. Pairs, singles and

Species Differences

There are more than 300 species of parrots. Although these species share some similarities, such as having four toes and hooked beaks, there are also differences among them. Our other common pets, dogs and cats, are one species, with different breeds that have been developed in captivity. A dog is a dog is a dog, whether it's a Pug or a Golden Retriever. A cat is a cat is a cat. But a parrot is a Cockatoo or a Lory or an Amazon or an African Parrot or a Parakeet. You get the idea.

Parrots, being different species that have adapted to different environments throughout the world, do not have one set of common behaviors or vocalizations. We are relying on studies of Amazon parrots for the information in this chapter. You should note the similarities and differences between an Amazon parrot and your own companion parrot.

flocks of juvenile parrots join together and share a tree or a grove of trees overnight. They disperse again at dawn to feed and play.) These differences in calls are like the languages that develop among geographically different groups of people. It's possible that juvenile birds who pair up and join a roost with one "language" learn that language to fit in. In that case, they are learning as adults. It's not the calls, but the learning that seems to be instinctive. This begins to explain why parrots learn our language when the flock they are fitting into is a human one. Certain instincts take over!

Observations of Cockatoos in Australia also provide evidence that parrots learn their calls. Two species of Pink Cockatoos, the Major Mitchell's and Rose-breasted Cockatoos, frequently claim a single nest hole. Sometimes hens of both species lay their eggs in a single hole. The Rose-breasted Cockatoos are smaller and often lose their squatting rights to the Major Mitchell's. They can't take their eggs with them, however. So sometimes the Major Mitchell's hatch and raise a Rose-breasted Cockatoo in the wild. These birds identify with their foster parents, behave like them, eat the same food and imitate their calls. It is reported that a fostered "Rosie" also will partner with a Major Mitchell's when he reaches sexual maturity and successfully rear a wild hybrid Cockatoo.

PRACTICE MAKES PERFECT

Both researchers noted that young Amazon parrots make softer and less frequent calls than adult Amazons. Video footage by Schindlinger shows a group of

Persisting Vocalizations in the Wild: 34

Amazona oratrix
Rio Corona, North of Casas, Tamaulipas Mexico

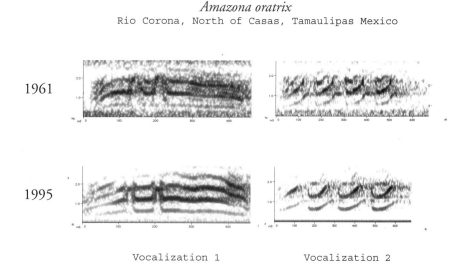

nestlings practicing vocalizations among themselves after they had been out of their nest for about two months. Wright noted that juvenile and immature birds called less often and had softer calls than adults. Here is another indication that wild birds learn to fit into their flock and learn their flock's calls.

REGIONAL DIFFERENCES

An aspect of Amazon vocalizations noticed by Wright was that different roosts had different vocalizations. Some roosts straddled the territory where there were distinct dialects, and it was found that about 10 percent of the birds in these areas were bilingual! As often happens when studies are just beginning, there are more questions raised than answers. Some questions we can ponder include:

> Is this a sort of parrot oral tradition tied to a roost area, or are there genetic differences between the groups of parrots with different dialects?
>
> Do visiting birds learn the established group's calls?
>
> Do calls change over time if a bird makes a mistake and that mistake gets passed on?
>
> Do Amazons travel between dialect groups?
>
> At what age do parrots learn their calls?
>
> How long do they continue learning?

Evidence of both dialects and languages in the Amazon populations was found. Schindlinger noticed that some roosts of Amazons in Mexico had similar calls but produced them with noticeable differences; this is what is meant by a dialect. The situation is comparable to the existence of High German and Swiss German, which are the same language but with regional differences.

For other roosts, there appeared to be a different language of calls used, with no similarity between the two populations. This is like comparing French and German, which are spoken by citizens of a neighboring population but are two distinctly different languages.

Caught on Tape

To learn more about Michael Schindlinger's studies of Amazon parrots in the wild, check out the web site www.sneakerfish.com/parrots/kw/. You may order a video showing wild parrots, including footage inside a nest cavity. Audiotapes with wild parrot vocalizations are available here, too.

Barra del Tordo

La Pesca

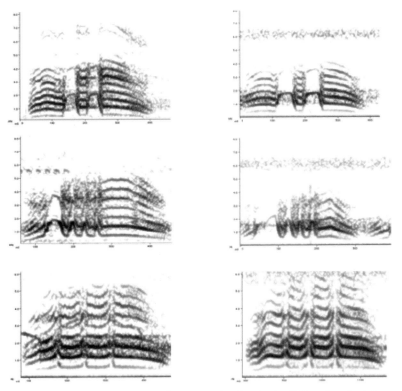

COURTESY MICHAEL SCHINDLINGER

Despite the small home ranges of pairs and individuals, Yellow-headed Amazon Parrot populations separated by 90 kilometers along the Gulf Coast share many of the same vocalizations. Certain population-level differences, akin to accents, can also be observed in the three common vocalizations depicted here in two groups of birds in Barra del Tordo and La Pesca.

Ciudad Victoria

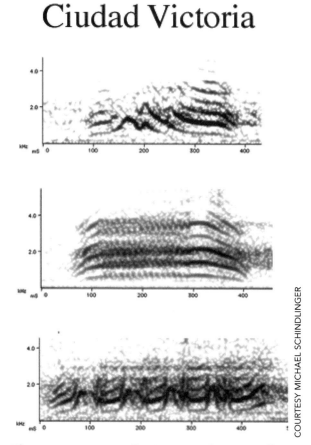

COURTESY MICHAEL SCHINDLINGER

These common vocalizations are from a Yellow-headed Amazon Parrot population recorded near Ciudad Victoria, Mexico, about 120 kilometers inland from the locations of the groups in the previous figure. This population does not share any common vocalization types with the coastal populations; it speaks not with a different accent but with a different language.

WILD BIRD MIMICS

Some birds are not very original in designing their repertoire, but borrow creatively from their avian neighbors. There are several species of wild birds who mimic the calls of other birds. Mimicry is a bird species copying or imitating the natural call of another, or several other species of birds and incorporating them into its own songs. Starlings and Mockingbirds are examples of species with this skill. Sometimes mimicry extends to mechanical noises or human speech. There is a difference among species in this ability.

Theories about why a species of bird would use calls from another species vary. Males may sing to impress the females of the species, or to define territory. It may even be a protection against predators.

Birds who mimic, for whatever reason, can seem quite interesting and pleasing to the human ear. They may even tease our companion birds. In Diane's neighborhood there are wild

Excellent Mimics

- Mockingbirds
- Superb Lyrebirds
- Starlings
- Thrushes
- Bowerbirds
- Warblers
- White-eyed Vireos

Mockingbirds who learn Cockatiel calls and have conversations with her small flock! Her reaction upon seeing a Cockatiel-colored bird circling her house, using Cockatiel calls, is one of panic—until she realizes it's not one of her birds at all.

Starlings both mimic wild birds and can learn to talk if kept as pets. A friend, Doris, took a Starling into her classroom, where it became quite proficient at saying "teacher, teacher," as well as entertaining children by eating bugs and worms.

A Fast Learner

Richard Lyon reports that an unusual event occurred on November 3, 1998, in his garden in Viewbank, a suburb of Melbourne, Australia. "Three recently fledged Magpies and the adult male were sitting at midday in Sugar Gums. In early afternoon I watched the adult male give a prolonged warbling subsong which consisted mainly of mimicry, with Grey Butcherbird being the main subject. It also gave a good rendition of the scream of a Yellow-tailed Black Cockatoo, and three extraordinarily good mammal imitations. The first, repeated several times independently, was of a person saying quite clearly, 'May I help you?' in an unmistakable American accent. To explain, my four-year-old daughter, Meg, and our next-door neighbours had been playing outside the day before with a toy telephone which said that. The imitation was perfect in terms of vowels, rhythm and intonation, though the consonants were missing or unclear. It was quite loud but clearly part of the subsong.

"The second mammal imitation was a horse, a brilliant rendition of a full-blooded whinnying neigh, rising and then falling in pitch, and repeated a second time after more Grey Butcherbird. The third was a dog, a deep 'woof-woof,' uttered once only. Perhaps it was all part of the young birds' education. I haven't heard the performance repeated."

MAKING BEAUTIFUL MUSIC TOGETHER

Another type of call found in the Amazon studies was the duet. A duet is a call performed by the two members of a mated pair of parrots. The notes produced by each member of the pair are sex-specific and are combined by the male and female calling alternately. The frequency and length of the notes change over the course of the call in an orderly progression. Pairs were observed performing duets near their nest holes.

Each pair creates its own duet, so that it has a distinguishing call different from neighboring pairs. The general style, or use of one or two notes, varied in the Amazon studies along the same lines that contact calls did, with bilingual birds using notes from each region.

Schindlinger noted that some parrot calls spanned two octaves in one tenth of a second. This type of vocalization is beyond the range of a human voice and is too complex for us to distinguish with human ears. We need to take into account that parrots are adapted to a different sensory world than humans.

Bring on the Band

Pairs of Amazon parrots create melodic duets together, and researchers have noted that at times an Amazon will vocalize seemingly for the sheer joy of it. Perhaps this is like our music, a life-enhancing rather than a life-preserving activity.

A parrot in his natural habitat is only one of the creatures vocalizing. It has been proposed by those in the field of bioacoustics that each natural habitat has a particular pattern to its overall noise level. When analyzed with equipment that determines sound frequencies and displays them, each type of living being in a habitat vocalizes at certain frequencies, and the sound frequencies produced by different

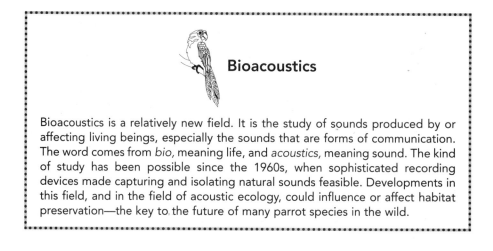

Bioacoustics

Bioacoustics is a relatively new field. It is the study of sounds produced by or affecting living beings, especially the sounds that are forms of communication. The word comes from *bio*, meaning life, and *acoustics*, meaning sound. The kind of study has been possible since the 1960s, when sophisticated recording devices made capturing and isolating natural sounds feasible. Developments in this field, and in the field of acoustic ecology, could influence or affect habitat preservation—the key to the future of many parrot species in the wild.

DIANE GRINDOL

Our companion birds, such as this Umbrella Cockatoo, are not that far removed from their wild cousins.

groups of animals do not overlap. Individuals chime in when others fall away, so the pattern is maintained. The overall vocalization levels remain constant. Myriads of animals synchronize in a symphony of sound to make this happen!

A specific area of habitat has a unique mixture of voices that vary by season but, researchers have found, does not vary over the years. Mapping frequencies of insect, amphibian, bird and mammal vocalizations, each occupies a range of frequencies and serves to create a sound pattern that is as unique as a fingerprint. The mix of voices is referred to as a *biophony*—a biological symphony—by Bernie Krause, a musician who records natural soundscapes.

Our parrots are not many generations removed from the wild and their cousins. They often have the same reaction to environmental conditions as wild birds do. Does your parrot match the noise level in your household, or adjust his calls so that he is louder and higher-pitched than the general noise level in the household? He's probably just maintaining the soundscape. You may want to consider turning down the television or the stereo, or moving your parrot to a quieter location.

POINTS TO REMEMBER

- Wild birds use calls for their survival and to establish social order.

- Contact calls are among the most common vocalizations of parrots studied in the wild, and are used to maintain contact between members of a flock or a mated pair.

- There are few studies of wild parrot vocalizations. Those done with Amazon parrots seem to show that social groups of the same species have distinct languages and that many Amazon calls are learned rather than instinctive.

- Parrots live in a much more aurally rich environment than people do, with the ability to differentiate and reproduce faster sounds with more variation than is possible with the human ear and voice.

- A parrot may naturally be inclined to fill empty sound frequencies in his environment, matching the noise level of a household.

Chapter 6

Who Talks and Who Doesn't?

One of the most interesting things about parrots, and some other kinds of birds, is that they can talk in our language. It's usually the first thing someone asks a parrot owner, and it's one of the first things new parrot owners try to find out how to teach their companion parrot, after the bird has eating and drinking down pat. If you *know,* are *absolutely certain,* you're *sure* that you want a talking bird, consider owning one of the species most likely to talk (see page 66).

Of the talking species, some speak more clearly than others, and some have larger vocabularies. Some parrots seem to learn new words for a longer period of time than others. If your budget is a consideration, you can still probably get a talking bird. Male Budgies can develop large vocabularies, and are lower-priced than some of the other parrot species.

Be aware that individuals within any species may vary greatly in their intelligence and aptitude for talking. Environment and teaching method also play a big part in a bird's ability to learn to speak—and you can optimize those no matter what species you have. Footedness (like handedness in people) may be a factor, and age is a factor in a bird's ability to learn new words.

You may consider, before launching into this project, the type, sex and age of the bird you are working with, the amount of time you have to spend training your bird, the bird's care, the bird's environment and also your goals in training your bird to talk. The method you choose for your bird's lessons will vary according to your goals and the time you spend with your bird, as well as the willingness of your family to participate. If you hardly have any time but your bird is talking anyway, you can pick up some clues in this book about how and why she's learning, and maybe channel that verbosity a little! Let's look at some of the variables.

THE BEST TALKING BIRDS

The stars of the talking birds include both African and Timneh Greys. Both are in the general family of African Grey Parrots. Sometimes the larger bird is called a Congo African Grey. The Timneh is smaller, with a horn-colored upper mandible and maroon tail feathers, but with all the talents of her larger cousin.

The largest Amazons are especially talkative, too. This includes the Double Yellow-headed, Yellow-naped, Blue-fronted and Panama Amazons. The Amazons listed below are the most known for talking and have been readily available as pets. Doubtless there are less common Amazons who also talk well.

Eclectus and Lories are talkative birds that haven't gotten much credit for that ability. People might be too blinded by their beauty: Both families of birds have gorgeous, iridescent, brightly colored feathers. Eclectus are fairly large birds with a distinct color difference between males and females. Males are green birds with bright, candy-corn yellow beaks. Females are red and purple birds. Wow! Generally the Grand, Red-sided, Vosmaeri and Solomon Island species are

DIANE GRINDOL

Simon is a Congo African Grey, one of the species of bird most noted for their talking ability. Wanda talks to him often, and Simon is exceeding her expectations with his vocal abilities.

A Double Yellow-headed Amazon will probably learn to talk. That's even more likely if she is happy and healthy!

available to U.S. pet owners. There are a number of species within the general families of Eclectus and Lories, and their talking ability probably varies. A chattering Lory might be a good guess for a talking bird!

Be sure to learn about the care requirements of the species of bird you choose. Lories, for example, need daily nectar and a lot of fruit in their diets. Their droppings squirt. That's a consideration in most households! Eclectus move deliberately and need an owner who understands that.

All of our avian companions need adequate housing, a balanced diet and regular veterinary care. This will help them live out their expected life span. A healthy, happy bird is more likely to talk, too!

Eclectus Parrots are some of the best talking parrots. They are unusual in that males and females are colored differently. This is a bright red female. The males are green with a yellow beak.

Generally, the best talkers can mimic the different voices of the various members of the family. These include:

African Grey Parrots

Blue-fronted Amazons

Double Yellow-headed Amazons

Eclectus

Lories

Timneh Grey Parrots

Yellow-naped Amazons

Talkative Species With Clear Voices

There are probably a few surprises for you in this list. A Ring-necked Parakeet or a Blue-fronted Conure might be the right size for your household and cost less initially than a larger parrot. Male Budgies also can develop huge vocabularies. They do tend to have high, fast voices.

Both Severe and Hahn's Macaws, which are basically green birds with long tails and some other identifying markings, are often kept as companion birds and are good talkers. They are also both miniature Macaws. There are two sizes of Macaws. You may be most familiar with the large Red, Green and Blue Macaws, which are all the large Macaws. But there is another family of miniature Macaws. Many species of parrots can learn to talk clearly, including:

Bare-eyed Cockatoos

Budgies (male only)

Conures

Hahn's Macaws

Indian Ring-necked Parakeets

Moustache Parakeets

Severe Macaws

Triton Cockatoos

Yellow-collared Macaws

Potential for Talking

Although none of these species is especially noted for talking ability, people have members of the species who do talk. Rather than mimic human voice qualities,

Moustache Parakeets can often learn to talk, and their speech is usually clear. Their cousins, the Indian Ring-necked Parakeets, are good talkers, too.

many have their own parrot voices. Still, they get their point across! This may be an indication of the difference in capabilities of an individual bird or may reflect the environment in which these individuals live.

Blue and Gold Macaws

Brown-headed Parrots

Green-winged Macaws

Grey-cheeked Parakeets

Hawk-headed Parrots

Lilac-crowned Amazons

Meyer's Parrot

Moluccan Cockatoos

Orange-winged Amazons

Rose-breasted Cockatoos

Senegals

Spectacled Amazons

Umbrella cockatoos

A Lilac-crowned Amazon may learn to talk. Or she may not. Joanna is a vocal bird and knows a few words, in addition to being a sweet companion.

Mediocre Talkers

These species get an A for effort. Some try to talk, but results vary and clarity leaves something to be desired. They have other desirable traits, though, that make them good pets for some people.

Caiques

Cockatiels (males only)

Pionus

Sulphur-crested Cockatoos

SPECIES THAT DON'T TALK

As soon as we dare to publish this list, there are bound to be people who report having one of these birds who does talk. To the best of our knowledge, these birds do not talk.

Budgies (females)

Canaries

Cockatiels (females)

Grass Parakeets

Rosellas

TALKING BIRDS WHO ARE NOT PARROTS

There are other whole families of birds who can and do learn to talk. Most have special care requirements and/or cannot be kept legally. In the United States we cannot keep native species as pets. Starlings are not native birds, so they can be kept legally in the United States. Native Crows, Jays and Magpies cannot, but members of these bird families native to other countries may be kept by aviculturists and pet owners.

Crows

Jays

Magpies

Mynah Birds

Starlings

FOOTEDNESS

Earlier in this chapter we listed the various birds who are commonly kept as pets and their relative abilities to talk, but there are a few other factors in choosing a bird who's likely to talk. One of these is footedness. In particular, right-footedness. Just as people are right-handed or left-handed, birds, who grasp things with their feet, usually prefer one foot to the other.

As it turns out, African Grey Parrots who use their right foot are slightly more likely to be better talkers than those who use their left foot. The use of the right foot is important, because parrots appear to use the different halves of the brain in much the same way that humans do: We divide the control of different kinds of activities between the left and right hemispheres of the brain. The difference is not great among parrots, though, and Greys who use their left foot are still great talkers.

AGE

The age of your bird also makes a difference. African Greys don't learn words before they are about a year old. A few may pick up a few words or make tentative efforts to talk before that time, but most don't learn for the first year. Studies have shown that most parrots learn a few words before they are one year old and stop adding to the total number of words in their vocabulary by the time they are six or seven years old. While they can learn new words after the age of seven, they tend to eliminate old words and add new ones. So it is still possible to train an old parrot to speak new words, but only if some words are lost.

Like many generalities in bird training, this one has exceptions that bring it into question. The big exception here is Alex, the African Grey. In his 20s he's still learning new things from Dr. Irene Pepperberg. Throughout this book you will find that scientists are pushing out the things we thought we knew to make room for the refinements that come as we learn more. Alex is one of the main instruments in this process. He may be learning in his 20s simply because he has never had a chance to stop learning. Learning has become a way of life for him.

TO MIMIC OR NOT TO MIMIC

One of the things you will have to decide early on is which of the various kinds of talking responses you want from your bird. Do you want a bird who just mimics? This might be called the "Pete and Re-Pete" style of training. You say "Pete" and your bird repeats "Pete" back to you. This is the simplest form of training and response. Your bird is simply acting as an echo. If you have a bird who's on the list of birds that don't talk very well, you might want to consider this method.

On the other hand, you might want your bird to talk on cue. This means that you have a more complicated task. You will need to develop a formal method of training that involves rewards when your bird does what you want her to do. This is not quite as simple as repeating, because you need first to define what you want your bird to do.

For example, you might want your bird to say "Pete" in response to you saying "Bob." This isn't so tough. You just need to get the idea across to your bird by associating the names "Bob" and "Pete" until she starts to get it. When she comes close, you give her a reward.

The reward can be anything she values, including food, a toy or simple praise. Food as a reward has a few problems. One is that hungry birds find food to be a good reward, but birds who are not hungry may not find it to be interesting. There are many problems associated with keeping your bird hungry, not the least of which is the moral issue of starving your bird. In most cases simple praise is the best reward, if it works. You may also routinely train your bird just before feeding time, so your bird is hungry but not starving.

The third kind of training for talking is cognitive training. This involves training your parrot to use language in context—perhaps to look at something and give an answer to some question about the item. The question can be anything your parrot can answer, such as identification, color, material, shape or which is bigger, smaller, the same color, the same shape or how many are in the group. This requires fairly intense training, and is described in Chapter 10. The time commitment is enormous. At the level practiced by Alex and Pepperberg, work in this area has been groundbreaking, and there is room for a great deal more study.

SHE WON'T TALK

There are some problems with talking birds that people often don't anticipate. Two of these are that a bird won't talk or that she won't stop making noise. The first problem is the easier of the two to evaluate and to solve. If your bird is one of the species that doesn't talk, then there is no surprise (unless you bought her before you got this book).

One reason an individual bird of a talking species may not talk is that she's too old and hasn't been encouraged to talk. It may be too late to teach this mature bird to do much talking. There may also be health or nutrition problems, or habitat problems that leave your bird depressed and less likely to talk. To see if this is the case, take your bird to a veterinarian for a checkup. This means you will have to spend a little money and you will have to compile as much of the bird's history as possible to enable your veterinarian to make a better diagnosis. Then follow your veterinarian's advice.

If the bird is a member of the species that doesn't talk or she has a bad history and is too old to talk, you may want to either trade her for another bird or accept her shortcomings and enjoy her other strengths. Many non-talking birds *do* communicate in other ways, and they make outstanding companions.

Finding a suitable home, if need be, is a humane process if you do a little work. There are many people who have birds who are too loud for them and who might want to trade for your quieter bird. This improves the lot of the people you trade with and the lot of the bird who was too loud. Loud birds who aren't enjoyed by their owners tend to be put in dark places and left alone a lot or abused in other ways. Removing a bird from that kind of an environment is good for both the previous owner and the bird. Parrot adoption and placement centers probably have suitable birds available to you.

SHE WON'T STOP TALKING

Noisy birds are exactly the opposite problem from those who won't talk. Usually there's a behavior problem that needs to be corrected. Frequently the problem isn't with the bird, but with the environment or the owners. This does not mean you aren't a good person. It may just mean you're unintentionally rewarding your bird for behavior you don't really want.

At this point you have two choices: One is to seek the assistance of a bird behaviorist and another is to find a new home for your bird. We encourage you to work with a behaviorist rather than pass on a problem bird. Consider your commitment to your bird and work on behavior modification. You can teach a vocal bird to whisper or talk instead of scream, for example. You can learn not to give your parrot dramatic rewards that perpetuate screaming behavior, as well. Start reading about enrichment techniques so that a bored bird has something to do.

There are a number of bird behaviorists in the United States who are good at parrot behavior modification. Some of them even work effectively over the phone. Consult with a local avian veterinarian or bird club to find someone in your area.

DIANE GRINDOL

If you are looking for a companion bird and know that talking ability is important to you, look for a species that is noted for talking. This is a Male Eclectus, one of the species known to talk well—perhaps even to rival African Greys in their talking ability.

ASSESS YOUR GOALS

Have you looked carefully at why you want to share your life with a talking bird? There are both negative and positive aspects of living with a bird who talks. Are you looking for scintillating conversation, a being to nurture and instruct or do you want to put on shows? Your goals will influence your training method, the type of bird you choose and how rigorously you train your bird.

If you want a bird mainly as a companion and can take or leave talking ability, then you should research the attributes of different species of the companion birds you find to be beautiful, desirable and affordable. Some birds in this category may talk; some will talk whether you train them or not; and others will not learn to say human words. In any species of parrot, there are surprising individuals who are motivated to talk and will learn. You may get lucky. If you end up with the parrot of your dreams, based on other criteria, you will certainly feel lucky no matter what your bird does or doesn't say.

If you are looking for a companion bird and know that talking ability is important to you, you should look for a species that is noted for talking. In addition, you must make the commitment to do some training with your bird. You will be happiest if your bird learns some of the words you want her to know. If you do some training, you are more likely to get the results you expect. A long time ago someone told you that you get out of something what you put into it.

According to the latest surveys, the effort you put into training will make the most difference for your Cockatoo, Cockatiel, Amazon or Conure. A study by Peter Snyder, Ph.D., of the National Aviary in Pittsburgh, Pennsylvania, shows different responses to speech training among different species of companion birds. He found that training did not affect vocabulary size for Macaws, Parakeets (including Grey-cheeked Parakeets) and African Greys. These birds are so skilled at talking that they naturally talked when their basic needs were met. Training made some difference in the vocabularies of Amazons and Conures. Cockatoos (including Cockatiels) made the biggest improvements in their speech ability when trained.

Perhaps you have higher goals. Rather than have a bird who randomly picks up what is said in the household, you want her to know some simple greetings and be able to identify her food. In this case, you must commit yourself to talking to the bird about these things and instructing household members to use the same words when they talk to the bird. Do you want to say "bye," "good-bye" or "see you later!" Do you want to call grapes "fruit," "round fruit," "green fruit" or "grapes?" Be consistent. Our companion birds often learn words that help them get what they want for themselves. What do they want? Your company, some food or a little entertainment. Your bird may develop the habit of talking to herself when alone, because that brings you in to see her. She may do this to practice her vocabulary.

If you want your bird to talk when you have visitors, you may want to teach her a few words that she says consistently on cue. This does not represent comprehension but makes you look good! This method of training is used by professionals in bird shows and requires that you schedule training sessions and work consistently with your bird. Your bird may be shy of newcomers. A bird doesn't want much from visitors to your home who are not part of the "flock." To show off your bird's talking ability may mean a lot of work to train her to talk on cue.

Let's dream a little. It's possible you have visions of working with birds at a theme park or putting together your own show. You could be the next bird trainer on *The Tonight Show*, or you may entertain at neighborhood birthday parties. If you do plan to put on shows, you may have to obtain larger species to work with. They are simply more visible to audiences. You may want to get some training yourself from a workshop, tapes and videos, or schooling at an appropriate program. Maybe you should volunteer or get a job for a summer at a commercial bird show to see if you really like it. If you put on shows, you will want your bird(s) to be highly trained and dependable, so you'll need to spend a great deal of time training them and getting them used to performing in public, with its many distractions. This type of training is responsive: The bird responds to a hand or voice signal and does not necessarily understand what is being said. Still, don't underestimate the bonding and communication that can develop between trainers and their birds. It's a very special relationship.

Maybe you are in love with the work Dr. Irene Pepperberg has done with Alex, the African Grey. Your companion bird could be trained to understand some things about her environment and to respond appropriately, as Alex does. Most of us do not have eight hours a day and graduate students to help in bird training. But the concepts can be used to some extent with your bird. Results will vary, depending on the species you work with, your individual bird's interest and intelligence and your own ability to work consistently with another person to achieve success.

Did you think saying "Polly wanna cracker?" several times to your bird is what speech training is all about. Hardly! We're beyond that. We know that parrots have some cognition, that they have an instinct to fit into our household flock by learning its major vocalizations and that they have the ability to talk. Teaching your bird to talk can be structured in various ways, depending on the level of communication or response you want from your bird. You might have a better idea now about the options. Reading over the description of training methods in the chapters that follow will give you an even better idea how they fit with you, your lifestyle, your bird and your expectations.

POINTS TO REMEMBER

- You have the best chance of success in teaching a bird to talk if she is a species that usually learns to talk, and if she feels like a member of the family.
- Talking parrot species vary in the clarity of their speech. African Grey Parrots, Eclectus and Yellow-headed and Yellow-naped Amazons generally talk most clearly.
- Some softbill birds, such as Mynah Birds and Starlings, mimic words as well as parrots do.
- Studies show right-footed birds may be better talkers than left-footed birds.
- Young birds may not start talking right away, and most species may get to an age where they don't add to the total number of words they can say.
- You need to decide whether you want your bird to mimic words, to talk on cue or to have some understanding about what she is saying. This affects the kind of training you will do with your bird.

Chapter 7

Pretty Polly
Parrots Perfectly

If you have a pet Starling and teach him to say a few words, does he still "parrot"? This chapter is about the words we try to teach our birds to say. You may want your bird to talk because you've always wanted a talking bird. You may want the company. It can be comforting to have someone to talk to. If that someone is your pet parrot and he answers back, all the better! You may train your parrot to talk because he can. We don't have the same option with our pet goldfish or the family Golden Retriever. (Ooops! Isn't that a bird dog?) You may not even train your parrot to talk, but he might just chime into the family conversation anyway.

Whether or not you intend it, a parrot may learn to say the words you repeatedly say to him. This is called *parroting* or *mimicking* or *imitation*—imitation because it's not the real thing. It's not "language" or "talking" in any sense that implies understanding or give-and-take.

It's much easier to train a bird at this level than to teach him to associate words with an object or an action. It has also been the level of training that has most frequently been used to train parrots over the years. Bird lovers know their parrots are capable of more than just parroting, but only recently has it been accepted that we can train them to use this ability. As far as we know, parrots can label items and their properties, and can communicate desires, although they cannot discuss a topic in-depth. The choice is yours about which type of training to do.

IT'S ONLY NATURAL

Field biologists have noted that parrots vocalize most in the morning and evening. A flock of parrots will noisily greet the dawn, then fly off in pairs or small groups to forage for food, tend eggs or chicks, play and rest. Their vocalizations during

75

the day consist, in large part, of staying in touch with one another, courting, establishing territory and tending to reproduction or pairing. Then they congregate in larger groups in the evening, calling long and loud as the sun sets gloriously in tropical orange skies. Or when the lights go out, or when dusk settles in your living room, or after the late show on TV. It wasn't the field biologists who made those last observations. It was Diane, who learned from years of Cockatiel ownership and setting timers to create dawn and dusk in bird rooms.

The point is that birds are naturally more vocal in the evenings and mornings. When you choose a time to teach your bird to talk, why not make it when he naturally vocalizes?

IMITATION

One of the standard, old-fashioned ways to teach your bird to talk is to repeat over and over a word you want your bird to say. For this method, choose one word. Conventional wisdom says that birds find it easiest to pronounce words with hard vowel sounds, like *t* and *p*. That doesn't explain why parrots often learn to say "hello," except that they commonly hear that word and get it out somehow. Diane trained Inca, a Blue-headed Pionus Parrot, to say "I love you," because that's a nice way to start the day. Training a bird to imitate a word goes something like this:

Person: I love you.

Parrot: (silence)

Person: I love you

Parrot: Brrr awwwwk

Person: Honey, have you signed that note for Johnny's teacher?

Parrot: (click, click, click, wolf whistle)

Person: Johnny, finish your cornflakes. I love you.

Parrot: (silence)

Person: I love you.

Parrot: Eyeeee awwwk awk

(Person leaves for work. Door shuts.)

Parrot: Luv yooooouu.

Even when parrots are not repeating a word to you, they are listening. There is also a learning stage in the training process when a parrot usually mumbles the intonation of what he's learning to say, or mumbles it or makes mistakes in pronunciation. A bird also often practices what he's learning, saying the word softly to himself. You should generously praise any attempt at speech at first, and gradually work up to rewarding only clearly spoken words or phrases.

The scenario we just described happens repeatedly, over months, as you are teaching a bird to mimic. It may take a day to a year for your bird to learn a new word. Some of this will depend on your bird's age and what species he is. It might also depend on whether or not your bird feels he's a part of your human flock and has a reason to learn what he perceives as your flock contact calls. It also depends on whether your bird is getting anything out of vocalizing. You can give him something to vocalize about by praising him, and reinforcing what he says by answering his vocalizations. Repeat the word he said, or answer with another, appropriate word.

We want to take a moment to reiterate this aspect of training. When you respond appropriately to your parrot for what he is saying, he is more likely to continue to try to say the word you want to teach. Your parrot is looking for results, and he instinctively wants to learn his flock's language.

Different species learn at different rates. People who raise both African Grey and Amazon Parrots remark that the Amazons learn to talk at a young age. The Greys tend to absorb information but actually talk at a later age. It might take a year for a Grey to say his first word, even though he has been listening all that time. Other birds progress through whistling or mumbling before they say a word clearly.

Parrots are natural performers and will learn to sing as well as talk. If your parrot isn't responding to words you repeat for him, try singing the words. Or try teaching your parrot a song. Many parrots can sing scales or a few bars of opera. Cockatiels are expert whistlers. Consider teaching a male Cockatiel, African Parrot, Starling or Mynah to whistle a few tunes.

Rewards for your parrot when he says a word can range from effusive praise to a highly desirable treat, like a small hulled seed, half a grape or another of your bird's favorite things. Other desirable rewards include a tickle, time to cuddle or a

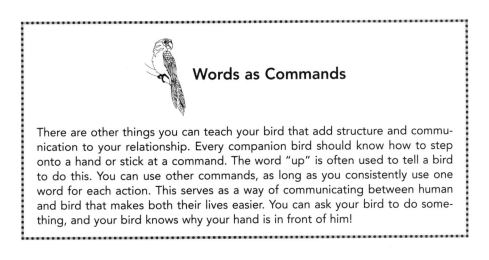

Words as Commands

There are other things you can teach your bird that add structure and communication to your relationship. Every companion bird should know how to step onto a hand or stick at a command. The word "up" is often used to tell a bird to do this. You can use other commands, as long as you consistently use one word for each action. This serves as a way of communicating between human and bird that makes both their lives easier. You can ask your bird to do something, and your bird knows why your hand is in front of him!

DIANE GRINDOL/COURTESY FEATHERED FOLLIES, LAFAYETTE, CALIFORNIA

Having a talking bird like this Ducorps Cockatoo can be a joy. Many talking birds are vocal birds, however. Be prepared for high-decibel natural calls and endless repetition of favorite words.

scratch. You can also associate a praise word with desired behavior, such as the word "good." A tip for teaching a bird words is to limit the number of things you expect him to learn. Teach him one word or phrase at a time. You might also consider starting with simple words. Start out with a one- or two-syllable word, then work up to longer words or a phrase.

You won't be intentionally teaching your talking parrot all of the words he learns. Parrots learn words that people say with expression. Often the unsolicited words a parrot learns are expletives expressed with emotion or body functions to which a family responds (use your imagination here!). Another category of words parrots pick up, perhaps because of the volume and expression and frequency with which we use them, is people calling one another. A friend's Macaw, who lived in a family with two teenaged girls, learned to say "It's not fair!" When teaching your bird, no matter what word you choose to teach, say it with expression and emotion.

This method of teaching your bird to talk is very casual. You simply say a word quite often, say it expressively and clearly, and repeat it to your bird whenever you're around him. There are no formal lessons involved.

People often report that they get tired of saying the word they are trying to teach a bird. You might reinforce lessons by playing a recording of the word between live lessons. Cassettes from answering machines or continuous loop tapes can be used to repeatedly play a word, or you could use a digital device or even an interactive or multimedia computer program to help you out while training.

You can see how well this method of parroting works if you walk into any pet store that has birds. There's a good chance the store bird says "hello" and his name, along with a few other phrases. He learned them from casual interaction with the public and his owner. Innumerable companion birds say at least a few words. The birds parrot a word, and amuse their owners or get a response. The response reinforces their use of the word. Communication and cognition are not a part of this method.

THE GOOD AND THE BAD

Once your birds understands the idea of repeating words, it's possible he will often repeat the words he knows. He's looking for a treat or reward, some praise or some feedback. There is both a downside and an upside to having a bird who says a few words. He does say them. He says them over and over. He says them all day. He uses the words. He repeats them. He mimics them. He whispers them. He yells them. It goes on and on. That's the downside.

The upside is that your bird is not screaming or trying to attract your attention in some other way. If you are making an effort to teach your bird certain words, and he's learning them, you are beginning to have some control over what your bird says. You know that if your bird is a talkative soul, he would learn something anyway! He would choose his own vocabulary from household noises and what the household says in excited tones. He might learn words you don't want him to say. Even with your patient lessons, this still might happen.

SIMON SAYS

One way to get your bird's attention as you are working with him is to mirror the bird's own calls. Why should this be a one-way relationship? You fully expect your parrot to imitate some of the vocalizations you make. Why not make this a cooperative adventure? There are probably a few bird calls you can approximate and use as contact calls to stay in touch with your bird as you work around the house.

This also teaches your bird to pay attention to what you say and to listen to your vocalizations. If you imitate his calls, those are familiar sounds to the bird—well, maybe, depending on how good a mimic you are! Even the very act of mimicking another species might give you some insight into what your bird is going through, and might inspire you to have more patience or to present your lessons differently or more often.

If your bird is having trouble with a particular sound, create ways for him to hear the difference. If "you're cute" comes out "you're cupe," say the words "cut" and "cup" very clearly for the bird, or use other examples. You may also try speaking to him in a voice that is close to his natural call. For example, use a high voice for a Budgie and a lower and slower one for an Eclectus.

Your bird may show his interest in talking by his actions. Do his pupils dilate and contract, does he stand up tall or stretch out his neck, or is he paying very close attention to everything that you are doing and saying? He's interested!

ASSOCIATING WORDS WITH ACTIONS OR OBJECTS

If you've lived with your parrot for a while now, you've probably noticed that he is an intelligent being. If you want him to go beyond merely mimicking words at random, consider teaching him the association between words, actions or objects. This way you can teach him to greet you when you come home, or to have a vocal interaction when you leave the house. Parrots can learn to name objects. They are especially motivated by food and toys, and by connecting with the members of their household flock, but there are infinite possibilities for using this training.

While training a parrot to parrot can be accomplished casually or with a couple of lessons a day, training him to make associations involves talking to your bird as though he is a young child. This is constant, you can probably make it a habit, and you'll probably have a few visitors to your house who think you're crazy! Then they'll think *they* are the ones who are crazy when they hear your bird ask for "apple" or "nut" or use other words intelligently.

Parrots can learn the difference between people in the household, and are able to learn the names of the family pets. They learn to call children and pets, as well as adult members of the family, whom they may refer to as "Mom" or "Dad." Parrots have learned to identify the weather and understand the concept of days of the week. Your commitment to your parrot's schooling may not be that high, but your parrot has that level of intelligence!

If your parrot doesn't reach this level of language use, don't despair. There are many different species of parrots, and they probably have different levels of intelligence. There is also probably a difference in intelligence among individuals within a species. Since we don't have Parrot Intelligent Quotient (P.I.Q.) tests yet, we can't figure out how responsive your parrot will be. It's possible that parrots

DIANE GRINDOL

This White-eyed Conure, Charlie, is a loquacious member of his household. He bawdily greets visitors and sends them on their way again with "good-bye." Talking parrots often also learn the names of the people and pets who make up their surrogate flock.

learn fastest at a young age, as well, when in the wild they would be learning survival skills and calls from their parents and flock. None of this has been studied with either wild parrots or with parrots in our homes; what we know comes from observations by parrot owners and a scant knowledge about some species of parrots in the wild.

Besides the difference between individual parrots and parrot species, you must decide about your level of commitment to training a talking parrot. There are some things a parrot will pick up on his own, and he may also learn words you say frequently—which seem to be a sort of flock contact call to the bird. Your bird could acquire this level of mimicry on his own without any particular training. Consistency and diligence are often required to reach the next level of training, in which the parrot can identify actions and objects.

TALK THE TALK AND WALK THE WALK

When you leave the house, you probably say good-bye to anyone who is remaining at home. When you come home, chances are you greet the rest of your family. With a parrot in the family—and he *is* a member of the family—you can do the same and get a verbal response. You will need to be very consistent in your greetings and speak clearly if you want your parrot to learn to associate your words with your actions.

Parrots are observant animals. You can't be sure what their cue is that you are leaving. People report that some parrots use the appearance of a coat or car keys to know that you are leaving, and say an appropriate phrase at that time. Others wait for the verbal "good-bye" from their human companions and respond to it.

Any greeting can be said with varying amounts of enthusiasm and with inflections on different parts of a word to create your own style of greeting. You could make your greeting singsong or long and drawn out or say it in a high or deep or "baby talk" voice.

Other actions your bird will recognize and you can develop communications about include entering the room, leaving the room, giving scratches or cuddles, taking a shower, preparing or eating food and time for a sing-along. What could you say, and say consistently, that identify these activities? Sometimes bird training challenges your creativity!

Use a consistent greeting when entering and leaving a room, as Gerry Stewart models here. It's very possible your talking bird will pick up your greeting and learn to use it appropriately.

Name foods for your bird. He can learn how to label things correctly, such as the fruits and vegetables pictured here. Of course you have to ask yourself, "Do I want a bird who can ask for what he wants?"

FOOD

One of the daily interactions we have with our birds is feeding them and eating, ourselves. There are many opportunities to teach your bird the names of foods or some table manners. An interaction with your bird about food might go like this:

> Person: Look, Sydney, I have a grape here. What a big, nice juicy grape. I like grapes, do you like grapes. Mmmmm mmm grape!
>
> Parrot: (Takes the grape.)

In time, you hope that your bird gets the idea that this fruit is called a grape. You also hope your bird gets the idea that there is a *particular* kind of fruit called grape. Diane knows a Macaw for whom all food is "apple," and he uses that label for any food. Sometimes a bird ends up creating his own word for food, or for a particular food.

THINGS

Parrots love their toys and are observant about their surroundings. Naming things is a relatively simple language concept you might try with your bird. There's probably more motivation for your parrot to learn to name things he can hold and chew up, or things that are important to him. You might have a harder time teaching "lamp" or "bulletin board" than "toy" or "chewy" or "ladder." Try to remember to

The parrot in this family learned to call and give commands to Mandy the Boston Terrier. Mandy benefited when he threw her treats!

use the same word consistently for each object, and to talk about the thing, whatever it is, so that the word appears often in your conversation. Remember to show enthusiasm when saying a word.

Since parrots see in color, you may also teach your parrot to identify colors. The more information you put into your verbalization about an object, the more the parrot will get out of it. You can train your parrot to recognize and identify objects and colors, just like Alex the African Grey, but associating things with their name, as presented in this chapter, is an informal way to work with your bird (alone if need be) and get results.

PEOPLE

Parrots can identify the different members of their flock, and will readily learn the names of everyone in your family if you make any effort at all to help them do so. Use your name, the names of family and friends and, of course, the parrot's name when speaking with him or when introducing him to people. Quite often names are learned in the context of our human contact calls, with the loud and enthusiastic call to dinner by mom or the various calls between spouses, siblings or housemates.

Parrots also learn household protocol. Diane knows a talkative Blue and Gold Macaw who yells "hello" and "come in" to people who come to the door and who calls family members when the phone rings.

PETS

The family pets are every bit as much a part of a bird's flock as his human companions. Quite often parrots, seeing family members call the dog by name and the dog appearing, learn a dog's name. More than a few parrots have kept dogs as their personal pets, as well, and have learned to throw food for the dog to eat or to give her obedience commands.

Any interaction between pets should be supervised. A Macaw Diane knows threw treats to the family dog, who never learned the parrot was enticing her close enough to his cage to take a nip at her nose. Not all parrot play is loving.

DIANE GRINDOL

Many parrots learn to call the family cat or to say "Here kitty, kitty."

HOME SCHOOLING IS IN VOGUE FOR PARROTS

People with the most aware and responsive parrots have learned to talk to their parrot almost continuously and intelligently. Verbal people seem more likely to have verbal parrots. When Diane sold male Cockatiels to families who kept only that bird as a pet and talked to him often, the Cockatiels usually learned to talk. This is despite the fact that Cockatiels, in general, can't be counted on to talk (although they pick up whistles readily). Many more Cockatiels from the same parents did not talk. The difference was the family situation and the amount of time spent talking with the bird.

Actually schooling your parrot to speak is a lot like talking to a small child. When children are babies they only babble or make eye contact, but we talk to them anyway and identify things for them. If you start talking to your parrot intelligently, or using baby talk with him, you won't get much intelligible response at first. It's possible your parrot will learn the meaning of several phrases over time and will learn to say a few of them, if he's inclined to verbalizations.

Even if your parrot never learns to say a word, your communication with him can be enhanced by speaking with him and paying attention to his reaction to what you're saying. Your parrot may not learn to say "bath time," for example, but may understand the term and get obviously excited about the possibility of taking a shower and the chance to groom those glorious feathers!

Some of the training aids you may consider include allowing your parrot to watch television shows made for children. These shows usually include a lot of repetition, music and colorful images—all things your parrot will enjoy. If he picks up some counting skills or learns to identify colors, you wouldn't mind.

If you want your parrot to associate words with either actions or objects, you don't want him to listen to a recording of one word over and over, or to learn too many words that are not in context. Therefore, most of the training responsibility falls on you and your interactions with the bird.

You can't expect to carry on long and meaningful conversations with your parrot, even if he does exceptionally well in learning to associate words with actions or objects. Nor will every phrase coming out of your bird's beak be something correct or appropriate. Parrots practice vocalizations to perfect them, saying a word to themselves quietly, or mixing up many vocalizations and prattling on to make a kind of parrot music. There are too many instances of parrots using words appropriately, however, to consign their chatter to mimicry.

GOOD BIRD!

There are many possible ways for a bird to respond to talking lessons:

- Your bird learns to say the word you are teaching him.
- Your bird says another word that sounds similar but is not the word you are teaching him.
- Your bird starts to learn many other words that are said regularly in the household, but not the word or phrase you are teaching him.
- Your bird turns words into garbled speech or whistles.
- Your bird does not learn to talk.
- You love your bird no matter what.

While you're giving lessons, be sure to appreciate your bird's beauty and personality, as well as the communication that is taking place between the two of you. Count this time as all-important socialization time that you owe your companion bird, a social creature. Your bird may or may not learn to talk, but is still an extraordinary companion who can be appreciated for his many qualities.

POINTS TO REMEMBER

- You can teach a bird to mimic a word you say often, clearly and with enthusiasm.
- Birds are most vocal in the mornings and evenings, so train your bird at those times, if possible.
- A bird can learn to respond verbally to your comings and goings.
- A parrot's vocalizations are not conversations.
- Favorite words for a parrot to learn are the names of food, toys, people and pets.
- School environments and television shows can be helpful tools for teaching words to a bird.
- There's no guarantee any bird or any species of bird will learn to talk; love your bird no matter what.

Chapter  *8*

Before You Start Talking Lessons

Whether you have been a bird owner for a long time or only recently were smitten, you have probably been to a theme park or zoo in your life. These places often have bird shows. Many species come out and perform tricks, act out a theme or play, or simply show off some of their natural ability. Usually a talking bird is included in the program, at least to say "hello!" It would ruin everyone's day if the bird with this part could not say "hello" on cue. Contrast this with your own attempts to show off your parrot's abilities to friends. Chances are good your own parrot vocalizes when *she* wants to, not necessarily when *you* want her to say something.

TRICK TRAINING

Most bird trainers use cues and rewards to teach a bird to perform a behavior when asked. If you want your bird to talk on cue, for any reason, you may wish to use this method. It will help you show off your bird for company, put on performances for your bird club or local parties or . . . who knows? You may start a new career. (If you do have aspirations for a show career, the choice of species you train may become important. There are many Conures, Cockatiels, Lovebirds and other smaller species who can learn tricks. However, it is usually difficult for these smaller birds to be seen by an audience.)

Using the cue and reward method, a bird responds to a hand signal, verbal signal or cue, and knows she gets rewarded for saying a certain word. There is no implied understanding by the bird of what she is saying. Clever show people usually make up a dialogue or skit to go along with the bird's vocalization, so it seems as if the bird is counting or answering a query. There's nothing wrong with such trick training.

DIANE GRINDOL

Think about your goals in trick training your bird. If you want to put on shows for an audience, a larger species such as this Yellow-naped Amazon Parrot is appropriate. If you are doing training for your own enjoyment and your bird's stimulation, a smaller Conure or Cockatiel is fine.

Cues do enable parrots to have some level of communication with their trainers, which fosters communication on other levels. Any kind of training is attention, which is appreciated by vocal, social parrots. Parrots with lots of energy and quick minds will usually enjoy the attention they get for performing; some are quite the hams, gloating in an audience's applause. Of course, most parrots enjoy their food rewards!

While many parrots are natural clowns and like showing off, if your particular bird does not like showing off, do not force her. Use another training method with that bird, or train a different bird to perform on cue.

LOCATION, LOCATION, LOCATION

Trick training is a more disciplined training than mimicry. You will need to set up a schedule for training, a training area, a bridge and a reward. You will have the best success with your training if you choose a relatively quiet training area free from distractions. Distractions qualify if they are distracting to either you or your bird. What are some distractions?

Distractions to Bird	Distractions to Trainer
Everyday Items	**Everyday Items**
Cage	Bed
Food dishes	Dishes need washing
Toys	New gadget or video game
Food	Food
Seeds	Brownies
Chicken	Pizza
Treat	Cookies
Breakfast	Breakfast
Flying Objects Overhead	**Unidentified Flying Objects**
Ceiling fan	Jet
Balloon	Abduction by aliens
Favorite Flock Members	**Family or Friends**
Spouse	Spouse
Child	Child
Dog or cat	Dog or cat
Other parrot	Friend
Enticing Objects	**Enticing Objects**
Balls	Stereo
Jewelry	Jewelry
Mirror	Television
Noises	**Noises**
Door slamming	Appliance running
Music	Music
Loud noises	Ambulance or fire truck siren
Microwave beeping	Microwave beeping
Telephone	Telephone
Attention Deficit	**Attention Deficit**
Distraction	Bills
Mirror	Relationship troubles
Chewing	Scheduling
Feather plucking	Worrying
Sex	**Sex**
Mate	Significant other
Favorite person	In the mood
Talking	**Talking**
Conversation	"Mommmmm!"
Radio	Conversations you can only partially hear
Music	Conversations you can't hear but are sure are about you
Teasing	Teasing

Obviously, no location is absolutely perfect. You need to do the best you can. Often, the training location most suitable for talking is a T-stand placed on the kitchen table. If your phone and too many bells and beepers, not to mention goodies, are located in that training area, try a quiet bedroom or the family room. The bathroom is relatively free of distractions, except for the occasional knock on the door.

Concentrate on the task at hand, be aware of your parrot's mood and willingness to work and listen carefully to what she is saying. You don't want to miss a correct response!

THE STAND

You could leave your parrot loose on a table or countertop, but you will have the most control and her undivided attention if she's sitting on a T-stand. A T-stand consists of a flat base and an upright pole with a perch fastened to it perpendicular to the pole. This forms a T shape, hence the name.

You will also be able to pay closer attention to your parrot if she is standing still. You will want to maintain eye contact with your parrot. Many species of parrots pin their eyes, or rapidly dilate and contract their pupils when talking, and you want to watch for this from a close vantage point.

If you or one of your family members works with wood, you can make a T-stand. There are also many styles available from bird supply companies, at bird stores, in bird catalogs and from companies who advertise in companion bird magazines. These range from portable stands to tall stands to tabletop versions. Some are also playgyms, with ladders and perches of various heights and places to hang toys. Remember to minimize distractions during lessons!

It's not necessary to have a formal or professionally made T-stand or perch for speech training. Alex the African Grey has done much of his work standing on the back of a standard metal folding chair. Diane tied a branch onto a footstool for Aztec the Blue-headed Pionus to stand on when he helped write this book. What's important is that you and your parrot recognize that place as one where training takes place. Much like setting up a desk and light to do homework, you are creating a work environment for you and your parrot.

Trick Training by Another Name

Operant conditioning is the technical term for training an animal to perform an action by offering her a reward. The behavior the animal then learns is called the *conditioned response*. In the vernacular, we refer to this method as *trick training*.

DIANE GRINDOL

A commercially made T-stand like this one Aztec is on, or some other perch for your bird, is good for speech training. Your bird will know it's time to work when she's on her stand.

REWARDS

As we've mentioned before, parrots vocalize to get a response. We see this with parrots who scream—one of the less welcome vocalizations from our feathered companions. When your parrot first started to scream, chances are good that her human companion either ran in to see what she wanted, or ran in talking excitedly or started scolding her. All of these actions are rewards to a parrot. She got company and you put on a good show in response to her screaming. Chances are, this scenario was repeated over and over, and the parrot effectively trained her human to provide what *she* wanted. When a parrot is trained to do what *we* want, when we want it done, she has to be very well motivated!

Bird trainers use food as a reward, which is one of the things a parrot cares about. For this reason, you probably want to schedule training sessions before feeding your parrot. Your bird will then be especially motivated to receive the treat/reward you have to offer. If you will be training in the morning, don't offer the bird her soft foods until you have worked on training. If you train in the evening, consider taking food bowls out of the cage one to four hours before the training session. Don't starve your bird, just work around the times she is most hungry. It is normal for wild birds to forage twice a day, in the morning and evening. Some bird keepers follow that schedule regularly, feeding their birds twice a day.

It's not difficult to find a food that Aztec, a Blue-headed Pionus, thinks is good to eat. For trick training, a smaller piece of this cracker, a piece of grated cheese or a half-hulled sunflower seed would work better. Small, quick-to-eat treats are best.

This doesn't mean your bird will only work for food! There are three things that parrots want. These three things are their joy in life, the reasons they scream and their best rewards for good behavior. The three things parrots want are food, attention and drama in the form of excitement and loud noise. Food, attention and drama.

Once your bird learns to learn, she will probably pick up new phrases or new trick behaviors quickly. She may even perform them for fun. As a trainer, however, you want to be sure that your bird will perform on cue, when the show's on. Having a cue-response system with a food reward is motivating for your bird. When it's show time, you can't wait until your bird is in the mood to perform.

The Most Rewarding Foods

Because the food reward is obviously an important part of trick training, it is important to choose a food your parrot likes. There are other considerations, as well. Whatever food you choose should be small enough for the parrot to eat it quickly. If you are feeding peanuts, cut them in half. Similarly, cut toast into cubes or break up crackers for rewards. If you offer small seeds, the bird may eat them quickly, but they leave a mess to clean up. Feeding hulled seed or curls of grated cheese avoids some of the mess. If you are worried about the high fat, and therefore high calorie, content of some of these foods, offer pieces of apple or half grapes.

POSSIBLE FOOD REWARDS

Apple	Meat, cooked
Baby food	Melon
Banana	Millet seed
Broccoli	Oatmeal
Cabbage	Papaya
Cantaloupe	Pasta, cooked or raw
Carrot	Peanuts, shelled
Celery	Popcorn
Cheese, grated	Pumpkin seeds
Cole slaw	Spices (anise seed, cumin, pepper flakes)
Cornflakes	
Cottage cheese	Sunflower seeds, shelled
Crackers	Toast cubes
Egg, hard cooked	Toasted oat cereal
Fish, baked	Walnuts
Granola	Yogurt
Grapes	

If you've thought hard and can't think of a single treat food your parrot likes that comes in small pieces, then you need to create a desire for a particular treat. Do this by offering your parrot a small amount of a treat food with her regular food each day. Give her some time to get used to this routine. When you can see that the parrot eats the treat food before her regular food, do not offer the treat food at meals. Instead, use it as a food reward in training sessions.

THE BRIDGE

In training parlance, the *bridge* is a specific sound that bridges the moment when the parrot performs a correct behavior and the moment the parrot actually receives a reward. It is the promise of a reward. Once the bridge acknowledges that a desired behavior was performed, the actual reward can come later. The sound means, "*This* is what is right, now you will get a reward."

Why do you need a bridge? It takes a while to fish a food treat out of a pocket and get it to your parrot, but a bridge can occur exactly as the correct behavior is happening.

DIANE GRINDOL

This Mitred Conure likes millet. That's probably a good treat to use when training her, but a reward would be one seed at a time, not a whole millet spray!

The bridge can be a clicker sound or any other sound, including a word. When you finally give a performance to a group, you will want it to sound natural. A word such as "good" is appropriate.

THE CUE FOR TALKING ON CUE

The last element you will need to think about when training your bird to talk on cue is the sign or word that you will use as a cue. This will be different for each word or phrase you teach your bird. The important thing about a cue is that it is consistent, so deciding on your first one or two will be helpful.

A cue can be either visual or verbal. Another decision! You may wish to use both a verbal and visual cue at first, then gradually change to just one of the cues.

Hand Signals

Visual cues are usually hand signals. Most often you are working closely with a trained bird and can hold your hand in different positions that are meaningful to your bird but do not distract an audience.

You could also use other parts of your body to cue a behavior. For example, you could train your bird to whisper in your ear when you hold a hand cupped over your ear. Or your bird could throw a mock tantrum if you cross your arms and pout. Make up something for your bird to say when you cup your hand over your eye, pretending to see something far away. What could she say when you hold a finger to your lips? Obviously, the possibilities are endless!

To get some other ideas for hand signals, watch the umpire in a baseball game or look up the signs used in American Sign Language.

TRAINING SESSIONS

You will want to have training sessions regularly. These can last as long as your parrot stays focused on the training. That, of course, varies. It may be as little as 10 minutes or as much as half an hour. You can have more than one training session in a day, if you would like to reinforce the day's lesson and progress faster.

Before you have your first session, you should have thought of a time and location that are going to work for both of you. Preferably this is when your bird has not eaten for a couple hours, or overnight, and it's a time of day you can consistently plan to interact with your bird. Your location is one that is relatively free of distractions for both of you at the time you plan to use it. You have decided on each of these elements of training:

T-stand or perch

Cue

Desired response

Bridge

Treats

Remember, as you train, to end every session on a positive note. End with a behavior your parrot can do well, so she can receive her praise and reward.

THE PET BIRD

With some luck, you have noticed that your bird is interested in talking, or that she is already picking up a few words and sounds just by being in your household. At the very least, she's a species that is known to be talkative, or she's a vocal bird—even if she's vocal but not producing words!

Now you want to direct her learning to specific words. You also want to be able to cue your bird to give a verbal response when you ask her to, not just when the bird wants something.

Is your bird healthy? If she is getting regular veterinary care, showers, socialization and a good diet, you probably are ready to start training. If you need to work on any of these or schedule a trip to the avian veterinarian, take care of your bird's health before embarking on training.

Is your bird comfortable in a variety of situations? If you do intend to perform on some level with your bird, you will want to start getting her used to being around lots of people. If you will mainly show off to visitors at home, make sure your bird meets people in your home and has a chance to settle down and observe them. If possible, invite people over with different hair styles and facial types. If you don't know people with these things, patronize a costume store or stock up at Halloween.

EXPOSE A SOCIALIZED BIRD TO THESE

Applause	Hair colors (various)
Bald heads	Hats
Baseball caps	Jewelry
Big hair	Mustaches
Children	Music
Earrings	Scarves
Glasses	

Children act differently from adults (most of the time), so it would be a good idea to introduce your avian companion to a few of the younger members of the human race. If you know you want to perform for crowds of people, take your bird to places where there are crowds of people. Do so at first with your parrot in a cage. If she has clipped wings and you get permission from an understanding crowd, let the bird sit on a tall T-stand during an event where there are quite a few people present. You could practice at a bird club, a bird seminar or a classroom, for example. Before your bird performs in public, she needs to get used to simply being in public. The public does some interesting things when it congregates. People clap, have moments of silence, a loudspeaker often comes on. So many distractions. You thought finding a training location was difficult!

Even if the "public" is just in your living room, you need to get your parrot used to working around distractions. If someone wants to meet your companion parrot, you should safely engage the bird's head, and allow a stranger to pat her

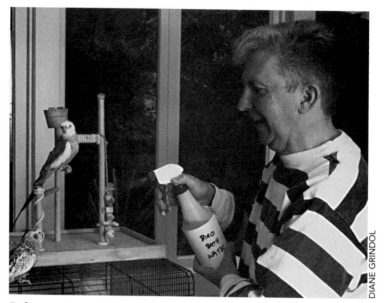

Before training can be effective, make sure your bird's needs are being met. This includes frequent showers.

If your bird doesn't like to be sprayed with water to bathe, consider alternative ways to keep her feathers healthy. This African Grey likes to "leaf bathe" in wet romaine lettuce.

> ### Where to Learn More
>
> Video series about trick training parrots
>
> Tani and Her Fantastic Performing Parrots
> Robar Productions
> 3767 S. 194th
> Seattle, WA 98188
> www.parrottricktraining.com
>
> Video series about training birds
>
> The Positive Approach to Parrots as Pets by Steve Martin
> (800) 834-9639
> www.naturalencounters.com/home.html
>
> Clicker Training for Birds
> www.geocities.com/Heartland/Acres/9154/
>
> Avian Publications
> 6380 Monroe Street NE
> Minneapolis, MN 55432
> www.avianpublications.com

back gently. If you are not even comfortable with this much interaction, make it known. Whole classrooms of children can understand that a bird can be looked at but not touched. It's often advisable to inform the uninitiated to move slowly around a bird.

THE PET HUMAN

Your bird may have you pretty well trained now to provide her with attention, snacks and entertainment. You're going to turn the tables on her and train the bird to do something that pleases you. Keep in mind that above all, you should both have fun. This mind-set will serve you well and will help to make training fun for your bird, too.

The other essential quality you will need plenty of in training sessions is patience. You will be repeating lessons over and over. You will be waiting for your bird to respond. You will repeat commands. There will be days when your bird is not interested. There will be days when you are not interested.

There will also be breakthrough moments when your bird understands exactly what you are trying to do and starts to work with you. I hope this happens early in the training process for the two of you.

Besides patience, patience and more patience, you'll also want to have discipline. You will need to train your bird at least daily, and may wish to have a couple of short lessons each day. Things will sometimes go well, and sometimes it will seem like there's not much learning going on. Remember that birds often listen and practice on their own before they say something. Don't give up in a few lessons if you do indeed have your bird's attention. There might just be some work going on behind the scenes!

You'll need ready access to your sense of humor, as well. This will enable you to see all the delight and joy inherent in training your bird. If you're open to it, your parrot will make you laugh—we promise. If you can keep your sense of humor, have fun and enjoy interacting with your bird, then it will all be worthwhile. Even if you're never center stage at a theme park, you've crossed the line into interspecies communication, and this will enrich your life.

POINTS TO REMEMBER

- You can use trick training techniques to teach a bird to consistently perform a behavior on cue.
- You should establish a regular time and location for training sessions.
- A cue can be a hand signal or a verbal command.
- A bridge is a verbal signal, such as the word "good" or a sound from a clicker, that tells birds they are doing the right thing and will be rewarded.
- Treats for correct responses should be small and should be desirable to the bird!
- Patience, diligence, consistency and a sense of humor are required of a bird trainer.

Chapter 9

Parrots Jump Into the Conversation

Parrots are learning from you, whether you teach them or not. Many are picking up on your actions and associating them with words, or noticing how they can get a response from you. No one tries to teach their parrot to imitate the telephone ringing, but when parrots figure out you come running at that sound, they often do imitate it! They take things even further sometimes, calling the resident teenager or family pet by name, or holding up their human companion's half of a conversation.

Parrots using appropriate language to communicate is being studied by Dr. Irene Pepperberg and The Alex Foundation. This has led to improved training techniques for those who wish to teach their companion birds some words and labels for objects. It has also led to increased recognition by the scientific community that parrots are intelligent animals capable of communicating on some level. That level is turning out to be fairly high, equivalent to the intelligence level of chimpanzees and dolphins.

To parrot owners, this has been no real surprise, although it's nice to confirm those suspicions in a public forum. Parrot owners, coexisting with numerous species, have noted that their birds use language appropriately. Responses to a survey about parrot language ability yielded many examples, which we will share with you here.

Parrots often learn to imitate the telephone and the microwave, which is no surprise. Both of those appliances cause people to run to them and give them attention. Parrots learn fast. (This is Gerry Stewart and Aztec, the Blue-headed Pionus.)

NEVER A DULL MOMENT! LIVING WITH TALKING PARROTS

This story comes from Maggie of the Risen Phoenix Aviary.

My favorite story is about a proven pair of Vosmaeri Eclectus that we got last summer. All through their quarantine we could hear them talking, but it was always soft enough that we couldn't make out the words. We heard them meowing like a cat, and a number of other things, but that was it. Eclectus are known to be good talkers, but it's also been our experience that they tend to talk more softly than Macaws, for instance.

We had our avian vet out to do well-bird checks on our birds. A poop sample was taken from each cage, and there were a number of birds that I wanted blood testing done on, since they were newer. Jack and Jackie, the new Eclectus, were on that list. We took out Jackie, who was not happy, needless to say, and was being very vocal in her protests. The vet assistant was holding on to her while the vet prepared to get a blood sample. Jack was still in his cage no more than 18 to 24 inches from us, watching intently. All of a sudden, Jackie paused for breath and all three of us heard and saw Jack, looking intently at his mate, shaking his head in a concerned manner saying, "Pray to God, say your prayers. Pray to God, say your prayers." The vet assistant almost dropped the bird!

When my Nape knows that I am preparing dinner, if I leave the kitchen and come back to where he is, he will keep repeating, "I want some." One day I was cooking something that I had to keep getting up to stir. He kept telling me "I want some," and I kept telling him, "It's not finished, Parrot . . . you have to wait." Again, I went to the kitchen, and came back empty handed, and he said, "I want some, I want some, I'm starving!!! Ohhhhhhh . . . I'm starving!"

Sue of Olympia, Washington, lives with a loquacious Timneh named Joel. He asks "Ready to go to work today?" as well as "Ready for breakfast? Ready for dinner?" When it comes to his own snacks, Joel can say that he would like an apple, orange, grape, cookie, cracker or chip. Joel is also into singing. He sings "Happy Birthday," which, of course, is appropriate on some days of the year! He also sings "We're off to see the Wizard, the wonderful Wizard of Oz."

GREYS KEEP THE CONVERSATION MOVING

Diane in Virginia says about African Grey, Meggie, "Every morning she uses the phrase 'Want some birdie bread,' which means she wants breakfast. The next phrase most often used is 'Don't you dare,' which means she is not happy with the current situation. She learned this because one day I noticed her body language indicated she might bite, and I said, 'Don't you dare!' She picked it up right away. If she wants to come upstairs she will say 'Wanna go upstairs' and then yell 'Diane.' 'Bye, bye, see ya later' is used every time a door opens to go outside. If you go over to her cage to tell her bye-bye, she will wave with her foot then say 'Wanna peanut, be back.'"

Carol of Colorado says this about her verbose nine-year-old African Grey: "When he was about eight months old, I'd gone to the doctor for an infected finger and came home with a white bandaged finger. The bird kept asking and asking, 'What are you doing? What are you doing?' Suddenly I realized he kept

DIANE GRINDOL

African Grey Parrots are renowned talkers. We've included many stories from people about their companion Grey Parrots.

looking at my finger and was asking what was wrong the only way he knew how. I explained I had a 'yow' but I was okay, and the questions abruptly stopped. I guess that's when the contextual speech began. Today, he would simply ask 'What's that?'"

An African Grey belonging to Linda of Texas has a colorful vocabulary. He may just live in a colorful environment. According to Linda, he says, "You stud muffin," "Bubba," meows like a cat, barks like a dog, sings "Me and My Shadow," calls the dogs by names and calls the ferrets.

Joel, a Timneh Grey who lives with Sue in Olympia, Washington, calls the cats who live in his household "Jeeves, hi, Jeeves" and "Daphne—hey, hey hey!!" or "Come on, Jeeves, Daphne." He is also polite to guests, asking "Wanna come in?" Once he's engaged, he asks "What are you doing—hug" and "What's going on?" He has a philosophical bent and occasionally says "Here we are."

Virginia of Florida says about her 16-month-old female African Grey:

She started out with a variety of whistles, which included the famous wolf whistle, and picked up a bunch of bird calls from a Mockingbird. She was imitating the microwave, the timer, alarm, etc., for many weeks before she began saying words. She meows and barks; the first because my daughter thought it would be funny, the second from the dog across the street. Just yesterday she began coughing. She sounds like someone in the last stages of pneumonia! If I had not learned that parrots don't cough, I would have rushed her to the vet.

I think that if I laugh at what she is saying or at the noise she makes, she repeats it and repeats it and repeats it. She does the telephone whenever she hears me go out the front door; so accurately that it gets me to run inside—which is what she wants! Occasionally she will do the telephone ring and then say "hello." I was worried (from things I had read) that all those whistles meant she would not talk. I now know that is not true. I suspect it is a natural progression.

Sandy of Ohio says her female African Grey, Moshi, "asks for water and for snacks. She also asks to get out of her cage. She calls the dogs and feeds them."

Susan of Virginia tells about her Timneh African Grey, an eight-year-old male, "I can ask him what he is doing and he will say 'Just sittin' here.' He says 'good morning' and 'good night' at the appropriate times. I was cleaning out my desk one afternoon and he said, 'hello.' I answered back hello and he said, 'Whatcha doing?' I said I was cleaning out the desk and he said, 'Come here.' I said no, that I was busy. He said, '*Come here!*' I got up and went to where his cage is, and he looked at me for a second and then said, 'Do you want a peanut?' Guess what? He got a peanut!"

Marnie from Ontario, Canada, has this to say about her 13-year-old male Timneh African Grey parrot:

He will repeat an entire phrase or sentence within minutes of hearing it. We interact with each other and have small conversations as you would a very small child, with him asking questions: "What cha doin'? Where ya goin'? What's at for?" On dusting day he has to know what everything is. He says "What cha doin' down there?" during my yoga workout and "Marnie, where'r you?" when I leave the room. He also says "No! Don't want to!" when told to get in his cage.

He taunts the cat with "Here kitty, kitty, kitty" (in my voice), come 'ere sweet kitty" (I've never called her "sweet" kitty). The cat comes (she's a sucker) and the little bugger makes a really loud, long, kissy noise. The cat gives him a look that would fry his drumsticks and he laughs this huge, rolling belly laugh!!

He calls us all by name, except my son, who he has decided is called Boy even though my son's name is the one he hears the most. He also calls my son "beep beep beeeeep"—the microwave sound.

COMING AND GOING

Laurie of Illinois has a Jardine's Parrot, a three-year-old male. She says, "Every morning when I am leaving for work he says 'Bye bye, see ya later.' And, when I am on my computer at night, typing away, I will suddenly hear from behind me, 'What are you doing?'"

Kathy of Colorado writes about her 10-year-old female Yellow-naped Amazon Beaker, "Whenever she sees anyone putting their coat on, she immediately begins saying 'Bye bye, I love you, see you later.'"

Carolyn of Florida writes about her first Eclectus, a 10-year-old male named Kiwi, "He uses 'Wanna go out?' to mean that he wants to change locations—to go in *or* out—which is my shortcoming, not his. I've never tried to teach him to say 'Wanna go in?' I have no doubt that he could learn it."

Lynn of Oregon says of her Umbrella Cockatoo, a one-and-a-half-year-old male, "He says 'hello' in greeting. He also uses it to mean 'I want something.'"

THE DYNAMICS IN MULTI-BIRD HOUSEHOLDS

If you only have one companion bird, we have two warnings for you. First, we know very few people with only one bird. They started with one, but then . . . . Second, as you read about people with more than one bird, you should realize that birds of different species are each housed in their own cage, and quite often the birds don't especially like one other and don't play together.

Sandie in California has African Greys, Cockatiels and a Lovebird. She says, "They pick up sentences that are repeated around the house, calling the dog, answering the phone, asking the bird something, telling the bird good night. They talk all the time, sometimes on cue. If I'm turning off a light, they say 'good night.' When I am fixing water to make food for baby birds, they will say 'baby birds.' The birds have learned from each other and repeat each other's phrases, bird calls, etc. The Lovebird whistles like a Cockatiel, the African Grey whistles like a Lovebird or the Cockatiel."

Cherrie in Alaska says about her Red-sided Eclectus, a two-year-old male, "He will ask for a bath if it's been more than three days since the last one. He says,

Questions of Sex

In most species of birds, you cannot tell the males from the females by their external appearance. Most birds need to have a DNA or surgical test done to tell their sex. Sometimes sex doesn't matter to the owner (well, the bird's sex doesn't), so they don't have this procedure done and really don't know if they have a male or a female bird. Of course, if the bird lays an egg, her sex is obvious! This leads to interesting names for birds when owners guess their bird's sex, but later find out the bird is really of the opposite gender.

'Bye-bye' only if I get my keys and coat out and head toward door. He says, 'What are you doing?' if our attention is diverted from him. He also asks 'How are you?' if we've come home after a long period of time, or if we do something really unusual or silly. I also have a White-capped Pionus who talks, with limited vocabulary but does use it in context. The two birds do not like each other and do not talk to each other."

Kathy lives with a Mynah, a Cockatiel and a Timneh Grey in Ontario, Canada. She says of her aviary, "The Mynah has learned a few words from the African Grey. Sometimes the Grey will say 'Be quiet, you idiot!' to the other birds if they're chatting away, but mostly will just chat along with them."

Esther in Michigan has Cockatoos, and says, "I have a second bird who is learning to talk from the first. They talk to each other and play peekaboo."

Debbie of Mississippi has a three-year-old Umbrella Cockatoo named Magic and a 12-year-old Double Yellow-headed Amazon named Em. She says, "When Magic does something bad, she looks at me and says 'I'm a *good* bird!' Also, when the Amazon came, Magic did not like him. They were both on the back of the couch one day shortly after Em's quarantine was over. Em reached out to bite the blinds—something Magic had been told a million times not to do. Magic looked at him and said, 'You're a *bad* bird! Whatchya doin'? I'm a *good* bird!'"

Carolyn of Florida writes, "My male Eclectus, Kiwi, taught my Yellow-naped Amazon, Casey, everything that he knows. They talked back and forth but, of course, it did not sound like a human conversation. Instead, they have a volley of words that they yell at each other. Sometimes it seems appropriate, such as when Kiwi would tell Casey to '*Be quiet please!*' when Casey was sounding off at dawn or dusk."

Thea in Nevada has an Eclectus, a Caique, a Senegal and a Canary. She says:

The Senegal is learning Caique! He has already learned all her whistles, and talks to her using them. Both the Senegal and the Eclectus tell the Canary he's a good boy when he sings! My family and friends have listened via the baby monitors as my alpha pair, Kiwi and Isis, talk to their babies in the nest. Here are the main things that they say appropriately to the babies:

"Hi darlin'."

"Is that good?"

"Want some, hmm?"

"Ah, sweetheart."

And they make the kissing sound when they are talking to the babies, just as I do to them. This is my birds' most touching use of speech. I've seen more than one damp eye among friends who have been fortunate enough hear the parents talking to their babies.

A Senegal Parrot can learn to talk and can also learn the calls of other birds.

Adriane of New Jersey says of her two Double Yellow-headed Amazons, a Severe Macaw and a Scarlet Macaw, "They all say 'hello' when I come home, 'nite nite' when they are being covered and the Severe says 'step up' when I open her cage. The scarlet says 'com 'ere' when she wants me to get her. My first Double Yellow-headed Amazon taught my second Double Yellow-headed Amazon everything she says. They both sing 'la la la la laaaa.' When I come home in the late afternoon I have a gab fest going on."

Jacklin of Idaho has an eight-month-old female Eclectus, Sarah. She says, "Sarah says 'gimmie a kiss.' If I say it first, she gives me a kiss; if she says it first, I give her a kiss. I have to mention that I am adopting a pair of bonded Eclectus Parrots. They are about seven years old and are named Popeye and Holly. From what I have been told, Holly doesn't talk at all and Popeye has a vocabulary of over 200 words. I am also told that he can sing 'I'm Popeye the Sailor Man' all the way through, including the 'toot, toot' at the end."

MINDING THEIR P'S AND Q'S

You really have to love birds to put up with some of their natural habits. You know about the mess they can create and their penchant for chewing on furniture. If a parrot really likes you, he will regurgitate on you. He isn't losing his dinner, he's saying "I love you!"

If your parrot isn't learning words, or if he's learning some undesirable vocalizations (such as screams or expletives), try converting them to laughter or song. It's much easier on human listeners! And we know how uplifting and infectious laughter is.

Says Kay of New York about her two-year-old male Lutino Indian Ringneck, "He laughs at my jokes!"

Jackie of Vermont says her 10-year-old Blue and Gold Macaw says "'I love' when she or he is sitting and 'feeding' me, which is generally considered an act of bonding. She says 'no, no, bad bird' after a round of raucous, loud playing."

Timneh Joel in Washington finds that flattery gets you everywhere. He says "I like your hat." He also appreciates treats and says "mmmmmm good." "Please" hasn't made it into his repertoire yet, but he can say "want some more!" to make his wishes known.

A five-year-old Green-cheeked Conure belonging to Tina of Illinois says "thank you" after receiving a kiss, being fed, going home or coming out of her cage.

Debbie of Mississippi has an Umbrella Cockatoo, a Double Yellow-headed Amazon and a Severe Macaw who have learned to ask for what they want. They want different things. Says Debbie, "The Amazon talks to get people to come back in the room with him. The Severe talks to get me to pet her. The Cockatoo talks so she can explain things to me."

Geri of California has two Grey-cheeked Parakeets, nine years and seven years old. She says, "My female tells me to 'c'mere' when she wants me. She tells my sister to 'c'mere' and then bites her!"

DIANE GRINDOL

Geri of California has a Grey-cheeked Parakeet who calls "c'mere" when she wants Geri. Are you sure you're ready for a parrot who can ask for what he wants?

IT'S A BIRD'S LIFE

Diane in Pennsylvania says about her older Yellow-naped Amazon, "I can and do hold conversations with him. He also sings a few songs. 'Somewhere Over the Rainbow' is his favorite. Most frequently he says 'Elmo's on. I want to watch Elmo.' Even my old Nape still learns new words and phrases."

Tiffany finds that reading body language is easier than interpreting her Conure's vocalizations. She says, "I've only figured out two of Mr. Noisy's 'words.' There's a two-tone phrase that means 'stop that.' And if I don't stop whatever it is I'm doing, there's a three-toned phrase, with an emphasis on the second tone, which I've translated as 'don't do that!' Wouldn't you know it, they both mean 'no.' Oh well! Good thing he's learning English faster than I am Conure."

Kristen of New Hampshire tells us about her two-year-old male Eclectus, Jessie, "Every night between 10 and 11 P.M. he says 'time for bed.' Around 11 he will crawl or climb back to his sleeping perch and go to sleep."

Sherri, who shared her life in North Carolina with an Umbrella Cockatoo, has these memories of Matilda:

> *First Incident: One day when she was about a year old, I was studying at the dining table. She was, as usual, right there with me. I realized she was chewing on the edge of a notebook and pulled it away. Unfortunately, she refused to let go, and wound up on the carpet beside my chair. I looked down at her, and before I could say anything she looked up at me and said, "Are you all right?" I started laughing; that was supposed to be my line—as a young, clumsy bird, I guess she'd heard it a lot!*

Second: One morning as I was putting on makeup with Matilda's supervision, I asked (just to make conversation), "Where's Steve?" She answered, "In the shower." He was.

Third: She left the bedroom one morning as I was getting dressed. After a minute, I called out, "Matilda, where are you?" She answered from the living room, "I'm right here!"

Fourth: I was vacuuming. Steve was outside. Matilda refused to get off my arm but wanted to bite the vacuum. Exasperated, I said, "Don't you want to go outside with Steve?" She said, "I love Sherri!"

Fifth: She once said "Hi, fish," as we walked past the aquarium. Another time she suddenly screamed in my ear, looked at me and said, "That's what the little guys [the Jenday Conures] say."

An Umbrella Cockatoo, Angel-brat, is a five-year-old female who belongs to Lisa of British Columbia, Canada. Lisa says Angel-brat "says 'hi' or 'hello' to greet someone. If she gets into trouble and I ask her what she is doing, she says 'Ida know. I love you'. She always tries to change the subject with lots of 'I love you's' when I am upset with her, just like a little kid! If I am sad or depressed, she will cuddle up against me and ask 'how are ya?' or 'how ya doin?' in a real worried tone of voice. When she wants something, she will yell 'mom,' 'mommy' or 'Lisa' over and over until she gets her way."

Kathy of Colorado writes about her 10-year-old female Yellow-naped Amazon, Beaker. "She will lift her foot and say 'tickle, tickle, tickle' (asking to be tickled on the foot). She laughs when we laugh. She says 'hello' when the phone rings, and 'hi' when anyone comes home after being away. When there are any loud voices in the house (as in an argument), she immediately begins to add her two cents' worth in an even louder voice. When one of the kids is upset, she begins to cry in a perfect imitation of a child crying."

Carolyn of Florida writes about her first Eclectus, a 10-year-old male named Kiwi, and about Eclectus in general. "Kiwi uses the word 'water' to mean drinking water, bathing, rain, and sometimes he says it repeatedly. It seems that he likes the sound of the word. As with all parrots, the wolf whistle seems to come naturally to the Eclectus. Eclectus

Yellow-naped Amazons like this one develop a comical, rollicking relationship with their human companions.

DIANE GRINDOL

are relatively new kids on the block among talking parrots. Some of the first-time viewer's questions are, 'Are they *real?*' and 'Do they talk?' Although it may sound too good to be true, these birds not only are strikingly beautiful, but they definitely are very good talkers too. It's a *win-win* option for parrot lovers—except maybe for the man in England with the Vos male who sings 'Yellow Submarine' from beginning to end at least twelve times a day!"

Steve and Shannon of Washington say of their male five-and-a-half-year-old Vosmaeri Eclectus, "He says 'mmmmm' if he likes his food, says 'go poop' to let us know he has to go, or has gone and is ready to be picked up. He is starting to say 'Let's go to bed' at night, because I take him to bed with me for about an hour every night while I watch TV—this is our quality time. He also knows what 'Go get the monkeys' means: He will go to the floor and play with his Barrel of Monkeys toy sometimes when we say it. He rarely says 'Here, kitty, kitty, kitty' anymore, since our cat died. He used to call her all the time. He says with great enthusiasm *'shower'* when the shower is running, or sometimes when we are in the car and it is raining. He also says 'water' when we go over a bridge. He has also created an interchangeable word, combining 'shower' with 'water,' that can't be described in text."

Digger is a five-year-old male Maroon-bellied Conure belonging to Lynne in Georgia. Says Lynne, "When he came into the shower for the first time he said, 'Digger is a wet bird.' When he turned his beak up at his fruits and veggies, I said, 'What do you want?' and he said, '*Special* yums!' (Special yums are seeds, fed only once or twice a week as a treat.)"

IT'S ONLY NATURAL

Among the most intimidating predators for wild parrots are the raptors—birds of prey. Many do hunt and kill smaller birds, and it seems pretty much instinctive, even for birds bred in captivity for many generations, to fear raptors or moving objects over their heads, such as balloons or overhead fans.

Blue-crowned Conure Chiquita belongs to Celeste of California. She says, "He learned to say 'scared' when he flopped to the floor or fell off his perch and I said to him, 'Are you scared?' Now if he falls, he says 'I'm scared.' On his own accord, he says he's scared when a hawk flies by the window but not when other birds fly past! He also has started saying it when there is loud gunfire or blasts on the TV. He often sticks his head in his food dish to amplify the sounds he is making!"

POINTS TO REMEMBER

- Be prepared for the unexpected when you have a talking parrot.
- Parrots learn to associate your comings and goings with appropriate words.
- Parrots can learn to ask for what they want—and will!
- It can be beneficial and reassuring to both parrots and their human companions to develop mutual communication.

Chapter 10

The Model/Rival Training Technique

To properly begin this chapter and understand the model/rival training technique, we need to get to know Alex the African Grey Parrot and Dr. Irene Pepperberg. Dr. Pepperberg is the world's foremost authority on the intelligence of parrots. Her work is entirely scientific, which has sometimes put her at odds with lay behaviorists whose interest in parrots either is short-term or is aimed primarily at trick training. Dr. Pepperberg's work is not short-term, nor is it designed to teach Alex tricks. She has worked with Alex for decades and has trained him so that he can respond to her in ways that answer questions about the intellectual capacity of parrots. To date, Alex has been a joy for her to work with, and he has not yet reached his intellectual limits. He just keeps learning new things and demonstrating his capacity to take the next step—and the next, and the next.

As far as we know, Alex is not an exceptional parrot. He was bought at a pet shop as a healthy young parrot. He was not given an IQ test. His training by Dr. Pepperberg has, however, been exceptional, and has resulted in most of the information in this chapter. Most of this training has been done using the model/rival training technique adapted by Dr. Pepperberg from earlier work by a German ethologist, Dietmar Todt. When you use this technique, you can teach your bird some really advanced material. She can actually be taught to count, identify objects, determine shapes and materials, and tell you what color certain objects are. In this chapter we set the stage for this advanced training. We owe this technique to Dr. Irene Pepperberg and her famous African Grey Parrot, Alex.

FIRST, YOU'LL NEED A BIRD

Not just any bird, of course. She needs to be your parrot, and by that we mean a parrot who has bonded with you enough that she's relaxed when you handle her outside of her cage. She can't simply be tolerating you by perching on the dreaded right hand, waiting for the equally evil left hand to come into biting range or getting ready to flee in a state of panic. This is the advanced stuff, and only students who are mentally ready for the material have much hope of success.

Second, your parrot needs to be comfortable in the company of someone else who will help you teach her some of the things she needs to know. It would be best if she were comfortable in the presence of a variety of other people who can help you teach. Since this technique requires two people a couple of hours a week, you may need to recruit more than one helper.

This matter of being comfortable in the presence of all the people involved in teaching is more important than it might at first appear. Even Alex, with all his exposure to students and the media, has a problem with new people. In the presence of strangers Alex will sometimes turn his back to the new folks and refuse to cooperate. This response may be a fear response, and it can last up to two to three weeks with certain strangers. Aside from this occasional response to strangers, Alex responds the same way to all of his trainers.

YOU'VE GOT TO HAVE FRIENDS

Wives, husbands, children if they're old enough and other people will do. The main qualifications for your helper are that he has the time, is able to follow simple instructions and has some small amount of acting ability. As we have already mentioned, all of your helpers need to have some history (at least two weeks and preferably longer) of cooperative interaction with your parrot. This rapport will be extremely valuable in helping your parrot maintain focus during training.

A PLACE TO WORK

You will need a place that is quiet and free of distractions for your training sessions. This can be in a number of locations, but it is a good idea not to offer your parrot a place of sanctuary to run to if she decides not to cooperate. There should be no human traffic in the area, at least at first, and there should be no other pets present. These early sessions are mainly intended to teach your parrot the methods you want to use to teach her lessons. You are all involved in learning how to learn, and how to teach one another, in the early stages.

Alex's teaching sessions are held in a laboratory with a lot of open space. The teachers sit on bar stools close enough to interact verbally and to exchange items that are used as toys. Your parrot should either be held by the teacher or put on a perch within easy reach, at eye level. All of you need to be able to reach and see

DORIS WILMOTH

Diane and Tom are in a comfortable location to work with Popeye, a female African Grey Parrot.

one another. It is particularly important that your parrot be able to see the interactions between the teacher and the model/rival. You also need to have a place to put the toys you will use in teaching, and to have a place to put toys out of sight when your parrot makes an improper response. Like the rest of us, parrots occasionally make mistakes.

TOYS!

The final thing you will need is a selection of toys. This is more important than it might at first appear. These toys are the things you will be teaching your parrot to identify, so you should really spend some time and thought on their selection. Usually, they shouldn't be food. During training, correctly identified toys will be offered to your parrot (and the model/rival) as rewards. If you offer food, it is often consumed, with one of two undesirable outcomes: You either run out of food or your parrot gets full and loses interest in working. There are exceptions to this food rule, such as uncooked pasta, but you get the point.

The toy should also be small enough to give to your parrot, if it is to be a useful reward for good performance during teaching. If you are interested in teaching your parrot to recognize colors, the toy should be a uniform and distinct color such as blue, red, yellow or green. This is to avoid asking your parrot to tell you whether a yellow and green piece of cloth is really yellow or really green. That kind of confusion makes teaching difficult for both you and your parrot.

Finally, the toy should be of a suitable material. It should be non-toxic, clean and sanitary. If it is of a material such as wood that is easily destroyed, you will need a large stock to replace the pieces your parrot turns to tinder. Some of the things that have been used in the past are leather, wood, paper, cloth, uncooked pasta, ceramic that won't chip or break and suitable metals such as stainless steel. We're sure you can think of more. If you want to color some of these toys, be sure to get non-toxic paint or food coloring, such as pastry colors. Once you learn the training technique, you'll think of a lot of new ideas.

Safe Materials for Toys

Leather. Leather can be cut into various shapes and dyed various colors using safe food coloring. Vegetable-tanned leather is safe if eaten and has a texture most parrots enjoy chewing.

Plastic. The best plastic for parrot toys is high-density nylon. Most parrots need to chew this tough plastic a long time to break off pieces. Brittle plastics or plastic shapes that allow pieces to be chewed off are not acceptable. High-density plastic is available in a variety of colors and shapes.

Wood. Wood is often used for parrot toys, but is usually thought of as disposable because parrots quickly splinter it into small pieces. One wood that has been suggested as being unsuitable for parrot toys is redwood, because it doesn't degrade if small pieces are eaten. Like leather and plastic, wood can be shaped and colored to make a variety of toys.

Cloth. Cloth can be a good material for toys—if care is taken to avoid tangling your parrot in loose threads. Chewing shreds cloth. If you use cloth toys, check them and your parrot often so you are sure no damage is being done.

Uncooked pasta. Pasta can be a good toy in a variety of situations if you are not concerned that it is being eaten. During training, it is acceptable if your bird eats the pasta. Pasta, with its many color and shape variations, is a good toy for parrots.

Metals. Some metal objects, such as those made of stainless steel, make good toys. Others contain elements such as lead and zinc that can be ingested as your parrot chews the toy. Make sure you know what the toy is made of, and don't assume because it is sold for birds that it is safe. All metal toys should be of a shape or size that prevents your parrot from eating them. You should check with your veterinarian or a poison center before offering your parrot metal toys, except for stainless steel.

Paper. Paper can be a great toy for your bird, depending on whether you care that it will be quickly destroyed. Many newspapers are now printed with non-toxic soy inks that allow your parrot to shred newspaper safely. When training your bird, you can use pieces of paper of many shapes and colors.

Toy Shapes

Later we will discuss teaching your parrot how to tell you the shapes of the toys you use. Before we can teach your parrot to tell you what shape her toys are, you need to decide what shapes you are going to teach her about. The names you use for these shapes need to be clear and distinctive, to keep confusion from complicating the teaching and identification process.

Circle. This shape is easy to make and recognize in almost any material. It is a good first choice.

Triangle. This is what Alex calls a three-corner. This is to differentiate it from a square.

Square. What Alex calls a four-corner.

Key. Alex identifies keys as part of his learning and testing. They are usually made of metal, but children's plastic toy keys are another good option.

Peg. This is another shape Alex identifies, but what he is actually talking about is a clothespin.

Colors

One of the great things about parrots is their color, but most people don't think about the fact that parrots can recognize colors and tell you what color things are. Alex routinely tells the colors of objects and selects or counts objects of specific colors when there are objects of many colors to choose among. Some of the colors Alex recognizes are blue, yellow, green and red, which Alex calls rose.

DR. PEPPERBERG'S MODEL/RIVAL METHOD

The model/rival method of teaching is the fastest proven way to teach parrots to identify new items or properties, such as color, shape, material or number. In this chapter we will work on identification of items. Later we will work on the properties of toys, such as color, shape and material. In even later chapters we will look at counting and finding specific objects out of a large number of objects.

The Model

One person plays the part of the teacher and the other plays the part of the model/rival. The point is for the model/rival to first show your parrot the proper response to a question posed by you, the teacher. That is, the model/rival first *models* the proper behavior.

For example, the teacher might hold up a piece of cloth and say, "What is this?" The proper response from the model/rival is to enthusiastically say, "Cloth!" The teacher then responds to this correct answer with lavish praise, always ending sentences with the word "cloth" such as, "That's right. This is cloth" or "Good, Tom. Cloth. The right answer is cloth." Using the word often reinforces the proper pronunciation and shows your parrot that the proper response is greeted with praise. And, just like human beings, parrots remember the last word of a sentence better than the words that came before. So you wouldn't use a sentence such as, "Cloth is the right answer. Good, Tom." If your parrot hears "cloth" at the end of each line of praise, she will remember the word better than if she hears it in another part of the sentence.

There are two things that are worth remembering at this point. One is that the model is always the rival of the bird for the trainer's attention. This means your parrot is in a constant state of wanting to get into the picture to be praised and to receive the great and wondrous toy. The second thing to remember is that some

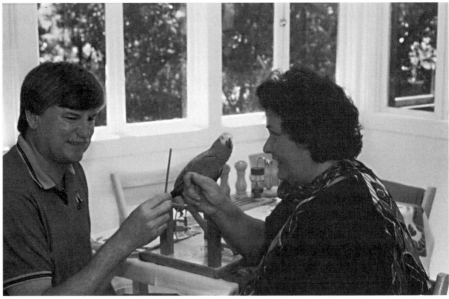

Tom is showing Diane (the model/rival) a green stick, as Popeye looks on. Diane and Tom are making a big deal about this stick and Diane is moving as if to take it. Eventually she says "stick." Popeye caught on and had to take the stick home with her!

Diane has successfully pronounced "stick" and has received her reward. As you can see, she is making the best of her new toy. Tom, all the while, is saying "stick" and congratulating her on the success of her efforts.

wrong answers need to be modeled. That is, you need to make some mistakes to show your parrot that not just any noise is going to get her the toy; she has to make a reasonable attempt.

After praise has been lavished on the model/rival, the real fun begins. She gets the cloth! Well, okay, maybe that isn't so much to you, but your parrot sees this as a really big deal. All that praise and a piece of cloth too. Now, there's something worth speaking up for! The model/rival makes a really big deal of playing with the cherished cloth for a minute before putting it down out of sight. If your parrot is paying attention, she just *has to* have that cloth.

The Rival

We now go to the sinister part of the training. We introduce rivalry. Once your parrot has seen the model in action, she is in a position to compete for the cloth. This means that even though the model/rival has so far been a rival for the attention of the trainer, your parrot has not yet actively entered the rivalry. Now she can actually get into the game.

She might try to say "cloth" or reach for it or make some random sound. Whatever she does, at least she has decided to get into the game. You want to encourage her, so offer her some attention and favor her with a reference to the cloth you are holding. You might say something like, "Polly, do you want this?" extending

JUDY MURPHY

When Popeye gets to take an active part, the real teaching begins. Popeye has said something resembling "stick" and is receiving her reward. All the while Tom is saying "stick" repeatedly, usually using it at the end of a sentence to give Popeye the idea that this is a really important word.

the cloth in her direction but out of reach, and wait expectantly. With any luck, your parrot will say something that in some way resembles the word "cloth." She might say "ka" or "ath" or some other part of the word "cloth" or even an unrelated word. Any sound will do to get things started. You simply want to get and keep her attention. Once you have her attention, it is the time for corrective action.

There are two forms of corrective action, depending on the sound your parrot produces. If the word is simply mispronounced, it is time to introduce the concept of "better." "Better" is your way of telling your parrot that the sound she has made is on the right track but not really what you wanted. As we said earlier, you are teaching your parrot how to learn. You may not get much of a return on your early efforts, but you will have taught her the tools that will make a great difference later.

To proceed from this point, you simply say the word "better" and wait for your parrot to make another sound. If she says the word "cloth," she gets all the praise reserved for a correct answer and then receives the cloth as a reward. The first time this happens, you have arrived at a new level of training your parrot! You have taught not only her the proper identification of "cloth," but you have taught her a new process that can be used for any new item you want to add to your parrot's vocabulary.

If, instead of clearly pronouncing the word "cloth," your bird continues to mispronounce the word, repeat "better" for two or three attempts. If the word is continually mispronounced, ask the model/rival to model the proper response again but this time include a lesson on "better." Show the cloth to the model/rival and ask, "What is this?" The model/rival then mispronounces the word—perhaps saying "oth"—and is told "better" by the teacher. Once the model gives the proper response, give the cloth and praise to the model/rival so your parrot can see.

Once your parrot has had a chance to see this modeling, give her another chance to produce the proper response. Finally, if some reasonable but not quite correct response is made, offer the cloth and say, "Okay, good try. Here's the cloth." Your parrot receives the cloth for her efforts, but only after several attempts. She will eventually understand that the correct answer yields her reward sooner and with more lavish praise.

The second kind of wrong response is a misidentification. The response is clear but obviously incorrect. For example, your parrot may respond "wood" instead of "cloth" (if she knows the word "wood.") Here the teacher responds with, "No, try again, Polly." If your parrot persists in identifying the cloth as wood, the model/rival steps in and correctly answers the question, modeling proper behavior and receiving praise and the cloth.

Remember, the rival is the evil twin of the model. Your parrot sees the model receiving praise and rewards for giving the correct answers, while your parrot receives nothing. To your parrot, the model becomes the rival and your parrot begins to compete for the toy. Early efforts may be short of the mark, but a good teacher and model/rival always let the parrot make several attempts and win whenever possible.

The following is an example of how a session of model/rival teaching might transpire. The parrot is Polly. The teacher is Diane, and the model/rival is Tom. The toy is plastic.

Diane: Tom, what is this?

Tom: Plastic!

Diane: Good boy! You get to play with the plastic. (Hands Tom the plastic.)

Polly: (Interrupting) Wa-wa.

Diane: Do you want this, Polly? What is it?

Polly: Pla-wa.

Diane: Better.

Polly: Pla-wa.

Diane: Tom, what is this?

Tom: Pla-wa.

Diane: Better.

What happens if the model/rival fails to perform? Tom is showing an attitude of disdain, and Diane is looking fondly at the unattainable stick.

Tom: Plastic.

Diane: That's right, plastic! Tell me what it is again. (Offers Tom the plastic.)

Tom: Plastic! (Takes the plastic.) Plastic!

Polly: (Tries to reach the plastic.) Pla.

Diane: Better. What is it?

Polly: Pla-wa.

Diane: Better.

Polly: Plast-wa.

Diane: Good try. Here's the plastic. (Offers Polly the plastic.)

As you can see, this example has most of the elements we have discussed in the model/rival technique. The proper behavior is modeled. The rival competes for the toy, stimulating your parrot to work to get the toy instead of allowing the rival to have it. With each attempt your parrot makes to get the toy, she is allowed to make a better attempt if her answer is less than perfect. If her answers continue to be less than perfect, the model offers the right answer again and gets the toy. These various parts of the model/rival technique can be used to teach many different behaviors.

CORRECTING POOR BEHAVIORS

There are a few behaviors that interfere with the pace of teaching the model/rival technique. Some of these might be the result of the environment the bird is trained in. Before applying any corrective measures to your parrot's behavior, be sure the fault lies with your parrot. If the training area has people or other pets walking through, it is likely your parrot is being distracted from the task at hand. It is important to inspect the area used during teaching and discover any influences that might interfere. If the environment is found to be acceptable, your parrot might need some help focusing on the task at hand. If your rapport with your parrot is not adequate, she may just be too nervous to settle down and participate in the training.

Earthquake

The earthquake is used if your parrot bites. It is a shaking of the hand or platform or perch your parrot stands on. It is a small shaking, depending on the degree of aggression your parrot exhibits. Be careful. We don't want to break a leg or dump your parrot on the floor. This is just a technique to break the connection your parrot has with biting and is not a punishment. We are simply trying to refocus her attention to our little bit of teaching.

After the brief earthquake, address your parrot by name and ask, "What's this?" Once her attention is off biting, you need to focus it back on you and the subject at hand.

Consistent Mistakes and Scolding

When your parrot makes a consistent mistake on something she has already learned, it is time for some negative feedback. "Nope" usually means the bird is having trouble with the concept or with controlling her muscles. We scold only when the bird has already learned the label and *then* persists in making errors during reviews. In this case you use the opposite of praise and scold your parrot. Saying something like, "No, you know better than that. You need to pay more attention," in a mildly scolding voice is adequate.

As with the earthquake, the point is to refocus your parrot's attention, not create a massive trauma. At the same time you scold your parrot, temporarily remove the toy from sight. This reinforces the idea that your parrot is not doing what you want.

ROLE REVERSAL

You need to decide whether you want your parrot to respond only to you or whether you want her to talk to everyone in the neighborhood. If you want your parrot to talk mainly to you, make sure you are always the teacher in your model/rival sessions. This is akin to being the captain of a pirate ship and not wanting the crew talking to your parrot and finding out about where the treasure is buried.

If, on the other hand, you want a more social parrot, recruit a number of potential helpers for your training sessions and take turns being the teacher and the model/rival. Parrots taught in this way, such as Alex, respond to a number of trainers and are less likely to develop quirky responses based on cues (that you may not know you give) from their primary trainer.

Parrots are highly social animals, and training them to become familiar with and offer appropriate responses to a large number of people is well within their normal behavior. This socializing is a good idea anyway, to minimize the amount of antisocial behavior, such as biting and screaming, a parrot may exhibit.

PRACTICE

We all need a little practice at the lessons we have learned, and your parrot is no exception. As your parrot picks up the names of items taught in 30-minute to one-hour sessions held two to four times a week, you can begin testing her on her retention of this valuable new information. You do this simply by holding the objects from the training sessions and asking, "What's this?" Each time your parrot answers correctly, you give the object to her and allow her to play with it until she tires of the play. Alex, for example, usually becomes bored with an object after one to five minutes.

One of the great things about practicing is that your parrot continues to fix in her mind the identity of each object she has learned about. It also entertains her, and the people practicing with your parrot. This kind of interaction is the main reason to have a parrot, and is essential to the success of a parrot-human relationship. Parrots who are kept in cages without adequate interaction with people often show self-destructive behaviors such as feather picking or self-mutilation. In training your parrot, you are enhancing her health.

During practice you can keep records of how well your parrot is doing. Each time you ask, "What is this?" you can record the success or failure of your parrot to answer correctly. If you have taught a number of words and variations, you can record them separately and see how she does on each item.

During the first 26 months of his training, Alex learned to use nine nouns: paper, key, wood, hide (rawhide chips), cork, corn, nut, wool (cloth) and pasta (bowtie macaroni); three color adjectives: rose (red), green and blue; two shapes: three-corner (triangle) and four-corner (square); and the use and meaning of the word "no." This is not the simple repetition we discussed in earlier chapters but the actual use and understanding of these words. Alex was able to use these words to identify, request or refuse more than 30 objects. If you can teach your parrot the way Alex was taught, you will have achieved real interspecies communication.

HOW ARE YOU DOING?

If we use Alex as the standard against which to compare your parrot, we find that 80 percent success in naming objects correctly the first time is quite good. However, we are looking at the success rate of a parrot who can tell a green key from a blue key and a yellow cork from a rose (red) cork, and who can pick out the yellow key from among a number of other objects including keys of other colors and other yellow objects. This is the kind of performance we might expect from a child.

The most common mistakes Alex makes are to forget to say that a green key is green or in some other way fail to completely identify the item he is asked to identify, or he says a word so poorly that he cannot be understood. In this first type of error, Alex gets at least part of the identification correct. In the second, he may be trying to say the correct word but doesn't say it clearly. Most of Alex's misses are near misses and not gross errors. I wish I could do as well on some of the things I have attempted!

POINTS TO REMEMBER

- You need a bird who is comfortable enough with you to relax and be trained.
- You need a quiet, peaceful place.
- You need a helper with whom your bird is also comfortable.
- Toys are teaching tools.
- Teaching is modeling.
- Correct errors as they arise.

Chapter 11

Advanced Concepts

Now that you have mastered the model/rival technique, you can start applying it to a variety of new concepts. When Dr. Pepperberg started her work with Alex, she had a number of goals in mind. Her work is purely research, but we can still learn from her published scientific work and emulate some of her goals with our own birds.

Her first goal was to determine whether parrots could use human language to identify and request objects. Clearly, she has shown that they can. Some of her long-range goals were to discover how far parrots could go in mastering language concepts such as words and sentences, color, shape and size, the idea of questioning, and other aspects of language. Finally, she wondered about the ability of parrots to take the language they have been taught and arrive at concepts they have not been taught, the way a child does when he puts familiar words together in new ways to communicate new things.

In this chapter we will depart from Dr. Pepperberg's work and look at some of the things you can teach your bird about communication, and how these lessons might affect the way you and your parrot interact. Some of this is just speculation. Other parts are based on the experience of parrot owners who have seen their parrots learn to communicate in new and novel ways.

What this means to you and your parrot is that you have a chance to talk to each other. You can find out what your bird really feels or wants. When your parrot can tell you that he wants a preferred food or a place to play, you don't have to guess what is important to him—you can just give him what he wants. Parrots who can tell you what they want and get it from you are better-adjusted pets. They are more able to fulfill their role as companions. With any luck, they may eventually be claimed as dependents on your taxes! They can even argue the case themselves.

We suggest you read and evaluate this part of the book, then take what works for you and leave the rest.

DIANE GRINDOL

Dr. Irene Pepperberg, working with Alex the African Grey and other parrots, has conducted research to find how well parrots can master areas of language such as color, shape and size and the idea of asking and answering questions.

THE BENEFIT OF "NO"

One of the real benefits of teaching your parrot to communicate instead of just to mimic is the word "no." Its one of the first things a child learns when he is just learning to talk. Hot stoves, electrical cords, cleaning supplies, the cat's tail and a variety of other things become "no's" until more specific meanings are learned. It's a great word. You say it, the bird says it, and everybody knows what it means.

The real success of this word with your parrot is that he will no longer need to use threatening or biting behavior to let you know when you irritate him. He can simply tell you "no." Can you imagine a parrot who simply tells you "no" instead of biting? Some of the situations where your parrot might say "no" include your efforts to pick him up when he would rather be left alone, offering the wrong toy or food when he would rather have something else, someone messing with his cage or ending a training session when he has had enough.

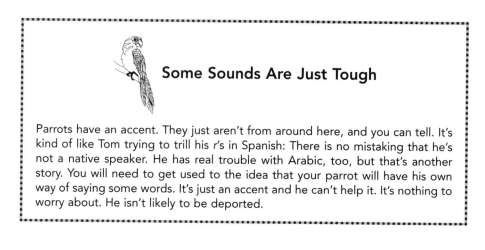

Some Sounds Are Just Tough

Parrots have an accent. They just aren't from around here, and you can tell. It's kind of like Tom trying to trill his *r*'s in Spanish: There is no mistaking that he's not a native speaker. He has real trouble with Arabic, too, but that's another story. You will need to get used to the idea that your parrot will have his own way of saying some words. It's just an accent and he can't help it. It's nothing to worry about. He isn't likely to be deported.

The other side of "no" is that once your parrot learns its meaning, you can use it too. Having a parrot who knows how to ask repeatedly for exactly what he wants may not always be what you want. Being able to end this repetition with a simple "no" is just what you need.

PARROT PRIORITIES

Keep in mind that birds aren't interested in everything just because we are. Parrots like noise and action and getting an active response to their many noises. Your parrot may have an abiding interest in the household pets, because his calling the dog gets the dog to come running into the kitchen. When their noises produce action, their world is perfect.

Another thing parrots like to do is tear things apart. This might mean your parrot is more interested in the material something is made of than its size, shape or color. Wood is much nicer to chew than stainless steel. It comes apart in interesting ways and then yields a whole new set of smaller toys. Who cares what color it is?

This means active communication with your parrot will be easier and more involved if you work with things that are of interest to your parrot. If you carefully observe your parrot, you will get some idea of what matters to him and be able to focus your attention there.

TOYS AND THEIR PROPERTIES

Toys are items that have a specific set of properties. What do we mean by that? Let's consider an example. A stick can be a toy. It's just a piece of wood; there doesn't seem to be much to it, but it will be different from other sticks in a number of ways. It may be longer or shorter, fatter or thinner, bigger or smaller, a different color, forked once or several times (with the number of ends depending on the number of forks), softer or harder and so on. Some of these properties are absolute, such as the color and number of ends, and others are relative, such as bigger or smaller, fatter or thinner, softer or harder and longer or shorter. Once you have taught your parrot to identify a stick, you might want to teach him to tell you which stick he wants by telling you the color of the stick or the number of ends the stick has.

What does this do for you? It opens a door into understanding your parrot. You can begin to keep track of his requests and other responses to the things you give him. For example, you might record the conditions under which he asks for a white stick rather than a black stick. Is something consistent here? Does he like black sticks at night and white sticks during the day? It's always good to explore your parrot's preferences. You get the chance to discover what you can do to enhance the life of your parrot, while finding more pleasurable ways for you to interact with him. If enough people make these kinds of inquiries and keep records, a scientific survey might reveal some general characteristics of parrot personalities.

Another great experiment would be to teach your parrot to count the number of ends on a forked stick, to the number four (you might have fun making these sticks yourself). Then, when he asks for a stick, you ask, "How many ends?" Keep track of his answers and see how complex a stick he prefers. Then, to make things just a little more complicated, put a variety of sticks on a table and let him take the one he wants. Does it match what he usually asks for? Is there a difference between the number of ends on the sticks he requests and the number of ends on

DIANE GRINDOL

What is your parrot interested in? The color or texture of an object may be intriguing to this African Grey. Parrots want the world to work for them, so work with treats and toys and behaviors that are interesting to them.

the sticks he takes when he has a choice? The kinds of answers you get may offer us some insight into the mind of your parrot. The kinds of choices he makes when he has to think about them may be different from those he makes when he just has to grab whatever he wants.

If you want some really juicy topics for your next social gathering, do the same experiment with your friends playing the role of your parrot. You might find some great parallels or differences, and the differences between thinking and grabbing when your friends make the choices might tell them a few things about themselves.

What about the comparative properties of toys? Your parrot can tell you that he wants the black stick with three ends, but telling you that he wants the longer stick is something else again—longer than what? Usually you simply present two sticks, one short and one long, and ask him which is longer. If he is clear on what you want and is responding well, he will give you the right answer. You can test him on a variety of samples of sticks and eventually find out how often he is correct.

Then you might want to test him with sticks that have different numbers of forks but are of the same length. Does he tell you that sticks with more forks are longer? Does he have a consistent response to this problem? Does he tell you that fatter sticks are longer when the sticks are of the same length? With enough of this kind of work, we might get new insights into the perceptions of parrots and how they compare to our own. It might help us bridge that gap in human-animal communication that currently keeps us apart.

After this exercise it's time to try something new. For example, let's compare soft and hard. Soft and hard are not the easiest concepts to use. If you ask some of your friends whether something is softer or harder than something else, you will likely get consistent responses. That is, until you get into the difficult stuff. Is cotton harder or softer than foam rubber? Is gelatin harder or softer than pudding? These more difficult questions get back to the problem with language in parrots that we have already touched upon: Do parrots and people have the same reference points?

If you can teach your parrot the concepts of softer and harder, you might want to try an experiment similar to the one described for longer and shorter. That is, you might want to let your parrot tell you what is harder and softer and then ask your friends to do the same. We're guessing that the human and parrot results will be different. Why?

There are several reasons. One is the way we test things for soft or hard. Humans might test with their fingers or rub some items on their skin. A parrot is likely only to take the items in his beak. In the process of evaluating soft and hard, we don't know what criteria a parrot considers important. It might matter whether the material compresses easily in the bird's beak. It might matter how easy it is to bite through the material. In comparing gelatin and pudding and cotton and foam rubber, the determination of soft and hard might be different depending on how your parrot decides what soft and hard are. It might be fun to get some idea how your parrot sees the world of soft and hard.

STUFF HE GETS ON HIS OWN

Parrots may learn things on their own. Some of these things may be categories, like the concept of stick we discussed earlier. Sticks come in many shapes and sizes, but they can all be called sticks. When we train our parrots to tell us about sticks, we train them to respond to the properties of sticks that interest us, for example color, number of ends, etc. Parrots may also create categories by themselves. If we pay attention, we can recognize the categories and reinforce and expand them.

One fascinating example of parrots identifying and responding to a category—in this case, gender—occurred with the flock of Cockatiels at the Department of Avian Sciences, University of California, Davis. Thirty-six pairs of Cockatiels were in a room. Access to this room was limited to a few people who were directly involved with these birds. Only people directly involved in the care of the birds were allowed to bring guests into the room. It was summer, and many of the guests who entered the room were wearing shorts.

As many of our readers are aware, male Cockatiels often whistle. In the case of this flock of Cockatiels, some of the males learned to wolf whistle and had taught the rest of the flock. After several weeks of the male Cockatiels whistling, one of the scientists working on the project noticed that this wolf whistle was reserved for women wearing shorts. He told this to a number of women, and was chided for his overactive male imagination. At that point he made a bet with one of these women that she would not elicit the wolf whistle from the birds unless she was wearing shorts. She showed up wearing long pants and, as predicted, was ignored by the males in the flock. But when she changed to shorts, they wolf whistled their little heads off. She lost the bet, but didn't seem to mind the attention at all.

We never discovered when or how these Cockatiels learned this particular behavior, but it persisted for a time, then was eventually lost. In any case, Cockatiels (at least the males) were able to work with two categories of information, gender and clothing. The Cockatiels would whistle at a woman they had never seen before if she was wearing shorts. The interesting part of this behavior is that the Cockatiels seem to have worked it out themselves. There was no one who had regular access to the Cockatiels who would admit to having taught them to whistle at women in shorts.

The bottom line is that the Cockatiels decided the name for a woman wearing shorts was a wolf whistle. As far as we know, they came up with it on their own.

SOUNDS THAT DON'T SEEM TO MEAN ANYTHING

As you might have guessed by now, there are sounds your parrot makes that aren't what you have taught him. In fact, your parrot probably makes sounds you couldn't have taught him; some parrot sounds are impossible for people to make. You might be able to give these sounds a useful meaning anyway. This is much like the

DIANE GRINDOL

Your parrot may make sounds that don't mean anything in English. Why not identify some as "words" and give them meaning for you and your parrot? (This is Ginny and Sammy, a Blue-fronted Amazon.)

technique you have been using to train your parrot, except now you already have the word and you need to teach the bird to associate it with the object or concept, instead of the reverse.

As each new sound comes up, make a list so you don't get confused or, worse yet, confuse your parrot by using the "words" inconsistently. Once you have identified at least one word, training can begin.

What you get out of this is a larger vocabulary for your parrot with limited training. The sound already exists, so you just attach a meaning to it. The problem with this kind of training is that you have to keep straight what these nonsense (in English) sounds means, if you are to communicate properly with your parrot.

EASY INCREASES IN VOCABULARY

There are two easy ways to increase the vocabulary of your parrot. One is to encourage action expressions and the other is to answer questions.

Action Expressions

Action expressions are phrases that direct some kind of action. For example, a parrot might say "Bring me water." It's easy to see that your parrot could request a lot of different things. Every time you teach your parrot from an action expression, you are teaching a new noun, so action expressions are an easy way to increase the number of nouns your parrot learns. There are a number of action expressions that come to mind in this process, but most of them take the form "bring me . . ." or "take me . . ." When you see your parrot stretching toward something or saying "bring me . . ." you can supply the appropriate word. Your parrot's motivation in this case is great, since he wants the item, and may want you to bring it to him again some time.

By using this method, you are not just increasing your parrot's vocabulary randomly. You are teaching your parrot about his favorite things and teaching yourself what his favorite things are. Isn't it nice that win-win can cross species?

DIANE GRINDOL

You can teach your parrot to ask for what he wants: "Bring me water," "Want nut" and so on. (This is Mercedes, a Blue and Gold Macaw.)

Answer Questions

A veterinarian recently took her Eclectus Parrot, Calvin, for a photo shoot. He's a well-socialized bird and is calm by nature, and in this case he was being held by the person he is closest to and was at ease. The photographer was setting up his lights and cameras and was moving a final set of lights into position when Calvin asked, "What's that?" Both the veterinarian and the photographer started to laugh. Calvin's use of the question was both appropriate and timely.

If we are teaching our parrots to talk to us instead of just teaching them to mimic, we need to get used to the question. Every time your bird asks a question, you should treat it as a serious question and give your parrot an answer. Just as with action expressions, questions give us some idea what is important to our birds. With that in mind, you might want to keep a log of what your parrot asks and, once you provide the answer, how often your parrot uses it. It's a window into his world and gives you a view of how big that world is. It affords you the opportunity to choose what you might add to his world that would interest him. You will be in a better position to enrich the life of your bird.

TESTING

After you have taught your parrot a few things, you may want to test how much success you are having. The first part of this process is keeping track of what you have trained your parrot to do. This may not be as easy as it sounds. You will need to record all of the formal model/rival work you have completed and also all of the more informal work you have done. This should include things like answering questions such as "What's that?" and the time you spent assigning meanings to the nonsense words your parrot produced.

Once you have completed this process, you will need to decide what you want to test for. For example, if you have a list of things you have trained your parrot to identify by using the expression, "What's this?" then you test your parrot by showing him the objects in question and asking, "What's this?" You simply tally up the correct answers and calculate the percent your parrot got right. You can do similar tests with the concepts of "What's bigger?" or "What's longer?" Most of the testing is simply a case of doing what you do during training and calculating the percent of correct answers.

This kind of testing helps you identify problems you and your parrot may be having in learning how to communicate. It isn't entirely scientifically correct, but you would need to read all of Dr. Pepperberg's work if you want to publish the results in a scientific journal. We're assuming you just want to know how well your parrot is doing on the things you are training him to do, rather than to break some new ground in parrot language skills.

You may want to test your parrot and record the results. This Thick-billed Parrot, the only living parrot native to the United States, lives at an educational institution. The extinct Carolina Parakeet was the only other parrot native to the United States.

Expectation Cueing

Expectation cueing is a situation in which your parrot has some idea what question is going to be asked from the kind of questions he has been asked so far during a training or testing session. This increases the chance he will give the correct answer even if he doesn't really know the answer.

Expectation cueing comes about in tests in which a single topic is tested. For example, if you're testing your parrot on his use of numbers, there is a fairly small range of numbers that your parrot can count. Eventually he might use numbers up to six, but in earlier tests he may have a choice, for example, among the numbers one, two and five. If he knows that he is being tested only on numbers, he has a one-in-three chance of getting the right answer if he simply sticks to one

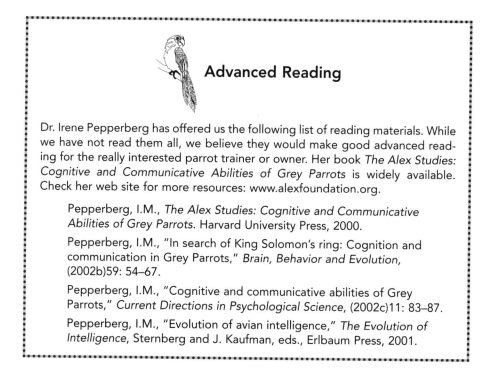

Advanced Reading

Dr. Irene Pepperberg has offered us the following list of reading materials. While we have not read them all, we believe they would make good advanced reading for the really interested parrot trainer or owner. Her book *The Alex Studies: Cognitive and Communicative Abilities of Grey Parrots* is widely available. Check her web site for more resources: www.alexfoundation.org.

Pepperberg, I.M., *The Alex Studies: Cognitive and Communicative Abilities of Grey Parrots.* Harvard University Press, 2000.

Pepperberg, I.M., "In search of King Solomon's ring: Cognition and communication in Grey Parrots," *Brain, Behavior and Evolution,* (2002b)59: 54–67.

Pepperberg, I.M., "Cognitive and communicative abilities of Grey Parrots," *Current Directions in Psychological Science,* (2002c)11: 83–87.

Pepperberg, I.M., "Evolution of avian intelligence," *The Evolution of Intelligence,* Sternberg and J. Kaufman, eds., Erlbaum Press, 2001.

number and repeats it as the answer to every question. He could than get 33 percent of the questions right just with this simple strategy. If he is actually trying to get the numbers right, a third of his answers that might be incorrect will appear to be correct simply by random chance.

In any situation in which there is a narrow range of questions asked, there is a chance of expectation cueing. To avoid this problem—and to avoid boring your parrot—all areas in which your parrot might be tested should be available to be covered in each test session. This maximizes the number of possible answers your parrot might give to a question. The odds of him getting a large number of correct answers by chance is thereby substantially reduced.

It is also useful to keep track of all the wrong answers and the correct answers given for each question. You might find that there is some ambiguity in the questions you ask, leading to an incorrect answer from your perspective. Your parrot, however, might be giving a different interpretation to the question and getting it right from his point of view.

POINTS TO REMEMBER

- "No" is probably the most useful word your parrot can learn. It can be used in place of aggressive behavior by both of you.
- Your parrot has an accent.

- Parrots have their own priorities; you will benefit from knowing what they are.
- Toys have specific and relative properties. Both can be used in communicating with your bird.
- Parrots will learn things on their own. Part of teaching a parrot to talk is learn what your parrot has learned on his own.
- Nonsense sounds can be turned into new words by assigning them meanings.
- You can teach new words by using action expressions to get your parrot to tell what he thinks you need to know.
- You can also teach new words by answering your parrot's questions.
- Testing your parrot can be a useful way to tell how successful your training has been and can give you perspective on what is important to your parrot.
- Expectation cueing can be avoided by making all aspects of your parrot's learning part of each testing session.

Chapter 12

Communicating and Playing With Your Bird

This chapter deals with some of the more advanced aspects of keeping an intelligent and talking bird as a companion. Not only is it fun to have a talking parrot, but there are ways your verbalizations can be used to make life easier for yourself and your bird. Beyond "hello," you can communicate with your parrot and can react to what a parrot is trying to communicate to you. We don't think of birds as being obedience trained the way a dog might be, but there are actually many areas of bird stewardship that are easier with communication.

Verbal interactions with our parrots are also a form of play. Birds have an endless capacity for play and would willingly play all day. Providing an enriched environment for your bird and coming up with appropriate games and activities are some of the challenging aspects of having a feathered friend. We'll give you some suggestions in this chapter.

COMMUNICATION MAKES LIFE EASIER

It's possible to have a relationship with a parrot in which there is some advanced interspecies communication. There are many ways to acknowledge the needs of your parrot and to tell her about your wishes. Some of these are verbal on your part. Even a non-talking parrot can respond to verbal cues and commands. A talking parrot can ask for what she wants, as well.

Entering a Cage

It is very useful to have verbal cues for your bird in your daily interactions. One of the very useful commands you can develop is a word that means "time to get

DIANE GRINDOL

This Blue-fronted Amazon is poised to go into her cage at a word from her human companion. It's very useful to have a verbal command for an everyday action such as entering a cage.

in your cage." This makes it easier for other people, such as a pet-sitter or relative, to care for your bird when you are away.

You choose the verbal cue to give your parrot for this action. The cue might be "time to go in," "back to your cage," "home" or "go in." Say it consistently for a while when you see her going into her cage. Praise her profusely for going in the cage as you say the word. You may even entice your bird to enter her cage by placing a peanut or other favored treat in the cage.

Be sure to practice this cue at different times of the day and when different things are happening in the house. It doesn't take long for a parrot to catch on. You can start saying your cue word and waiting a moment to get a response. If your bird doesn't respond, guide her into her cage.

You can also accompany your cue word with a hand signal or action of some kind. You could tap the top of the cage, sweep your hand into the cage or point to the cage, for example. The keys to shaping a behavior are to be consistent in your words and action, and to praise your parrot profusely when you observe the desired behavior. A talking parrot may begin to use the cue word to ask to go back to her cage.

Good Night

Once you establish a good night routine with your bird, she can ask to go to bed. The whole routine usually involves going to the bird, getting her back in her cage as we discussed above, covering the cage and turning off the lights.

Birds need more sleep than most people—10 to 12 hours per night—so our schedules do not always coincide. Many people therefore have a sleeping cage for their bird in a separate area of the house that can be quiet and dark when it's the bird's bedtime. The consequences of sleep deprivation for your parrot range from grouchiness and nippy behavior to increased breeding behavior that could trigger chewing and biting for territorial reasons, as well as egg laying in females.

The routine for putting your bird to bed can include a word or phrase you repeat throughout the process, such as "good night," "nighty night," "sweet dreams" or "bedtime." Your bird then knows it's time to settle down and go to sleep. If she talks, she can ask to go to bed when she's getting tired. You are giving her the tools to communicate with you.

If your bird doesn't talk, watch for actions from your bird that signal the same thing. Diane's parrot Aztec doesn't say a word, but he communicates in very understandable mime. If he wants to go somewhere, he leans in that direction or takes off on his own. If it's bedtime, he's up on his roosting perch and dozing. Diane responds to his body language, and talks to him even when she knows she will not get a verbal response. Aztec obviously understands her.

No Hassles Moving Around

Our birds are built to fly speedily from one place to another. Many companion birds have clipped wings, however and rely on humans for transportation around the house. It's easiest when both you and your bird cooperate to move smoothly and accomplish this without a hassle. When a bird doesn't understand where you're going, she may jump off your arm, refuse to go in her cage or head back the direction from which you were coming.

A bird is immobilized when you hold your hand over her back, keeping her wings at her side. That sounds simple enough. But to a bird this can be a very threatening action. Birds are prey animals, and when they are restrained their instincts tell them that they are about to become someone's lunch.

With your reassurance, a bird can learn to be restrained in this way. Start in small steps. Practice putting your hand near your bird's back, then over her back, actually touching it. Use a word that will mean you're on the move with her. Next, start gently putting pressure on your bird with your hand, and eventually progress to holding down her wings and walking a few steps. This method of transportation will become second nature to you and your bird over time.

Of course, there are other ways you two can move. You can securely hold her toes with a thumb while she's perched on your hand. She can climb on a stick at your command, and be whisked to her cage or a play stand. The important thing is to start talking to your bird while these actions are taking place. Use a word or phrase consistently as you perform these actions. That's how you communicate with your bird. It eliminates the surprise factor for her. When she knows what you want and what you are doing, she is less likely to feel that you are being unpredictable or even threatening. And when she has words or actions she can use to make requests of you, her life is less frustrating.

This male pearl Cockatiel is learning to have a hand laid over his back. Eventually, this will be a useful action for returning him to his cage.

Going Up

Occasionally, when Diane's Cockatiels are out of their cages and milling around the top of them, a startling event happens. The event is startling to the birds, such as a cat looking in the window, a loud noise or even an earthquake (Diane lives in California). This stimulates a bird's natural flight reaction, so there may be up to a dozen Cockatiels spread out in various parts of the house to which they've flown in their excitement.

Fortunately, the Cockatiels all know the command "up the ladder," and when they hear it they head for long ladders placed near their cages that extend from the floor up to the first bars of the cage.

To teach this, at first, Diane placed each bird on the floor, went to him, said "up the ladder" and pressed the ladder to him. Cockatiels naturally want to get up off the floor, and they willingly climbed on. Diane then placed the ladder so it leaned against the cage, and each bird was returned home that way. After doing that a few times, she started saying "up the ladder" and guiding the bird toward the base of the ladder, which she now knew was a way up off the floor and home.

Now "up the ladder" means the birds seek out the ladder on their own. It's great to be able to give them a cue that gets everyone back to safety. Almost everyone. Sometimes one of the Cockatiels gets behind a piece of furniture and has to be retrieved. You can establish a similar routine with your bird. This has made a big difference to new owners of chicks who have limited mobility, such as one little beauty who lives with a 92-year-old woman.

Getting Carried Away

Most companion birds will have to get into a carrier at some point in their lives. Your bird will need to travel to the veterinarian safely, may come with you to work or might need emergency accommodations on a trip or in the event of a natural disaster. Use a word, command or hand signal consistently to mean "get in the carrier," and your bird will learn to calmly enter a carrier. You'll need to practice this daily for a few weeks. Just get in the habit of using a carrier to travel between rooms in your home or up and down stairs. Or start taking your bird on errands with you.

It's nice when a bird doesn't associate getting in a carrier only with a trip to see the avian veterinarian. Take your bird on walks in her carrier or on car trips to friends or out to the store. Remember to take precautions in extreme weather. Don't plan trips when it's too hot or too cold for your bird.

Lassie Come Home

We think of obedience commands such as "come" as being only for training dogs, but this is a useful command for a bird to learn as well. What would happen if your bird ever got outside by mistake? Most companion birds are not familiar with the environment outside their house and can't find their way home. Remember, birds are very visual. Many birds don't have a homing instinct either. Cockatiels, for example, are nomadic by nature, and many parrots forage over a vast territory in the wild and don't instinctually stay within a small area. For some reason, many companion birds who fly onto a high perch outside don't necessarily know how to get down out of a tall tree or off a phone wire. You'll want to have a command for your bird that means "come to me." And you'll want to use it before local predators catch on that your bird is vulnerable.

Start using your "come" command whenever your bird is heading for you. Praise your bird for coming to you. Say, "Good come, come on, you're a good bird to come to me." Since your bird knows how to step up on your finger, give the "up" command when your bird is a few inches away, which requires her to come over to step up. We think it's especially important to use both a hand signal and a voice command for "come," in case your bird is far away but still within bird vision.

DIANE GRINDOL

Did this Meyer's Parrot arrive at her destination via a carrier? Communicate with your parrot about getting into a bird carrier using a phrase such as "let's go." Make sure you take her to fun destinations in her carrier, as well as to those necessary trips to an avian veterinarian.

Think what fun a talking bird will have turning the tables on you with this command! I can just see them learning "come here," "come cage," "come kitchen," "come couch" and so on, to call you to a location. What's next? Are we going to suggest you teach your bird to sit, stay and heel?

Want Some?

If we are observant, our birds try to tell us what they want. In fact, that's usually what they're doing. Our avian companions don't try to please us the way a dog does. They want to satisfy their own wishes and ensure their own survival. Because they are prey animals, some of their actions are dictated by their instinct to survive.

Offer your bird a dish of water or a treat food and ask her if she wants a drink or if she wants a bite. Often shaking the head means "no." If that's not the case with your bird, notice what reaction she does give. There will be times the answer is "yes" and your bird will take a drink, grab the treat or bite into it.

As you make these offerings, name the treat. Your talking bird can learn to say what she wants. Your non-talking bird will learn to identify favorite foods. Diane has no doubt that Aztec knows what a "nut" is, and he answers yes or no using body language when offered a drink from a cup.

Grooming Is a Breeze

Bird grooming consists of keeping the wing feathers and nails trimmed. You can combine verbal commands with your actions to get into a grooming routine that does not involve a lot of stress for your bird. Wrapping a bird in a towel every once in awhile, with no explanation of what's going on, can be traumatic for our prey species pets. However, being conditioned to having her wings and feet handled regularly can make grooming chores just part of everyday life for your companion bird.

Some birds naturally extend their wings to show off. That seems to be a regular and natural behavior for many Macaws and sometimes for Cockatoos. Your bird will learn to do this behavior on cue if you start using the same word consistently when you see her do the behavior. To prepare your bird for clipping her

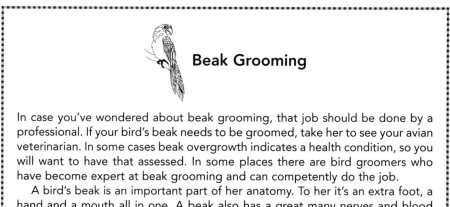

Beak Grooming

In case you've wondered about beak grooming, that job should be done by a professional. If your bird's beak needs to be groomed, take her to see your avian veterinarian. In some cases beak overgrowth indicates a health condition, so you will want to have that assessed. In some places there are bird groomers who have become expert at beak grooming and can competently do the job.

A bird's beak is an important part of her anatomy. To her it's an extra foot, a hand and a mouth all in one. A beak also has a great many nerves and blood vessels in it. And of course, the beak is attached to a bird's tongue, another important part of her anatomy. You do not want to accidentally cause permanent harm to your bird by making a mistake while grooming a beak.

Most healthy birds do not need much maintenance on their beaks. Many never need any beak grooming at all. Performing birds might have their beaks shined up so they look good on stage, but the typical healthy companion bird doesn't need regular beak grooming as a general rule.

wing feathers, also start handling her feathers when her wings are outstretched, and sometimes pull her wings up to get her used to the handling and restraint. Go through all the motions you'll use when trimming a wing feather, except actually doing it. This is good practice for the actual act, so that wing clipping is not stressful for your companion bird.

With smaller birds, regularly play games with a towel or practice the restraint you will be using when clipping wings. Even our smallest birds can get used to being picked up with a hand over their back, being held in a towel and being held against your chest while you extend their wings to inspect them.

One low-stress way of trimming a large parrot's toenails is to ask your bird to put her foot through the bars of her cage, or to hand you her foot when she's on the back of a chair. Then use a metal file to file at least one of her nails. She can learn "next," "foot" or some other relevant command so that this becomes routine.

Danger!

A bird, whether she verbalizes in English or not, can learn that you have exclamations that are designed to keep her safe. One of these Diane uses to talk to her (non-verbal) Pionus is "hot" to warn Aztec that a serving of food is still too hot to eat. She first used this when he dived into a plate of steaming spaghetti and was unpleasantly surprised by how hot it was. She uses "hot" to stop him from tasting hot foods and imbibing hot drinks.

In your everyday life, perhaps "stop," "no," "watch out" or "tsk tsk" would be useful phrases to use when a bird is too near a predatory animal, a hot stove, an open window, a poisonous plant or some other danger.

Fetch, à la Bird

You know how the game of fetch works with a dog. You throw a stick or a ball and the dog brings it back to you. Then you start over. This goes on endlessly if you have a retriever breed!

Birds can become quite adept at a form of fetch, too. The rules are a little different with them, though. You give them an object or a group of objects with which to play. This could be bottle caps, small craft sticks, buttons or beads. Then the bird throws an object overboard, off the top of her cage or over the edge of a table. She will then most likely go to the edge and look over, eyeing the item below. This seems to be an important part of the ritual.

You fetch the object and return it to the bird, then the game starts over again. Birds happily do this with more than one item, such as a whole selection of colored sticks or a whole bowl of freshly cut veggies (this is to be discouraged). You can have fun teaching your bird how to throw items into a specific container or from a specific area. Maybe you will be training a birdie basketball star.

Verbalizations you can use in this game include naming objects, asking your bird to get a specific object, or using a word to tell her that you are about to play this game. There are also exclamations of fun and joy you can associate with throwing objects and with watching objects fall: "Wheeeeee, ohhhhhhh, oh-oh!"

This leads us to our next topic, play.

THE IMPORTANCE OF PARROT PLAY

A companion bird is sensitive and enthusiastic. A bird is also a challenge, for she is highly intelligent, yet is often caged. Like any being, a companion bird benefits from intellectual stimulation and interaction. Most birds live in flocks in the wild, so socialization is especially important to them. Birds spend some time foraging for food, but also usually find time for exploring and playing with foliage in the environment or with their flock members.

Guess what? When you have a companion bird, you're the flock! You provide the environmental enrichment your parrot needs. Your bird depends on you for playtime and fun, as well as for the basics of care.

Variety Is the Spice of Life

There are many ways birds have fun. Part of your challenge as a companion bird owner is to be meticulously observant of your bird's activities. Note what she does when she's happy, bored or exploring. What kind of activity keeps her occupied? What can you do to enhance that kind of experience and give your bird a challenge? What will keep both of you engaged in the relationship? Your companion bird will appreciate the efforts you make to put variety into her life.

As you observe your bird, you will note that different species have different natural abilities and behaviors. Individual birds have individual play personalities and preferences as well. If you have an Amazon Parrot, for example, you may have more verbal than physical interactions with her. Amazons participate in a duet behavior in the wild that you can turn into a verbal game at your house. Start talking or singing to your Amazon regularly, encouraging your bird to take up part of the song as her own or to say a phrase back to you. Your duet can be nonsense or a chattering banter. Of course, African Grey Parrots are verbal as well. Rather than boisterous repartee, a Grey likes learning and will think it's a game when you start naming objects for her and getting her physical puzzles to work out.

The engineers of the bird world are Cockatoos. Objects that fit inside one another are very attractive to a Cockatoo. If you can find stainless steel nesting tools or hardware, or sets of gears for your Cockatoo, you'll have a bird who's entertained for hours. Other natural behaviors of Cockatoos are to thread items through each other. You might want to provide your Cockatoo with safe, short lengths of rawhide laces and chain or beads to see what she can do. Of course, the ultimate Cockatoo occupation is chewing! Expect to provide your Cockatoo with plenty of opportunity to chew by supplying her with untreated lumber, whisk brooms, baskets made of natural materials and woven or fiber chew toys. Chewing and preening are closely related behaviors. Help your young Cockatoo learn to preen her own feathers without chewing them. If you have a preening toy for your Cockatoo made with strings, allow play only under supervision. Strings can get tangled around a bird's legs or neck, and metals other than stainless steel can result in heavy metal poisoning. Play safety is important!

Some of the small parrots love snuggling. These include Lovebirds, Caiques and many Conures. To a Lovebird, traveling around in your pocket or under your collar is a treat. In their cage, these birds like a snuggling place or a nest box for roosting. It's not unusual for a Conure to like being turned on her back or to play on her back with a toy or ball you provide. Lovebirds and Quaker Parakeets instinctively shred materials and build nests. For these birds, provide palm fronds, clean hay or loosely woven baskets they can shred. You and the birds will have hours of entertainment.

This Maroon-bellied Conure, like many Conures and Macaws, likes playing on her back.

Budgies are high-energy little parrots. They naturally bop each other on the beak when playing, so you can lightly flick your Budgie on the beak with a fingernail as a form of beak wrestling that is interesting socialization for your bird. None of the members of the parakeet family are cuddly, but many are social and verbal. A male Budgie or a Ring-necked Parakeet will readily learn to talk. You can also teach the birds tricks, or set them up with toys in an aviary large enough for flight, creating a colorful, never-ending source of fascination that is better than television for entertainment!

Cockatiels are low-energy, peace-loving birds with a few quirks of their own. Males drum on perches or other surfaces in a macho display. You can join them by thumping back and making it a game. Cockatiels are good at ringing bells in time to music or other inspiration, or sitting quietly with their bells on their heads! Of course, being out of the cage and sitting on or near their favorite person, as well as some scritch time, are Cockatiel favorites as well. Cockatiels also like to undo knots on their rawhide lace toys and move colorful beads around on other toys. Cockatiels appreciate food toys such as broccoli flowerets, cooked corn on the cob or the seedy core from a green pepper as a foraging toy. A whole carrot to tear apart is equally entertaining.

Many toys and games are interesting to all species of companion birds. Time out of the cage is an important way to socialize your bird and give her more exercise. You can formalize time out and contain the bird mess as well by making acceptable play areas. Set up a perch or blanket in each area where a bird can play. Going for a ride, a picnic or other supervised time outside the home can be fun for your bird. Be sure the bird is securely in a carrier or has on a bird halter, and don't leave a feathered friend unsupervised.

Of course, the ultimate entertainment for a bird is doing what comes naturally—flying. If you can provide a daytime or summertime aviary for your bird that is large enough to fly in, your bird will stay in top shape. Smaller birds can be allowed flight times in a house or apartment. Birds with clipped wings still need exercise. Take time daily to hold your bird's feet and encourage her to flap by moving your arm up and down. You can also devise ways for your companion bird to exercise in going about her daily business. Make sure food and water are at opposite sides of a cage, or devise a play area that is accessible with a ladder or through flying or hopping. Train your bird to come to you and to return to her cage, giving you ways to exercise her.

As simple a thing as occasionally redecorating a cage offers entertainment and alleviates boredom for a companion bird. New natural wood perches give your friend bark to chew on and strip. A new bouncy perch, rope perch or swing offers something different. One of the safe play areas in your home could feature a special perch or swing. A play area can be as simple as a blanket, towel or newspaper spread on the floor. Put out toys or a toy basket for your bird and spend some time

DIANE GRINDOL

Encourage your bird to flap by moving your arm up and down. She really needs the exercise! (This is a Red-fronted Macaw.)

playing. Some species are comfortable on the floor, including Cockatoos, Greys and Cockatiels, while others will feel safer off the floor, on a bed or table. Macaws like to wrestle and play rough with their owners during play time. Other birds may just like to explore or will want gentle petting. Greys may exhibit their instinctive digging behavior. Verbal birds will like talking into hollow containers in which they can hear an echo.

As an adventurous soul, you can also include your companion bird on car trips. Start with short trips. Take your bird in a carrier or a small cage, with no hanging toys that could become harmful missiles on a bumpy ride. Strap the carrier in. Many birds enjoy riding in a car and are even welcome sometimes at your destination. Time in the car can be spent singing or vocalizing and talking about the sites you're seeing. It makes the occasional trip to see the veterinarian less stressful. Not every car ride ends up at that scary place! If you start taking longer trips, look for hotels or motels that accept pets and plan your trip around them. Of course, you must be sure to only take your bird out in weather that is neither too hot nor too cold and to carry a water bottle to spray your bird if she does heat up.

Young birds and older birds who have lived sedentary or boring lives may not know how to play. This is where your responsibility as a flock-mate comes in. When a companion bird doesn't know how to play, you can teach her. If a toy

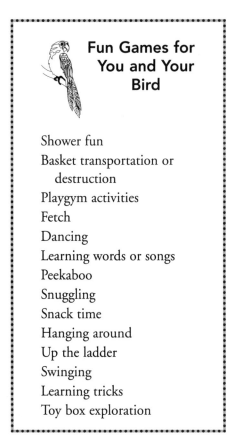

Fun Games for You and Your Bird

Shower fun

Basket transportation or destruction

Playgym activities

Fetch

Dancing

Learning words or songs

Peekaboo

Snuggling

Snack time

Hanging around

Up the ladder

Swinging

Learning tricks

Toy box exploration

is scary for a bird, don't immediately assume she doesn't like it. A bird is a prey animal, and natural wariness saves the lives of her wild cousins. A companion bird can be conditioned to accept items that initially are scary. Leave the toy or perch outside the cage but within sight of your bird for a few days. When she no longer notices the toy, move it closer. When this is acceptable, put the toy on your bird's cage, on the outside. Then at last you can move the toy into the cage.

You can model how to play with a new toy for your bird. Before it's in the cage, exclaim over the toy, jiggle movable parts, ring bells and enjoy the toy. A bird who doesn't know how to play with toys needs lots of these lessons from another member of the flock. Any movement toward a toy should be rewarded with verbal praise or even a favorite treat. At first, that might just be touching the toy outside the cage.

Your bird may enjoy holding on to a rope you swing around or a long ladder you flip over or twirl around. Go slowly and teach this activity in stages for the greatest success. First get the bird used to being on the conveyance (blanket, rope or ladder), then to being jiggled on the conveyance. Then lift her and finally, start moving the blanket or rope or ladder so your bird is riding on it and eventually flapping too.

Interaction between you and your bird is pleasurable for you both. You can teach your bird "up" or teach her a trick. You'll both enjoy the interaction and sense of accomplishment. Birds who have learned from their owners and are understood by their owners are fulfilled birds with a sense of how to communicate between our species.

I've only mentioned a few of the many ways in which you can provide your bird with an enriched environment. Put on your own thinking cap, think like a bird and look around. There's a world of entertainment out there, and a lifetime of enjoyment because of it!

POINTS TO REMEMBER

- Interspecies communication can make life easier for you and your bird.

- To teach your bird a phrase for a regular activity, such as going into her cage, consistently use that phrase every time you do the activity.

- Birds are intelligent animals and need play and variety in their lives or they will not thrive.

- Different species of birds, and different individuals within each species, have their own preferences for play. Watch your bird carefully to see what she likes to do.

- Birds are flock animals and need social interaction with us—their flock members.

Chapter 13

Problem Solving for Vocal Birds

This chapter is sort of like a list of errors in a computer or technical manual. Error 234 means you left a colon out of an address. Error 64 means you lost your network connection. Error 3001 means your hard drive is no longer working, and that's big trouble! Some of those errors are easy to fix, others involve installing new parts. Some involve calling to the technical support department of the manufacturer.

With parrots, there are few errors that involve just changing one small thing for a quick fix. There are some that require technical support. If you try to replace parts, you might find it doesn't work too well! If you replace the whole piece of equipment and start with another parrot, that might not work either; you and your environment created the parrot you have, so the problem could just reoccur.

TALKING PARROT PROBLEMS

Chances are really good that you've been training your parrot, or he's been training you, for quite some time. Your parrot has an innate need to learn his flock vocalizations and to have his needs met. Some parrots are downright manipulative when they learn what gets your attention! Think about what gets your attention. Is it the phone, the microwave or your spouse? What sounds or words does your bird imitate?

PROBLEMS WITH VOCAL PARROTS

Screaming

Using foul (or is that fowl?) language

Vocabulary includes undesirable word(s)

Imitation of bodily functions

High-volume sounds or words

Forgetting words

Boredom

Not learning new phrases

You may have actually created your bird's bad behaviors as well as his good ones. This happens over time, and the behaviors can be changed over time. They start to change when you take responsibility for the actions that caused them. It will take some thinking to figure out what happened, and it will take some more creative thinking about ways to fix things. There are probably several options in your situation. How do other people handle problems with their vocal bird?

This Blue-fronted Amazon is responding to his owner's attention by talking. You may actually be inadvertently rewarding bad behavior by giving lots of attention and interaction to your parrot when he's doing something undesirable, such as screaming.

PRAISE THE PARROT

One of the simple concepts you can use to change parrot behavior is to ignore unwanted behavior and praise good behavior. This promotes the repetition of a good behavior and the disappearance of a bad behavior. If the behavior you don't like is your parrot saying a certain word, you can make the vocalization disappear by not reacting to that word. This is what it means to take responsibility for your bird's learning. How have you reacted in the past to a swear word or a noise imitating a bodily function? You probably reacted with a loud exclamation of your own, started laughing or went over to the bird and started talking to him. You might have been chewing him out, but he got some attention and a show!

With your new strategy of ignoring an unwanted behavior, you will show no reaction when your bird says a swear word or imitates a burp or other bodily function. You'll have to clue in family members and guests as well, who might spontaneously "reward" this behavior with attention. You might even take it a step further and turn your back on your bird or leave the room.

Shannon of Washington has a male Vosmaeri Eclectus who breaks all the rules. You can't believe everything you read! Shannon responded to our survey question, "Do your birds talk or vocalize when you don't want them to? How do you deal with that?" by replying, "Only the wolf whistle. This seems to be his way of saying he would like your company. Sometimes he does it when we sleep in on weekends. My husband just yells at him to 'shut up,' and that does the trick. I know this tactic does not work with most parrots, but ours does not like to be yelled at, or yelling in general, and he will let us know this by involving

Wanda is praising Joanna for being good. It's sometimes difficult to remember, but rewarding good behavior is positive reinforcement for continuing a desired behavior.

himself in our domestic disputes, which usually cracks us up and stops the argument."

The second step in this process is to praise the bird for saying things you want to hear, and for just playing quietly and being a good bird. This is sometimes hard to remember to do, since you're rewarding something that's not exceptional but is desirable. Reward your bird by paying attention to her, saying "good bird" or offering a special treat.

It's more difficult to ignore screaming than it is a single word, but you can change behavior by doing just that. Ignore a bird when he screams and remember to praise him for being quiet. Diane ignores her Pionus by walking around his cage with her back to him and not giving him any of the attention he seems to want.

This will be especially effective if you have thought about it and discovered how the screaming behavior was first created. Do you normally come running when your bird screams, or do you give her something as a bribe to be

This Gold-capped Conure has her mouth full! Many people learn to simply ignore the screams of their Conure companions.

quiet (the bird's reward), or do you scream back, putting on an interesting and entertaining show for your intelligent companion?

Esther in Michigan says of her Citron-crested Cockatoos, "The second bird does more flock calling than I appreciate. I give reassurance when appropriate; otherwise I ignore and praise when he's quiet or talking."

It's also important to remember that physical punishment is not an acceptable way to work with your bird. Parrots aren't physical with each other. People have tried squirting water at a bird who is vocalizing loudly, but this can make it difficult for the bird to accept a bath, which is a necessary part of a bird's week. The bird will appreciate the squirt or could lose trust in an owner for being dealt with in a physical instead of a cerebral way.

Tanya of Kentucky is pragmatic. Her Gold-capped Conure, Sagan, and Lesser Sulphur-crested Cockatoo, Jack, do sometimes scream. When they do she ignores it. "They are not punished for screaming or talking at any time."

PRESTO CHANGO

If your bird is saying something you don't want to hear, another option is to change the word or vocalization into an acceptable word, change screams into words, or change loud vocalizations into softer ones. You will need to model this behavior for your bird. Next time you hear an unacceptable word, start reacting to it as if it is really what you want to hear. Instead of "Mandy" (the old girlfriend), you could say "candy," "randy," "manu" or "manly." Talk to the bird about how "manly" he is or tell him that his favorite treats are called "candy." You could also use the model/rival technique. Have a family member or friend participate. They will be rewarded for saying the new word, but you will say "no" or ignore the old, unacceptable version.

Similarly, if the main thing you object to about your bird's vocalization is its volume, you can model acceptable behavior by starting to whisper to your bird. Owners report that sometimes it drives them nuts to have an African Grey learn a Cockatiel's call, a baby's cry or a Mockingbird's repertoire, then repeat it at full African Grey volume. Think again about how you have reacted in the past to loud outbursts. Chances are you were loud yourself, or you ran over to your bird. It's not a natural reaction to stay calm and whisper to your bird. But try it!

Taco, a female Solomon Island Eclectus, and her companion, Tiki the Cockatiel, live with Tena in Colorado. Tena says, "Taco does sometimes talk loudly when we have company and she is not the center of attention. We just tell her in a whisper to be quiet and whisper to her, and she will then start whispering rather than being loud."

THE BIG COVER-UP

Yet another possibility for excessive screaming is short periods of "time out." Parrot style, this means time spent covered up and in their cage, away from their favorite companions and the rest of the flock. This can lower the energy level of your parrot's vocalizations and help your shattered nerves. You will probably want the cover to be thick and dark.

Ellen of Calgary, Alberta, lives with Guccia, a 22-year-old Eleanora Cockatoo. She says, "His talking is always pleasant but turns to screaming when put in his cage and he thinks it isn't time or is unjustified. We try to ignore it for the most part and will take him out if he is quiet for 10 minutes or so. Sometimes if he has been screaming for 20 minutes straight and we can't handle it any more, we will cover him."

Thea in Nevada has one Eclectus, one Caique, one Senegal and a Canary. "When the Caique screams excessively, we put her down for a nap like a child."

Set a timer for 10 minutes or less. Your bird is not sitting in the dark thinking he was bad and promising to never do it again. He's also not counting the time.

He doesn't equate a longer time out with a more grievous offence. Your bird probably doesn't care a whole lot about pleasing you. But he cares about his own needs, which include food and fun. By covering your bird, you are simply changing the scenery and putting your bird into a situation in which he's not likely to vocalize. You're communicating your displeasure and hoping the bird gets it. You're removing fun and attention, which are two things he craves.

Don't forget to praise him for appropriate behavior. When your bird is playing, vocalizing softly or carrying on pleasant conversation, reward him with praise or a little play. Expect the best from your bird!

Debi in California has four African Greys, a Double Yellow-headed Amazon and several male Cockatiels who vocalize. When they are screaming and making car alarm and smoke alarm noises, she gives them two warnings, then they are put into their cage and covered. With the fourth Grey she only has to give her the "evil eye" for her to be quiet. Giving a parrot the evil eye is staring at her without blinking, with a stern expression on your face.

DRIVEN TO DISTRACTION

Covering the cage is one kind of distraction you can use while you're working on curbing unwanted vocalizations. There are others. A distraction can effectively stop an undesired behavior, while creating industriousness and quiet on your bird's part. Distractions include things to chew and eat. They also include a new activity, like being covered or going somewhere with you—even if it's just to a different room. They might include starting up a whole new conversation. You can model this behavior, too. If you have a screaming bird but you're having fun playing with a new bird toy, the bird might just change the focus of her attention to the toy.

When Marnie's 13-year-old Timneh Grey is noisy, she does a contact whistle or distracts him with a toy or a piece of fruit or something else to keep him busy.

Be sure to note what time your bird is repeatedly vocalizing. What's going on in the room? Is this a sunup and sundown situation? Is there something in the room that the bird is vocalizing about? Try using distraction in a situation where you would normally expect noise, and offer the distraction before the noise begins. This includes coming home in the evening. If you give your bird a treat, some veggies or a chew toy when you come home, you can listen to messages, change clothes and attend to your chores before giving your bird some attention. Diane's friend found that leaving corn on the cob in her parrot aviaries overnight limited morning noise, because it kept the parrots busy destroying the corn and cob, instead of notifying the neighborhood that it was dawn.

Use a similar strategy with phone calls. Before you make one, give your bird a chewing challenge, such as putting newspaper or twigs on top of his cage that must be pulled through the cage bars and shredded. See if this keeps him occupied, even with the distraction of your animated conversation on the phone.

Lisa of British Columbia, Canada, has an Umbrella Cockatoo named Angelbrat who often talks, sings, barks or otherwise makes noise when Lisa would like some quiet. To deal with it, she asks her Cockatoo to please be quiet, then tries to distract her with a treat or a toy. This usually works.

Also take a look at whether your bird's needs are being met. Are there ways you can involve your parrot in more of your activities? Honestly, is your bird getting plenty of attention or could she use a little more? Attention isn't always hands-on; usually just being near you is exciting enough. Diane has a Pionus named Aztec who is helping to write this book right now. Aztec screams less now that he has perches in many rooms and is involved in many of Diane's daily activities.

There are bird shower bars that can be tacked on tile walls, windows and mirrors, so your friend has a place to be with you. There are portable playgyms and T-stands that contain the mess a little. You can make a toy basket with "foot toys" that goes with you to other rooms. It doesn't hurt to make sure your bird knows how to play on his own, but providing love and socialization are important, too. When your bird is sitting quietly or playing with his toys, remember to praise him.

THE DECIBEL LEVEL IS A FACTOR

Birds seem to feel a need to keep up with the level of noise in their environment. Diane sold a Cockatiel chick once to people who complained that he was a noisy bird. He certainly hadn't been before leaving home, and he was very young to have learned many bad habits. Upon further investigation, it turned out the bird's cage was on top of a television set. The Cockatiel constantly chattered to keep up with the constant chatter on television! Another bird who was her companion Cockatiel, Charlie, rang his bell to compete with the booming voice of the local Tupperware salesperson—which did nothing to promote sales. Charlie also rang his bell in time to classical music.

Noise level is a factor when your bird is around sound equipment, a television, in busy households, when the vacuum is running, when a faucet is on and when there's someone on the phone. Even if there's construction in the neighborhood or a loud storm, you might notice a higher noise level from your parrot.

Red-sided Eclectus male Reggie, who belongs to Kathy of Georgia, sometimes gets loud. "Turning the TV or radio off will usually quiet him down," Kathy says. "If he's in his cage and I'm home, he'll call for me. If I'm in another room, he'll call for me."

Debbie of Mississippi has an Umbrella Cockatoo named Magic who can scream very loudly at times. "If I'm on the phone, I either put her back in her cage or I

DIANE GRINDOL

This Bronze-winged Pionus has accompanied her owner to the living room and is sitting quietly on the couch. Taking your parrot with you as you move from room to room is one way to provide her with more socialization and keep screaming behavior to a minimum.

leave the room (if she's already in her cage). If I'm not on the phone, I'll do my best to ignore it unless it gets really bad. Then she gets put back in her cage."

Your options are to be aware of what's causing the bird's noisiness and do nothing—just be aware. Or change the level of noise. Or move the bird to a less noisy location. Depending upon the size of your living quarters, the control you have over household noise and your willingness to make changes, the perfect situation for you will be very individual. Maybe you could try some whisper modeling with family members.

ANSWER YOUR PARROT

Your bird is often looking for a response when he vocalizes. What could be more natural than responding? Try to respond in a way that acknowledges that the bird is using words that have meaning. For example, if your bird says "hello," say "hello" back and maybe tack on a "how are you?" Let the bird know that you are fine, are suffering a backache or have the sniffles today. This will serve to enlarge your bird's vocabulary and give him attention as a reward for talking. It will also help the bird to retain his vocabulary.

Lynne of Georgia lives with a five-year-old male Maroon-bellied Conure and a three-year-old Severe Macaw. When asked if her birds vocalize when she doesn't want them to, she replied, "Of course! When I'm spoken to, I answer."

It's natural for parrots to live in a flock. In the wild, a bird is never separated from his flock or his mate. People become a captive bird's flock, and we come and go in our homes. It can be helpful to have a contact call to let your parrot know you're within earshot and okay.

Remember that positive reinforcement keeps a behavior in existence. At the beginning of this chapter, we mentioned that ignoring a vocalization is one way to make it go away. Answering a vocalization is a way to keep it around. There are numerous accounts of a bird saying something once and not repeating it. If you hear your bird say something for the first time (something you want him to say), be sure to make a big deal out of it, praise your bird and answer what he said, including using the word or phrase he said. If you treat a new vocalization the way you treat an unwanted bit of fowl language—by ignoring it—it will go the way of the expletive. Which is, hopefully, away!

Marti, a 15-year-old Mexican Red-headed Amazon (also called a Green-cheeked Amazon), belongs to Kay of New York. Kay says Marti calls to her when she's out of the room—sometimes loudly. Kay calls back or goes in the room to reassure her she's still around. So Marti keeps calling.

Answering a contact call is a behavior a bird expects from members of her flock. Birds spend time out of sight of one another, and when they do so they use contact calls to keep the flock in aural touch. Many people have found that developing an acceptable contact call for themselves and their bird aids in communication and keeps down the volume of screams a bird might otherwise choose as a way to keep in touch. Thea in Nevada, for example, has trained her three birds to say "hello" for contact calls.

What contact call could you use? When you leave the room, you could whisper or whistle, or use the word "hello" or the phrase "I'm here" as your contact call—telling your bird you are still within earshot even though you are out of sight. You may have already subconsciously established such a routine, or your bird may one-sidedly have decided upon a call. Try imitating your bird's contact call as a communication, if you wish. This talking thing can go either way: You can learn bird, or your bird can learn to speak your language.

ATTITUDE IS EVERYTHING

Another aspect of natural behavior in birds is that they greet the dawn and call as they settle in to roost at night. If you were to travel to your parrot's native habitat, you would find flocks of birds vocalizing at these hours. Another way to deal with your bird's vocalizations is to tolerate them as expressions of his well-being and love for life! Many of our avian companions have only been out of their natural environment for a generation or two. Our more long-term avian companions, such as Cockatiels and Budgies, who have been in captivity since the 1850s, have still not lost that trait.

Your attitude is important. You can decide to be stressed and work at changing a behavior, or you can enjoy your parrot, interact with him, acknowledge his nature and enjoy your bird for what he provides you in the way of companionship and entertainment.

Lee of Pennsylvania says her Blue and Gold Macaws do vocalize when she doesn't want them to, but "I usually enjoy their vocalizations."

Ellie has a Sun Conure in New York. When asked if her bird vocalizes when she doesn't want him to, she replied, "Does it matter what I want?!"

Mary Beth in Texas has Quaker Parakeets who screech at sunup and sundown. "I tell them to talk, not squawk. Nub usually answers me with an expletive. So I figure it is something that he has to do."

WHY CAN'T WE ALL JUST GET ALONG?

Sometimes a bird will decide he doesn't like one member of the family and will scream at that person. There are a variety of reasons for this, including the attitude of the person your bird dislikes and your own attitude toward that person. Other causes include a history of abuse from a person who looked like the person in your family the bird dislikes. Part of the cure is for the person who is the focus of the noise to begin to establish a relationship with the bird. This isn't always easy. Sometimes the parrot's fear or dislike of the person includes biting as well as screaming. Sometimes the bird believes he is defending the rest of the flock from this despised interloper. Think of a pleasurable activity the bird can enjoy, such as shower time, an afternoon snack or a verbal duet. Only the person the bird initially dislikes should do this activity with the bird. That's one way to gain his trust and affection. Engage in this activity with a positive attitude.

One of the other ways to get past this initial stage of difficulty is for the disliked person to get two perches, each about two feet long. The bird is then encouraged to perch on one of the perches and allowed to sit there. The bird will usually either go to the end of the perch as far from the person as possible, or he will move to attack the hand holding the perch. If the bird moves away, put the other perch out for the bird to transfer to it. Keep repeating this process until you have the bird moving nearer to the person with each change of perches. Eventually the bird will move closer and begin to form a better relationship with the person he once despised.

If the bird moves to attack the hand holding the perch, move the other perch in a position to intercept the parrot before he reaches the hand. Keep the parrot near the end of the new perch farthest from the hand. As the parrot moves to attack again, repeat the interception with the other perch. Eventually the parrot will reduce his moves to attack the hand holding the perch and begin to calm down. This process takes time and will require that the person who is involved be willing to make friends with the parrot who's working so hard to rid the household of him. It's fortunate that most people can learn to come to terms with the problem long enough to teach the parrot a new way of interacting.

POINTS TO REMEMBER

- Vocal birds learn unwanted sounds, from electronic noises to bodily functions, and undesirable words.

- If you ignore unwanted verbalizations and praise good behavior, you can change a parrot's behavior.

- You can model what you want your parrot to do and say to change his behavior.

- A bird's vocalizations often match the volume of noise in a household. You can adjust one or the other, or tolerate the noise level.

- Answer your bird's vocalizations to retain his vocabulary and to teach him more words.

- Some vocalization is natural and is an expression of a parrot's joy of life. This is especially true of morning and evening vocalizations.

Chapter 14

Parrots Who Don't Talk

If your parrot does not talk, you may find yourself feeling one of several ways about it:

- You are happy that you have a relatively quiet parrot.
- You're fine; you did not expect your bird to talk.
- You are resigned about your bird's lack of talking ability.
- You are unhappy that your expectations were not met.
- You still have energy and enthusiasm for teaching your bird to talk. You'll keep trying.

If your bird does not talk and you've tried consistently to teach her over some months (years?), you may have face up to the reality that your bird does not talk in English. Not right now. Maybe never. No matter how hard you wished she talked, she does not. Accepting that fact and working at other aspects of the parrot-human relationship can be rewarding. There's probably something about your parrot you have grown to appreciate. Does she snuggle, laugh, share meals with you? Is she gorgeous, amusing, flirtatious? Even parrots who do not talk *do* communicate, so building trust and communication can give you something to work on that pays off for you both.

This chapter lists the things you can change in your environment to get your bird interested in talking. They're meant to improve her health and happiness so that she is inspired to talk. These steps may also improve her life without improving her talking ability—which means they are definitely worth a try.

COVERING THE BASICS

First and foremost, consider whether the basic needs of your non-talking bird are being met. Find out if she's healthy. When was the last time you took your bird in to see an avian veterinarian for a well-bird check? Although birds don't need regular vaccinations the way dogs do, it's still a good idea to have an avian veterinarian examine your bird regularly, weigh her and perform lab tests. (For advice on finding an avian veterinarian, see Chapter 1.)

Most talking birds are prey animals and naturally try to hide their illness, since looking sick could result in being eaten or being driven from their flock. For this reason, an avian veterinarian will usually take samples of your bird's blood and droppings for analysis by a lab. A bird could have a low-grade infection that could make her feel bad enough to clam up. It's only possible to know that through lab tests.

Your observations as an owner are important to your veterinarian, as well. If a talking bird stops talking for no obvious reason, a trip to the vet is a good idea.

MAKING A PARROT FEEL AT HOME

You may not have thought of your parrot as a rain forest creature who is adapted to your living room, but that's pretty much what you have—except for the adapted part. Your parrot is a rain forest creature still adapted to life in the rain forest (or savannah or tropics or cloud forest). As the companion of a caged animal, you have taken on the responsibility of providing her with all of the aspects of the rain forest not normally found in a living room. Those include sun, rain, abundant food and branches to destroy. There's usually plenty to do and lots to learn in a rain forest habitat. Is there plenty for your parrot to do and learn and explore in your home?

For the most part, we've provided our birds a way to be safe from predators. Their instinct to flee from potential danger may still be strong, though. Even after 150 years in captivity, most Cockatiels who live in outside aviaries know how dangerous a hawk flying overhead can be. They react accordingly. Without knowing what's upsetting her, your bird may be quite frightened of household decorations or furniture that are over her head. This could be a clock, balloons, an overhead fan or a knickknack shelf. If your bird does not seem comfortable where she's located in your home, try moving things around or move the bird to a different location. You also may give her a safe area in her cage or behind a sheet of plywood, or a grouping of toys. Your parrot is most likely to talk when she is comfortable, happy and healthy.

When Diane started to hang a bright orange plastic chain as a plaything for her parrot, he reacted with extreme fear. He's at least two generations removed from the wild (four generations on his mother's side) but still seemed to know that a long, brightly colored wiggly object could spell danger—it could be a snake. Take a second look at your bird's surroundings. Pretend you are a bird, looking out of her cage or off her play stand. As a prey animal, would you be comfortable? Is there always a cat prowling around your cage, or are you safe in your cage? Are fingers and snouts and paws intruding into your space, or is the cage a safe place? You may have to create an off-limits area around your bird's cage if little fingers are being poked at a bird. This kind of teasing could inhibit talking.

Though we think of our parrots as being rain forest birds, they are adapted to many different habitats throughout the world. It might be fun for you to read more about the natural environment of the species you keep for a pet. Cockatiels and Budgies, for example, are from a dry desert region in Australia. Other parrots are grassland birds, and others, such as the Derbyan Parakeet, a native of the Himalayas, are high-altitude birds.

RAIN, RAIN, COME AGAIN

In the rain forest, and in most wild habitats, it rains! When you provide your companion parrot with frequent showers, she will be happier and will start to gleam because her feathers are well cared-for. Showers are a part of making a parrot happy. In hot weather, they are especially appreciated. How would you shower a parrot? Use water alone. Forget the soap. But there are many variations on that theme. They range from splashing in the kitchen sink to sharing your shower.

A tried and true method is using a plant sprayer. Fill it with warm water and set it on a light mist. Spray your parrot from above, simulating rainfall as much as possible. For a larger flock of birds, there are garden sprayers available that you pump up to build pressure for spraying. If you go this route, be sure to use it only for water for your birds. Don't ever use a sprayer that has ever contained fertilizers or pesticides.

You may be able to teach smaller birds to take a bath under a water faucet. You want to adjust the water so it is neither too hot nor too cold. Alternatively, you may be able to offer your bird companion water in a dish or in a saucer for bathing. We know a couple of people who have birds who "lettuce surf"—they take baths in wet lettuce. Perhaps in the wild they would delight in wet leaves on a tree branch!

If your parrot is large, or if you want to save time, you and your bird can shower at the same time. Simply being in a misty bathroom is good for your bird's feathers and sinuses. If she gets sprinkled, all the better. There are special parrot perches made for showers. The curtain rod is convenient, too. Be sure to keep the toilet bowl closed when your parrot is with you. Bodies of water are enticing but dangerous to a bird. If you have a flighted bird with you, be aware that she might fly into the mirror. You could cover the mirror to avoid this.

Review the basics to make sure your companion bird is happy. Does she have plenty of playthings and mental stimulation? This Peach-fronted Conure is turning someone's wristwatch into a toy.

Obviously, you should regulate the temperature of water so that it is comfortable and safe for your bird.

LET THE SUN SHINE IN

You may allow your parrot time outside in a cage, or on a perch outside if she is well supervised. Access to sunlight helps birds manufacture vitamin D_3. If you are feeding your companion a formulated diet, she's probably getting enough vitamin D_3 from that source. Many companion bird owners offer their birds full-spectrum lighting anyway. This is lighting that emits rays that contain the entire spectrum of sunlight—which normal incandescent or fluorescent lighting does not. There are special bulbs available that do, however.

DIANE GRINDOL

A companion parrot can benefit from regular exposure to sunshine or full-spectrum lighting. This Red-lored Amazon is catching some rays.

Lighting is one of the things that makes a parrot's environment more natural and will add to her sense of happiness and well-being. Her natural colors will be shown off to the very best advantage too, making you even happier to watch your bird's antics.

R&R

How long is your parrot up each day, and is she getting enough sleep? Parrots should probably have 12 hours of sleep a day. If you are staying up to watch the late show, your parrot might not be getting enough sleep to be alert and to vocalize.

Like people who are sleep-deprived, parrots who aren't getting enough sleep are grouchier and nippier. Diane has known of Cockatiels with a Dr. Jekyl and Mr. Hyde personality who are sweet during the day but who nip their owners in the late evening when they're up past bedtime. In the long term, a bird's health may be compromised and she could develop infections or behavior problems.

Some birds, including Cockatiels, are stimulated to exhibit nesting and breeding behavior when they are awake for long hours each day. These birds are adapted to the desert and don't have a breeding season. They breed whenever conditions are right to bring up their chicks in what they expect to be a harsh environment. Regulating daylight hours regulates breeding behavior, which includes territorial biting, chewing on wood and laying or incubating eggs. That's a nice benefit for pet owners!

You may consider putting your bird's lighting on a timer, to provide her with long nights. Be creative in your other provisions for your parrot's well-being. Can you leave her covered later in the morning, let her sleep in a quieter room, or work with other household members to provide a suitable schedule?

PARROTS ARE SOCIAL BUTTERFLIES

You have a bird adapted to living in a highly social flock. When your parrot joined your family, she probably bonded to other birds in the household (if you have other birds) or she decided to include the humans in the household as members of her flock. You want that flock status if you wish to have a talking bird. It seems one of the reasons parrots talk may be to learn flock calls. In our homes, the flock calls are phrases we repeat often and sounds that elicit a desired response, such as calling the flock together. I guess garbage truck beeping is part of the morning cacophony to a parrot and bears repeating.

DIANE GRINDOL

Cockatiels especially need to receive enough sleep (12 to 14 hours per night) so they don't become nippy at night and so that long days do not stimulate breeding and nesting behavior. These are male Pearl and Cinnamon-pearl Cockatiels.

You can teach your parrot more of these flock calls by using them deliberately. "Hello," "good-bye" and "thank you" are simple ones. Do you maintain social contact with your parrot even when you're out of sight? Her flock buddies would, and you may wish to come up with a contact call of some sort.

WHERE IS YOUR PARROT IN THE PECKING ORDER?

If you sense that your parrot is not talking because she doesn't perceive herself to be a very important member of the family, you can increase her self-esteem by trying one or all of the methods we are about to describe.

Letting clipped wings grow out increases a parrot's agility and ability to control her own body. Of course, you will have to be very careful not to leave doors or windows open. If you don't dare let a parrot have free flight in your house, you could make sure she has a less drastic wing clip the next time this is done.

Allowing your parrot to have some time on a high perch is another way to increase her sense of self-importance. In the wild, the higher-ranking birds get to sit in the higher branches of a tree. Parrots can be manipulative if given half a chance, so you may or may not want to try this one! Be sure your parrot needs the extra confidence, or consult with a parrot behavior consultant about your particular situation.

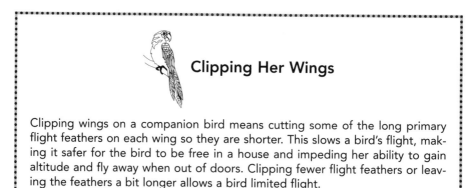

Clipping Her Wings

Clipping wings on a companion bird means cutting some of the long primary flight feathers on each wing so they are shorter. This slows a bird's flight, making it safer for the bird to be free in a house and impeding her ability to gain altitude and fly away when out of doors. Clipping fewer flight feathers or leaving the feathers a bit longer allows a bird limited flight.

The number of feathers clipped and the amount clipped off each feather varies by species and individual. Long-tailed, slim-bodied birds like Cockatiels and Conures are aerodynamic and need more feathers clipped shorter to curtail their flight. Stocky, short-tailed birds like African Greys and Amazon Parrots benefit from a less drastic wing clipping.

Birds replace their feathers at least once a year, so usually wing clipping needs to be done at least that often. Your avian veterinarian can perform this service, as can a bird groomer. You can learn to do it yourself, as well, with good instruction from an experienced individual the first time.

You may have expectations about your parrot's talking abilities that she simply cannot meet. Especially in the beginning, a bird may not say words clearly. Some species don't have clear, humanlike voices. Bugsie, a Senegal Parrot who belonged to Peg of California, says "bagel-bagel" when he means "tickle-tickle." It took Peg a long time to figure this out! Once you figure out what a parrot is saying, react to it to encourage the phrase. You can also say the word clearly yourself, so your parrot can improve her pronunciation.

I WANNA

Parrots who are taught to talk using any method, or none at all, are most vocal when talking produces something they want. If you can make a game out of giving your untalkative parrot treats or affection, that's a step in the right direction. A game you could try with food is to eat some in front of the bird, naming the food over and over. When the bird obviously wants the food and makes a sound, go ahead and give her some. You're hoping that sound she uttered will eventually turn into an actual word.

Chiquita, a Blue-crowned Conure who belongs to Celeste of California, is typical. He says "wanna see the babies" when he wants to go to the window and watch wild birds. He also says "come on" to mean he wants to come out of his cage or get off his perch to play with his family.

Our survey respondents were very clear that their birds asked for hugs, attention, cuddles or food. Angel-brat, the Umbrella Cockatoo, talks to get attention. She calls her owner Lisa by name or calls "mommy" when she's hungry and needs more food in her dish. Similarly, Jennifer of South Carolina has a Quaker Parakeet who talks when she wants to be fed because the rest of the flock is eating.

IT MIGHT TAKE SHERLOCK HOLMES

Diane was visiting friends once and was the first to tell them that their Budgie was talking! She had heard the high-pitched, fast chatter of the Budgie and realized that what the household thought was noise was actually a series of words. They learned to listen to what their Budgie was saying after that.

Does your bird talk even though you don't recognize it yet? Susan of California lives with a Grey-cheeked Parakeet and a Brown-headed Parrot (one of the Poicephalus, a small African species). She says she generally knows what her birds are saying, but they talk with "overtones of scratchy little bird" and other people need her "translation" to understand what the birds are saying.

Part of having a talking bird may be listening. Frank, who belongs to Rose-breasted Cockatoo Julie, describes the process very well. "Now she has begun to speak in extended gibberish and we can't understand what she's saying. It sounds like she's speaking long sentences. Every once in a while a new expression materializes

Listen carefully to your bird's vocalizations! Initial attempts at speech are usually mumbling sounds. Budgies talk in a high, squeaky voice and may be saying words you don't recognize unless you listen closely.

out of the gibberish and it may or may not be added to her standard repertoire. Can others tell what she's saying? Not right away. It's like baby talk: Only the parents can tell. Sometimes I'll hear something that my wife can't and I'll tell her, 'There it is again! Did you hear it?' Soon Julie is saying it very clearly, even though strangers might not catch it. Julie has her own voice. She does not mimic the timbre of a human voice, but she's got the cadence and expressiveness down pat."

Remember that birds pick up the intonation of a phrase before they can clearly say a word. Listen for that in your parrot's vocalizations before you give up on her.

There are other instances when a bird mumbles or whistles a word softly to herself before she says a word to another being. Listen to the mutterings of your parrot as she nods off to sleep or when she's by himself for a while. Some owners spy on their bird from outside a room, or if you are serious about this, you could have a video camera running. A voice-activated tape recorder may also catch your talking parrot chattering.

If your bird makes any attempt at a vocalization, reward her with praise or a treat. A squeak or grunt could well turn into the clear word you expect—eventually. Remember to have some patience with your bird. Most birds listen for a while before they actually say a word. It's important for you to keep talking to your bird, whether or not you are getting the response you think you should!

THE COMPETITION

Many birds vocalize to establish their territories and show off their vocal prowess for potential competition. If you have just one companion bird, or a particular bird is the only one of its species in your family, you can provide this competition with a mirror. This might mean occasional access to the bathroom mirror, or providing your parrot with a mirrored toy or mirror of her own. This works especially well with the smaller parrots, such as Cockatiels and Parakeets. It doesn't promote cognitive vocalization, but it does provide practice time.

If you give a bird a mirror or a mirrored toy, be sure to choose a product made especially for birds. Normal mirrors may be a source of lead. They also are fragile. Bird toys are made of non-toxic materials or are constructed so they cannot be pulled apart by busy beaks. In addition, choose a mirror made for the size of bird you have. A Cockatiel mirror does not need to be as indestructible as one made for an Amazon Parrot or a Macaw.

DAVID WROBEL

A mirror can stimulate talking and provide companion-ship for a single bird.

SING ALONG

Our companion birds are very musical, and we've already mentioned that they enjoy vocalizations that are expressive. If you aren't getting any results from talking to, at or with your bird, try singing. Develop songs about "thank you" and naming the various fresh fruits and vegetables you provide your parrot. Sing "hello" and "good-bye" and see what happens. Or at the very least, find an interesting tune you can sing for your bird often, and also play a recording of the song.

If whistling is more your style than singing, you could try teaching your nontalking bird some intricate whistles. Remember that wild birds can make and hear quite involved vocalizations. They can hear and should be able to repeat many complex whistles. Your aim should be to make these whistles the flock call.

Your bird will only sing as well as you do. Diane once sold a Cockatiel to the owner of a woman's clothing store. She was quite proud of the whistles he learned. She was embarrassed, however, when a musical patron remarked to her that the bird whistled off-key. She knew who he learned that from!

CONSULT WITH A PROFESSIONAL

If you would like some expert advice about your non-talking parrot, there are parrot behavior consultants who specialize in helping people deal with their parrot problems. These people are not found in every community, but there are several throughout the country with years of experience and a track record of success, and more people are offering these services each year.

A parrot behavior consultant is someone with abundant life experience in handling parrots, who will counsel you about your parrot's behavior problems. He or she suggests changes you can make in your own attitudes and behavior, and/or different methods of handling your problem parrot. The result is often a parrot and a family who adapt better to living with one another.

There are no certification programs a parrot behavior consultant must pass; they are self-taught as a result of their dedication to parrots and their human companions. The field of parrot behavior was first developed by Chris Davis, and Sally Blanchard popularized the study of parrot behavior through her "Parrot Psychology" column in *Bird Talk* magazine and later through her own publications about parrot behavior, the *Pet Bird Report* and the *Companion Parrot Quarterly*.

You can usually arrange a phone interview with a parrot behavior consultant. If there is one practicing near you, he might be able to come to your home and see what kind of environment you have set up for your bird and what kind of interaction you have. When consulting with a parrot behavior consultant, be sure to provide as much information as possible, and be very honest about your bird and her situation. Also, follow the directions the behavior consultant gives you, and respect his business by paying promptly and calling him during his business hours (in his time zone!).

One place to find contact information for many of the country's behavior consultants is to find out who is speaking on the topic of parrot behavior at upcoming seminars. Another way is to look at ads in the back of the popular magazines listed in Appendix B. You may also ask bird club members, parrot owners or your avian veterinarian.

COMPARE NOTES

Another way to find more information about talking birds, and about why your parrot isn't talking, is to share with other parrot owners. Other people with the same species may have clues to your bird's behavior. Talking to several people with the same kind of bird might give you insight into whether you have a late bloomer, or if one of the sexes talks more than another in your bird's species. In many cities there are bird clubs, which usually meet monthly and offer a chance to talk to bird owners, learn from speakers and peruse an informative monthly newsletter.

CONTINUING EDUCATION

You can attend local and national seminars—most are listed in the companion bird publications as well as on the Internet. If you have a chance to attend a regional or national meeting, do so. It is an excellent opportunity to talk to rooms full of other parrot enthusiasts. Usually the speakers are available to chat with at a meal or in the hallway as well. Make a point of meeting and sharing with as many people as possible, and you will learn about your bird and companion birds in general.

There are a few ways to get the most out of attending a seminar or convention. Have a plan before you go to find out the answers to a few specific questions. For example, plan to find out everything you can about a certain species or a particular behavior problem. Be open to insights from the planned lectures and the people you meet. Even if you go with someone else, agree to sit alone, next to different people, for each lecture. This will give you the chance to talk to new people throughout the event. If you really enjoy a speaker, take time to invite that person out for coffee or to exchange business cards. Invite other seminar attendees to explore the town with you. Look up a zoo, park, aviaries or sites in the city where the seminar is held.

Take business cards. Even if you don't have a business, you can have inexpensive calling cards made up at office supply stores or can print some on a home computer. Be sure to include your name, bird interest, phone and/or fax contact numbers and e-mail or web page information. Don't include your address, unless you have a post office box. For safety's sake, you don't want to advertise where you live when you have birds. When you get home, evaluate your success. Did you meet new people? Were your questions answered? What would you do differently the next time?

There are also national societies that specialize in many companion bird species, and they have regular newsletters and, usually, annual meetings. Often breeders as well as pet owners are members. These societies are the most likely to be informed about projects regarding conservation of the species in the wild and any research about relevant health problems, behavior or intelligence. To get the most information about the species you have, these societies are a good choice.

Finally, there are several organizations that unite bird owners and breeders throughout the country or even internationally. They offer publications and/or conventions. A few of the specialty and national and international organizations are listed in Appendix D.

There are also lists on the Internet to which you can subscribe (you'll find some suggestions in Appendix B). These are a series of e-mails to a group of people with the same interest. You might decide to join a list about behavior, the species of bird you own or bird care. You would then start receiving e-mails to your own account from other members on the list. You can exchange information, make friends and share your experiences. One of the important things to remember, however, is that anyone can contribute to a list. You aren't getting professional advice, you're sharing opinions.

A TRUE STORY

Even if you did the best you could and acquired an African Grey or one of the other species who usually talk, you could end up with a bird who doesn't talk. This happens. Here's a true story, sent to us by Helen.

> This is a story of a lady and two Greys. The lady bought one female Grey and named her Cami because she was a Grey Cameroon. Cami was a baby, still being hand-fed. A couple of months later, this lady purchased a male Congo Grey, also being hand-fed. Since he was about four months younger than Cami, he was referred to as Baby, until the name stuck.
>
> This lady had a pet shop, and hoped that by the time these two grew up together and reached breeding age, they would be tightly bonded and would provide her with saleable babies. Meanwhile, they lived at the pet shop because (as anyone who owns their own business knows) so did the lady, unless she was home asleep. This gave them the opportunity to be socialized, spend their waking hours with her, and grow up together. Good plan, right?
>
> Did a parrot ever cooperate with people plans? Naw! As they grew, Baby rapidly became the larger and more dominant of the two. Instead of bonding, he bullied Cami, and by the time they were two years old she had been pretty

much relegated to the bottom of the cage while he took over the rest. The lady kept hoping they would eventually bond anyway, but by the time they were three, Baby started physically bullying Cami, and this lady could see they would have to be separated.

What to do? She did not have space or money to provide two cages spacious enough to properly house a Grey. After much agonizing, she chose to offer one to me. She could not bring herself to choose, so she just told me to chose one and whoever was left would be fine with her, because they were both her babies.

There was, by this time, a lot of talking coming from this cage. (Did you think I would never get to the talking part?) It was obvious that Baby was doing most of the talking, but Cami was heard to talk, as well. Now it was in my lap—what to do, what to do? Being soft of heart, I fell for the underdog—the poor little girl who was living at the bottom of the cage. I chose Cami and brought her home.

The first three days, all I heard were squeaky toy sounds. (Have you ever seen anyone enter a pet shop and not squeak the doggy toys?) She did call for Amber a lot (the owner's daughter) and say "hello." After she realized she wasn't being boarded temporarily and mom was not going to come get her again, she quit talking altogether. Oh, she picked up a foreign language from our Conure, and learned to whistle every tune we whistled around the house, but no words.

After about six months, she was starting to quietly try out some words to herself if no one else was in the room. Sometimes if I heard "hello," I would call "hello" back to her from wherever I was, but rarely did she answer me. We did play a musical follow the leader, though, in which I would copy a note she had whistled, then she would go a note higher—I would copy that, and she would offer me another note, or a combination of two to copy, and so on. We would do this for long periods of time. Still, no words.

About this time, we took Baby to our home to "baby-sit" for about a month. I won't go into what-all he said and did, but the upshot was that as soon as he came, Cami quit talking altogether and hasn't talked since.

Cami is a real sweetheart. Hubby and I can both handle her, she loves me to cuddle her right before I tuck her in at night, she is rarely loud even when she's whistling back and forth to us . . . but no words.

She will be four years old this spring. Will this lady ever talk? I mean, if this gal thinks just sitting around and looking good will get her room and board in this family . . . well, she's absolutely right! But shhhh—don't tell her! We want her to think that talking is a requirement!

POINTS TO REMEMBER

- A healthy bird will vocalize more readily than a sick bird.
- Provide baths, lighting and a good night's rest for your parrot to stimulate happiness and talking.
- Parrots want a response for their vocalizations. They appreciate food rewards and praise or socialization.
- Try singing or whistling instead of talking to your companion bird.
- There are parrot behavior consultants who can offer you professional consultation about your non-talking bird.
- Even if your bird never says a word, love her and enjoy her.

Chapter 15

Starlings, Mynahs and Other Birds

The birds we will discuss in this chapter are known to imitate human speech, but are not parrots. As a group, they are *softbills*—as opposed to *hookbills,* which are the parrots. These softbills include Starlings, Mynahs, Jackdaws and Crows. Yes, Starlings, the little black birds out on your lawn with the speckled coats. Mynahs are an "exotic" species, meaning they are native to other countries, and have a long history as talking birds and as pets and aviary birds in the United States.

Softbills are entirely different kinds of birds than parrots. Their beaks are designed to eat fruit or bugs. Starlings love mealworms as treats. Their droppings are correspondingly runny or smelly. Bathing is important to Mynahs. If you are considering keeping any of these birds, be sure to find out about their care requirements and provide for them accordingly. We'll give you an introduction to their care and talents in this chapter.

HISTORIC STARLINGS

Starlings are remarkable in that they have found their way into some historic situations. Pliny (a natural historian and scientist who lived from A.D. 23 to 79) wrote about Starlings who mimicked Greek and Latin and "practiced diligently and spoke new phrases every day in still longer sentences." Shakespeare chose a Starling in *Henry IV, Part I* (Act 1, Scene 3) to disturb the sleep of the king. He had Hotspur propose teaching a Starling to say "Mortimer," the name of an earl Henry distrusted.

Wolfgang Amadeus Mozart bought a Starling on May 27, 1784. Three years later he buried the bird with great ceremony. Mourners with heavy veils marched

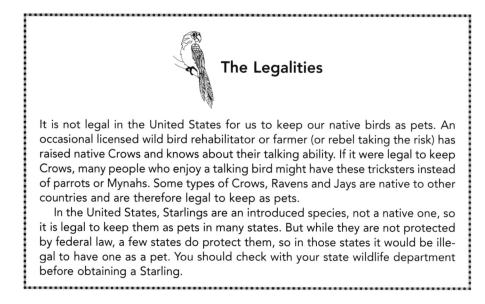

The Legalities

It is not legal in the United States for us to keep our native birds as pets. An occasional licensed wild bird rehabilitator or farmer (or rebel taking the risk) has raised native Crows and knows about their talking ability. If it were legal to keep Crows, many people who enjoy a talking bird might have these tricksters instead of parrots or Mynahs. Some types of Crows, Ravens and Jays are native to other countries and are therefore legal to keep as pets.

In the United States, Starlings are an introduced species, not a native one, so it is legal to keep them as pets in many states. But while they are not protected by federal law, a few states do protect them, so in those states it would be illegal to have one as a pet. You should check with your state wildlife department before obtaining a Starling.

in procession to the graveside to hear Mozart recite a poem he had composed for the occasion. Mozart bought the bird because of the music the bird sang to him when they first met. It has even been suggested that he composed *A Musical Joke* in honor of the Starling's penchant for rearranging the things he heard into nonsense. A review of the piece called it, "awkward, unproportioned, and illogical," saying that the "amateur composer . . . had lost all control." That sums up mimicking by the Starling quite nicely.

Fewer than 200 Starlings were introduced into Central Park in New York from England in the 1890s. That population has grown at least a million times to its present North American population of more than 200 million.

Starlings as Mimics

Mimics in the wild do a really good job of regularly inserting some of their neighbors' songs or calls into their own songs or calls. Other kinds of birds don't seem to have any particular ability to mimic in the wild, but Starlings are good at it.

Wild Starlings have a repertoire of about 26 to 27 songs. The male uses these songs to attract and stimulate the female to mate with him and to produce eggs. It's all clearly worked out. The male sings and attracts the female. The more he sings and the more songs he sings, the more likely he is to attract a mate. The same is true with egg laying. The more he sings and the more songs he sings, the sooner she lays eggs. It's all quite simple.

Within this basic framework, however, the Starling is an adaptable bird. Most Starlings have pieces of the songs of other birds in their neighborhood mixed into the songs the males sing to their mates. In many areas the Starling will mix about 15 to 20 songs from other species into his own 26 to 27 songs. It gets a little hard to tell what came from the Starling and what came from his neighbors.

This flexibility in mimicking the songs of other birds seems at odds with the rigidity of singing in Starlings. Starlings will sing for about 25 seconds at a stretch (called a *bout*), during which time they sing their songs in exactly the same order over and over. As you can imagine, their songs are really short. They even seem to have rules that group certain kinds of songs together. For example, you will not hear a rattle type song that isn't preceded by or followed by another rattle type song.

Talking in Starlings

What does all this have to do with talking in Starlings? There are a few things that seem to be consistent in Starling talking that relate to their behavior in the wild. One is that you can expect your Starling to put anything he learns to say together with anything else. Context may or may not matter to a Starling. One Starling was heard to say, "Basic research," when he was trying to untangle himself from a string. Another was heard to say, "I have a question," while his foot was being treated for an infection. Were these comments in context? They might be if you or I had said them, but a Starling is not likely to know what basic research is. We might want to ask a question if we were being treated for an infection, but I doubt that a Starling is likely to have a specific question in that situation.

On the other hand, there are many reports of Starlings consistently making contextual statements. For instance, the sound of car keys being rattled always led one Starling to say "good-bye."

Wild Starlings are natural mimics and borrow from the songs of other birds.

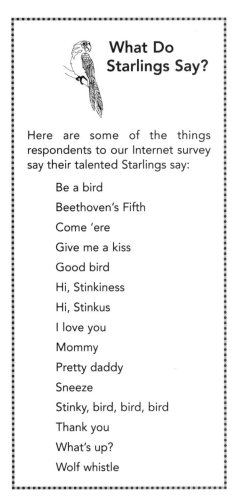

What Do Starlings Say?

Here are some of the things respondents to our Internet survey say their talented Starlings say:

Be a bird

Beethoven's Fifth

Come 'ere

Give me a kiss

Good bird

Hi, Stinkiness

Hi, Stinkus

I love you

Mommy

Pretty daddy

Sneeze

Stinky, bird, bird, bird

Thank you

What's up?

Wolf whistle

Diane of California (not the author) shares her life with a seven-year-old Starling. Stinki whistles for the dogs when he hears them bark, knowing Diane will whistle to the dogs as well. He also says "ermie" or "erm" for wormie or worm when he sees Diane getting a container of mealworms out of the fridge (a favorite treat for Starlings). Stinki also makes up medleys of whistles and spoken words.

It's also possible that what the Starling says is simply incomplete. One Starling used to sing, "Way down upon the Swa-" without ever adding "-nee River." His owners corrected him thousands of times, to no effect. Other Starlings will sing a bit of one thing and then change to another. There seems to be no particular rule or trend in the rearrangements of what a Starling hears and learns.

On our Internet survey, Starlings received high marks from their owners for their personality and talking ability. Although Patricia would not recommend Starlings for the general public, she feels they are delightful companions under the right conditions. Further, she says, "I wouldn't trade Charli for the best-talking African Grey on earth (and I'm 'God Mom' to an African Grey!)." She believes Starlings are misunderstood and even hated. Some people would like to have them eradicated, or consider them to be filthy birds. It surprises people when they see Charli and understand he's the same kind of Starling you find in the wild.

Stinki's mom, Diane, says, "Thank you for asking about birds besides hookbills! You would think sometimes that nothing else existed besides hookbills. I do breed Budgies and have a pair of Cockatiels. They are fun, but the Starling has great personality and talking ability."

Learning to Talk

Starlings and some other birds seem to learn in a social context. That means what is going on is as important as what is being said. Konrad Lorenz, a famous ethologist, recorded one famous example in Jackdaws. His pet Jackdaw, who used to fly free in the area, was not seen for several days. When he did return, his foot was injured. The foot was tended, the bird recovered and seemed to be fine. Months later when the Jackdaw was startled by a small boy, he screamed (in German, of course), "We got him in the trap!" It appears that this emotionally charged event resulted in the Jackdaw learning a new phrase after hearing it only once.

In a related matter, Pliny was said to have recommended beating a parrot with an iron rod to teach him to talk. Of course, we absolutely do not endorse the use of iron rods or beatings to teach a bird to talk, but it does illustrate that the value of a social context was recognized long ago. In Dr. Irene Pepperberg's work with Alex, she clearly manages to put Alex in a social context that has some emotional content. Alex must perform if he is to receive the reward that is in front of him.

What Social Context Is Useful?

Dr. Pepperberg has a clearly defined social context in teaching Alex that works really well. Whether this kind of teaching will extend to Starlings, Mynahs or Crows remains to be seen. There are, however, some factors in the learning environment that you can easily regulate. One of these is the location of your bird. If you want your bird to imitate you and your family—that is, to mimic human speech—keep him in the company of humans. In one set of experiments with Starlings, some birds were kept mainly in the company of humans and some mainly in the company of other birds. As you might expect, the birds kept mainly with humans learned to mimic humans and those kept among birds picked up the vocalizations of birds.

Patricia in Wisconsin has a very social relationship with her Starling Charli. "He goes into what I call his 'recording mode' when I say something he likes. If he is on my hand, he will turn his head so an ear is as close to my mouth as possible. I will repeat whatever I said that caught his attention, a couple of times. If he says something to me, I will repeat it back to him."

The second aspect of social environment is to keep conditions consistent. If you want your bird to pick up the words you would say at home, keep your bird at home. If you want your bird to learn the things he hears on television, set his cage near the television. It may prove difficult to get your bird to say exactly what you want him to say in any case. As we have already noted, some Starlings will take parts of the speech that is offered to them and recombine them as they choose.

It appears that Starlings may be able to do some other kinds of choosing, as well. One Starling, after hearing the question only once, learned to say, "Does Hammacher Schlemmer have a toll-free number?" This may not be what you want your bird to say, but once they have the expression in their brains, Starlings are not easy to convince to say anything else.

MARGHERITA WARHURST

Squeekie the Starling singing. Squeekie is 12 years old. He does the charge whistle and the wolf whistle, imitates a noisy closet door and quacks like a duck. He can also say "Mama," "mom," "mummy," "mommy," "Squeekie," "komme schon" (German for "I'm coming"), "schwind" (German for "fast") and "squeek!"

Accuracy of Sound Reproduction

Some birds have a remarkable ability to reproduce the human voice—so remarkable that people think another person is speaking, and respond accordingly. In one experiment with Starlings, people listened to a tape of the birds talking and were asked to comment. In almost every case the listeners asked which of the voices were human and which were the Starlings. In all cases the voices were the Starlings!

In one household, the Mynah constantly called both of the children and the cat. The children were often fooled and came when the bird called. The cat soon refused to come unless he could see the person calling him.

Patricia has a pet Starling in Wisconsin. She also has five parrots. In her household, Charli the Starling is the only talker! Patricia and others do understand what Charli is saying, unless he is in the process of learning a new word. At first, he mumbles and garbles words. But by the time he has perfected it, the word or phrase is intelligible. So are the coughs and sneezes he imitates as a consequence of his human flock getting colds. Patricia says Charli continues the Starling tradition of imitating other birds by chirping like a Parrotlet and doing "a mean Budgie cussing."

STARLING CARE

In the wild, insects make up a large percentage of a Starling's diet. This is different from either parrots or Mynahs, so diets made for either of these types of birds are not appropriate to feed to a Starling. Instead, Starling diets are based on dog food. Mix either kibble or canned dog food with poultry mash made for laying hens, avian vitamins and hard-boiled eggs to feed a Starling. For recipes, see the web site www.starlingtalk.com/diet.htm.

Treats for a Starling include vegetables, fruit and mealworms. Offer a Starling leafy greens, cooked yam, broccoli, hard-boiled eggs, grapes, cherries, cottage cheese and cooked cereal in addition to his dog food diet. Starlings will eat mealworms, which can be purchased in many pet stores or ordered from suppliers. They should not be offered earthworms, however.

Companion Starlings, who live up to 20 years, need both socialization and exercise. Starlings appreciate free flight time out of their cage. They are inquisitive birds who get into things, so spend some time bird-proofing the room where you'll let your Starling out. Starling droppings are messy, although it is easy to clean up after them. Starling owners report that they cover furniture with a sheet while their feathered friends are out of their cages, and they keep tissues and wipes handy to pick up droppings.

Starlings are not cuddly birds. Your companion Starling will probably not like to be petted or handled. He will still bond with you, though, and will fly to you for treats and to play games. Talking to a Starling is an excellent source of entertainment for both of you.

Cages should be roomy enough to allow flight. In addition to perches, toys and feed dishes, Starlings also enjoy having a wooden shelf on which to rest and may appreciate a wooden sleeping box or other enclosed area in which to sleep. Starlings will like playing with a toy box of interesting and colorful objects such as buttons, molted feathers from other birds, small bottle caps, measuring spoons, junk mail, wadded paper, parakeet toys and cat toys. You can also plant grasses and safe, non-toxic plants in potting soil for your bird to play in and eat.

Starling sleeping boxes or lofts should be at least eight inches square and should include a two-inch-square opening and a perch for the bird. They can be made of wood, cardboard or plastic. They could be specially made for your bird, or you could use a plastic container turned on its side and mounted securely to your Starling's cage.

As with any avian companion, you are responsible for keeping your Starling safe and happy as well as healthy. Before acquiring a Starling, research his care thoroughly and be sure you are ready for the responsibility involved. If you can offer your Starling a healthy lifestyle and the socialization and free flight he craves, then go ahead and join the ranks of Starling fans who delight in their rambunctious, talkative and inquisitive charges.

MYNAH THE MIMIC

Mynahs are members of the Starling family. Usually one of the subspecies of Hill Mynah or the Javan Hill Mynah is kept in captivity as a talking pet. In contrast to the European Starling, the Indian Hill Mynah is uncomplicated in the wild. While the Starling mimics almost anything he hears and incorporates parts of it into his song, the Mynah uses only a few calls in the wild. The male Mynah has about 12 calls that he shares with the other males in his area. The same is true of the female, although her 12 calls are different from the male's. The idea that a Mynah would turn out to be a good mimic is not necessarily in line with what we know of their natural history.

However, for parrots, Mynahs, Crows and Ravens, their abilities to mimic human speech in captivity seem to be related to the fact that they acquire some of their calls in the wild. Their natural calls and vocalizations are not all instinctive. In fact, it seems that parrots and Ravens, at least, develop language groups and possibly individual identifying calls. This means these birds are receptive to learning their flock calls after they have fledged (left the nest). If the bird is in a human flock, he learns human calls.

The Mynah is a remarkable mimic. He has been kept in households for years as a favored pet, primarily because of his ability to mimic human speech. The most common species kept is the Indian Hill Mynah. They are bright black, with white-tipped wings and yellow wattles.

If you wish to teach a Mynah to talk, you should acquire a young, hand-fed bird who is likely to become a part of your flock. By three to four months of age, your Mynah should begin saying his first words. It's still possible to teach a Mynah to talk if you acquire an older bird.

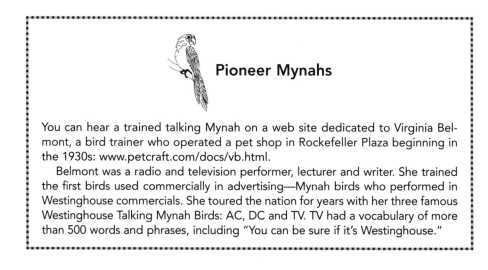

Pioneer Mynahs

You can hear a trained talking Mynah on a web site dedicated to Virginia Belmont, a bird trainer who operated a pet shop in Rockefeller Plaza beginning in the 1930s: www.petcraft.com/docs/vb.html.

Belmont was a radio and television performer, lecturer and writer. She trained the first birds used commercially in advertising—Mynah birds who performed in Westinghouse commercials. She toured the nation for years with her three famous Westinghouse Talking Mynah Birds: AC, DC and TV. TV had a vocabulary of more than 500 words and phrases, including "You can be sure if it's Westinghouse."

Waldo is an 11-year-old Mynah. He didn't begin to talk until he was six months old and stopped learning by the time he was one year old.

Teaching a Mynah to talk is similar to teaching a parrot to talk. You can follow the guidelines in the other chapters of this book. Briefly, you will have the most success if you live in a talkative household, if you interact a lot with the Mynah, and if, when you are teaching a phrase, you say it with enthusiasm. Of course, this means the bird will also learn some enthusiastic phrases you didn't mean to pass on. Mynahs who live in human households are often allowed some time out of their cage to socialize with their humans. They can learn new words in the cage and out, so don't forget to talk to your Mynah while he's in his cage.

Mynahs have talking spells when they spout off every word they know, and they can talk back and forth with their human companions, but be aware that Mynahs don't reach the level of association between objects and language that parrots do. Virginia Belmont trained her Mynahs to talk on cue in the middle of the 20th century (see the box on page 186), but not many people have achieved that level of training with Mynahs.

Mynahs have clear voices. Our survey respondent Kathy, who lives in Ontario, Canada, has a Greater Indian Hill Mynah as well as a Timneh Grey Parrot and a

BUDDY NELSON

Vinnie, a five-year-old Mynah, sits on a dish in which he bathes. He learned many of his vocalizations from a CD. His phrases include "my goodness sake!" "oh by gosh by golly," "hello Vinnie," "good morning" and a very good impression of the telephone ringing.

Cockatiel. They all talk, and Kathy says, "Everyone can tell what all three of them are saying. They are clear talkers. However, the Mynah has the mimicking ability down pat. The Timneh African Grey is a good mimic, too, but not as clear or true to the voice as the Mynah, and the Cockatiel has a very clear, cute, parrotlike voice."

Kathy has made a cassette of her own voice saying different words and phrases that she plays for her birds, but she says, "I believe they learned the most words from just listening to everyday chatter in our house." Her Mynah has learned a few words from her African Grey as well as from human household members.

Mynah Care

Mynahs are softbill birds and require different care from parrots. They need a diet that's high in protein and low in iron. Iron storage disease is a common problem in these birds. To minimize iron absorption, do not feed Mynahs spinach or raisins, which are high in iron. They also should not eat foods such as citrus, which are high in acid, in conjunction with other foods, because it causes the retention of iron.

Mynahs get a Mynah pellet as a basic diet, with a variety of fruits and vegetables. Mealworms and crickets are treats to them. Mynahs should be housed in spacious cages or aviaries, as they are active and like to hop around. Toys are appreciated and can include parrot-size swings, rings, bells and other colored or shiny, hard toys. You'll need to wash their toys as well as their dishes when you clean their cage.

Mynahs also like to play inside paper bags, cardboard boxes or nest boxes. Mynahs may bathe several times a day and need to be provided with a bathing bowl. When Mynahs drink, they can't suck up water but must fill their bill then tilt their head back. Be sure they can do so from the water container you provide them.

Mynahs crouch down on a perch, facing straight ahead, to sleep. This is in contrast to many parrots, who tuck their heads in the feathers of their back.

Beolino ("Beo" is the German word for Mynah) lived to be at least 18 years old. Beolino was very tame and went everywhere with his owner.

Waldo bathing. According to owner Elayne of North Carolina, "We can't keep a water bowl in his cage (he drinks from a hanging bottle) because if I had even a bottle cap with water in it, he would try to get in it."

Mynahs need to bathe regularly. This is Waldo after his bath.

CROWS DO MORE THAN CAW

Although it is now illegal to keep native crows in the United States, "The Old Crow Tamer," the author of *The Lost Folk Art of Taming Crows,* was kind enough to share his observations about companion crows. People who have a license to rehabilitate wildlife occasionally feed Crows, and there are people who would like to see native crows become legal as pets.

The Old Crow Tamer says Crows are natural mimics. They learn to copy not only human speech, but the telephone ringing, appliance buzzers and the sounds of other household pets. He says he had a Crow "that barked so much like our family dog that you had to be looking at one or the other to be sure which one was barking."

Repeating words and saying words with enthusiasm are the key to teaching a Crow to say words. This is exactly how we would advise teaching a parrot, so use all of the hints in this book to work with a Crow, should you find yourself with one. Most Crows can be trained to talk, and it doesn't seem that there is a difference between the sexes. In any case, unless a DNA test is performed, there's no way to tell the difference between a male and a female Crow.

Crows are babies until one year old, and that's about when they begin to mimic. The Old Crow Tamer suggests starting speech training slightly before that age. In his youngest months, provide loving kindness and develop a bond with the bird. Once again, to have the incentive to learn human speech, a Crow must associate his humans with his flock. A Crow will be fully grown at two years old.

If you are interested in Crows, learn more about their care and the species that may be legally available to you. Appendix B lists a few books about their intelligence. If nothing else, you can have a new appreciation for some of our native wildlife!

Softbill Bird Care

To find out how you can obtain a softbill bird, such as a Mynah or an exotic Crow or Jay, and to learn more about softbill care, there is information available at these web sites.

www.softbills.com

www.geocities.com/Athens/Atrium/1424/Corvine_advocacy.htm

www.mynahbird.com/

www.starlingcentral.net

www.starlingtalk.com/

www.starlings.net/

www.starlings.info/

www.shades-of-night.com/aviary/birdpet.html

birds.cornell.edu/crows/index.html

This is a five-year-old handfed Pied Crow named Aristotle. She says "hi," "hello," "good girl," and "Stotle" (short for Aristotle). Pied Crows are not native to the United States, so they are considered an "exotic" species of Crow and are legal pets.

ROBERT J. RUSH

CRAVIN' A RAVEN?

The most famous Raven of all, the subject of Edgar Allan Poe's poem (see below), demonstrated that Ravens can talk—but again, in reality they only will do so if raised as a member of a human flock. They are intelligent birds who, like parrots, learn calls and develop language groups in the wild.

Ravens have a firm foothold in Native American lore as mischievous and intelligent beings. Among Northwestern tribes, there is a legend that Raven was the first shaman who put the sun in the sky, regulated the tides and even created the human race.

Visiting Raven territory and living with a Raven have their exciting moments. We found a story of a camper who was befriended by a Raven. The bird accepted crackers as snacks, flew beside his new friend on a hike and generally accepted a closer relationship than we usually expect of a wild bird.

Wildlife rehabilitators who have shared their homes with Ravens talk about their practice of stealing desirable objects and of hiding food around the house. "Bert constantly searched for good hiding places for his loot. Not just any place would do. Several had to be tried out before he was satisfied," Gabriele Drozdowski wrote in "Bert and Kong: Ravens in the House" (an article that appeared in the March/April 1999 issue of *AFA Watchbird* magazine). "Once I thought my

Excerpt From *The Raven* by Edgar Allan Poe

Open here I flung the shutter, when, with many a flirt and flutter,
In there stepped a stately Raven of the saintly days of yore.
Not the least obeisance made he; not an instant stopped or stayed he;
But, with mien of lord or lady, perched above my chamber door—
Perched upon a bust of Pallas just above my chamber door—
Perched, and sat, and nothing more.
Then this ebony bird beguiling my sad fancy into smiling,
By the grave and stern decorum of the countenance it wore,
"Though thy crest be shorn and shaven, thou," I said, "art sure no craven,
Ghastly grim and ancient Raven wandering from the Nightly shore—
Tell me what thy lordly name is on the Night's Plutonian shore!"
Quoth the Raven, "Nevermore."
Much I marveled this ungainly fowl to hear discourse so plainly,
Though its answer little meaning—little relevancy bore . . .

knife was gone for good, but three months later I discovered it behind some books on a shelf. I had been searching for hours. Not for the knife, but for the source of a horrible stench in the house, which turned out to be a decomposed anchovy stashed away for a later snack—between the pages of Webster's dictionary."

It is unlikely that Ravens could be considered desirable avian companions. They are a challenge, to say the least. Yet they are another one of the wonders of the bird world, an intelligent species from which there is much to learn about nature and ourselves.

POINTS TO REMEMBER

- Because they are not native species, it is legal to keep wild Starlings as companion birds.
- Starlings are excellent mimics in the wild, and talk if raised by people.
- Mynah birds have clear voices and mimic accurately.
- The softbill birds require very different care from parrots, so be informed.
- It is not legal to keep native Crows or Ravens as companion birds, but there are some legal exotic species in these families that can be kept as pets. Their intelligence makes keeping them a challenge, though.

Chapter 16

Going to the Birds

If you have a developing interest in birds, you might want to include some bird shows in your travel plans. If you do, there are a wide variety of theme parks and aviaries where shows are performed. They're located all over the world. In fact, you could inquire at any zoo or theme park you plan to visit. It's possible there's a bird show if there are animal acts offered as entertainment. Birds, with their bright coloring, intelligence and outgoing personalities, are favorite subjects for trained animal shows.

If training your bird appeals to you, you can get more instruction yourself from professionals. You may get what you need from books and videos on the topic, or you may be able to attend a seminar given by a successful bird trainer. These seminars offer valuable insights and firsthand observation of handling techniques that you can incorporate with your own companion bird. You may be considering a career working with animals if you are a younger reader or even may be looking at a second or third career. There are schools with degree programs in animal keeping and training. (If you're interested in a career in animal keeping, training or wildlife education, look for resources in Appendix B.)

IT'S SHOWTIME!

There are many places where you can see bird shows. There are two public aviaries in the United States: the National Aviary in Pittsburgh, Pennsylvania, and Tracy Aviary in Salt Lake City, Utah. If you really want to learn more about all birds, it's a good idea to visit either of these parks. Be prepared to expand your world and learn more about the incredible diversity of avian species on our planet! During the summer months there are shows at Tracy Aviary.

Parrot Jungle in Miami, Florida, is especially interesting for the parrot lover, with free-flying Macaws and beautiful landscaped grounds. There are also some well-known international bird parks. You'll find a list of American and international

Birds and bird information turn up in some of the most unlikely places. There are free-flying birds in the Frederik Meijer Gardens in Grand Rapids, Michigan, as well as this instructional sculpture featuring oversize bird eggs. Find out more at www.meijer gardens.org.

bird parks and aviaries, with contact information, in Appendix B. But that list, and the list of bird parks, is by no means complete. If you plan a vacation somewhere, search the Internet or talk to your travel agent about places to see birds or to watch bird shows. Be sure to mention that you are interested in parrots. There are specialized tours for birders, or bird-watchers who are interested in a variety of wild bird species.

Another place to see bird shows is a zoo. Throughout the country, zoos welcome visitors, and many of them have animal shows to entertain you. Not every bird featured in shows is a parrot, either. Often raptors are included, or another interesting species at least walks across the stage, so you can see it and marvel. Hornbills and Emus have parts like that, and the raptors often fly. As do the parrots. Imagine the training involved in allowing your bird free flight, and being pretty sure she will return to you.

After reading about talking on cue, you have some idea about the training birds have received in order to perform. People who make a living by putting on bird shows are the professionals at this art. With your background in beginning training, you can learn a lot from watching a bird show. Note what hand signals are given, the bridge (the word "good" or a click) for the birds when they perform correctly, and how often treats are given as rewards. What treats do these professionals use? Are you getting any ideas for your own work?

DIANE GRINDOL

Professional shows feature many species of birds. The show may feature a dialog that tells a story, such as on this Western set at Marine World in Vallejo, California.

You may also note how many birds are involved in the show and what species are used. Chances are good the large, showy birds are performing. It's not that the smaller birds can't learn interesting behaviors but simply that they are not as visible to audiences. How many birds are performing? Often in professional shows, each bird learns just a trick or two. In fact, several birds learn the same trick or two, in case one bird doesn't want to work that day. The show must go on!

These types of shows are also put on at theme parks and some hotels. If you plan any kind of family adventure, it might be worth checking to see if there's a bird show. Parks with bird shows include Busch Gardens, Sea World, Great America, Six Flags and Universal Studios. Usually there are birds at Rain Forest Café locations as well, although they don't perform. Of course, you could try talking to them and you may get a response! What are these birds picking up from being in an active, exciting public location?

Zoos and Theme Parks With Bird Shows

These are locations where bird shows have been held. Many of the zoos listed also have excellent aviaries. Inquire before you visit any zoo or park, as shows may be seasonal.

Akron Zoo
Akron, Ohio
(330) 375-2525
www.Akronzoo.com

Blank Park Zoo
Des Moines, Iowa
(515) 285-4722
www.blankparkzoo.com

Bronx Zoo
New York, New York
(718) 220-5100
www.bronxzoo.com

Caribbean Gardens
Naples, Florida
(239) 262-5409
www.caribbeangardens.com

Cincinnati Zoo
Cincinnati, Ohio
(800) 94-HIPPO
www.cincyzoo.org

Columbus Zoo
Columbus, Ohio
(614) 645-3550
www.colszoo.org

Denver Zoo
Denver, Colorado
(303) 376-4800
www.denverzoo.org

Detroit Zoological Park
Royal Oak, Michigan
(248) 398-0900
www.detroitzoo.org

Florida's Silver Springs
Silver Springs, Florida
(352) 236-2121
www.silversprings.com

Houston Zoo
Houston, Texas
(713) 533-6500
www.houstonzoo.org

Los Angeles Zoo
Los Angeles, California
(323) 644-6400
www.lazoo.org

St. Louis Zoo
St. Louis, Missouri
(314) 781-0900
www.stlzoo.org

San Diego Zoo
San Diego, California
(619) 234-3153
www.sandiegozoo.org

San Diego Zoo's Wild Animal Park
Escondido, California
(760) 747-8702
www.sandiegozoo.org/wap/

Toledo Zoo
Toledo, Ohio
(419) 385-5721
www.toledozoo.org

Tropicana Hotel and Casino
Las Vegas, Nevada
(888) 810-TROP
www.tropicanalv.com

BIRD BUSINESS

You expect more from your own bird than the professionals do at a theme park, when it comes down to it. Don't you want your bird to know all the tricks, not just specialize in one or two? She can. Several private bird shows have been started by people who trained their avian companions to do a few tricks, then decided to share what they learned with larger audiences.

You can see these local masters of avian training at work at birthday parties, school assemblies, Renaissance or craft fairs. There are a few magician or theatrical acts that incorporate birds, because the performers have some interest in birds. The purposes of local performers may be to inform, educate or entertain.

Joe Tyler's talking African Grey is part of a stand-up comedy routine he performs at nursing homes, libraries and schools in the Reno, Nevada, area. One of their teachers even made a book of their work. Tani Robar and her Fantastic Performing Parrots perform at her bird club's annual bird fair, at bird clubs and national bird conventions, and also at other functions. Joanie Doss and The Amazing Amazons have kept people entertained in Alaska, and now in Oregon, for many years.

DIANE GRINDOL

This is what it looks like to have a bird in training—you have Macaws flying through your kitchen! There's a T-stand for talking training in this kitchen, too.

Chris Biro dresses up as a pirate for his local shows. His colorful costumes and huge Macaws awe audiences and add spice to events they attend, as well as educating children about birds, conservation and recycling to make our planet a better place.

Bob Bartley of California is another performer who dresses in period costumes and has incorporated his long-time companion, Gypsy, into his performances. Gypsy is a beautiful scarlet Macaw. They travel to events where both their talents can be showcased, such as Renaissance Faires.

The people we've mentioned have counterparts throughout the country.

Tani Robar performs here with her Caique, Cassie. With Tani's other personal companion birds, they've made videos that show you how to train your birds.

Chris Biro giving one of his educational presentations dressed as a pirate.

Bob Bartley and Gypsy perform throughout the country, mainly at Renaissance Faires.

You'll need to keep your ears open for places where they are performing, or ask bird club members where you can expect to meet some of them. To become one of these people, all you have to do is start networking and ask to be included in a show at a school, library or event. Practice by giving a show for a bird club or your family, so you can get some frank criticism of your performance and make necessary changes before you go big-time. Then make a few posters and business cards, and you're off!

Other people are not so much performers as educators. Bird breeders can give schoolchildren a chance to hold baby birds. A baby Macaw is not so little! Young birds are more gentle and trustworthy than older parrots, and they benefit from being socialized. Educators can also explain the mysteries of eggs and expose children to a whole world of birds they might not have known existed.

Anyone with a well-trained and socialized bird can do classroom visits. Birds are very different from our dog and cat family pets, so learning how to interact with them, train them and talk to them expands a child's world. You never know when you're planting the seed for a future forest ranger, conservation program director, aviculturist, writer, artist, zoologist or veterinarian. Usually it turns out someone in the class has a bird at home or lives in a family who also raises birds or is keenly interested in the rain forest's wildlife.

LEARN FROM THE EXPERTS

A few bird trainers offer private lessons or seminars to teach people about working with their own birds. Participants range from the very beginning companion parrot owner up to zoo employees. You'll find a few places where instruction is offered listed in Appendix B. You may inquire of your favorite bird performer about workshops, or arrange for them to come to your own city to give lessons to a small group of interested bird owners.

There are also several national organizations for bird owners that hold annual conventions. Quite often there's a bird trainer present, providing entertainment or giving seminars or presentations. Most parrot trainers use vocalizations in their acts, as well as teaching their birds to perform numerous behaviors that complement an amusing story line.

Going to a convention or show gives you the chance to meet other people who are as interested in birds as you. It also gives you the opportunity to ask an expert the questions you have been wondering about.

DIANE GRINDOL

Moorpark College in Moorpark, California, houses "America's Teaching Zoo," where you can learn to train animals and give educational presentations. Students also put on shows for the public. This student is teaching a talking Double Yellow-headed Amazon a cue.

202 Teaching Your Bird to Talk

For a membership fee, national organizations also usually have some type of publication to provide continuing education. National organizations usually are composed of a network of bird owners who are valuable resources for you. For a list of organizations that sponsor seminars, look in Appendix B. Also search your local newspaper for other seminars near you, and check the calendar listings in national magazines and local bird club newsletters.

MAKING A CONTRIBUTION

Bird clubs are also organizations to which you can contribute either time or knowledge. When you get a lot out of owning birds, you often wish to give back to birds of the world in some way. You may wish to volunteer at an event, raise money for conservation or research, or set aside a monthly contribution to a worthy cause.

Through the strength of individual contributions, great strides have been made in avian medical research over the last few years, and there are opportunities in other bird-related research and conservation projects. For example, there is still a lot to be learned about parrot nutrition and parrot behavior. Feather plucking is still a mystery syndrome. Birds probably have allergies, but this hasn't yet been fully researched. We don't have vaccines for some of the major avian diseases. Tests for some diseases and requirements for effective dosage for treating different species are still being worked out. With the increasing widespread acceptance of acupuncture and herbal and homeopathic treatments, there are whole new disciplines of avian health care to explore. This is a time when you can contribute much to our knowledge of birds by supporting appropriate projects.

This is also another way you can help birds. Dog and cat owners keep breeds that humans created. Pugs and Great Danes don't exist anywhere in the wild. There are still wolves living in native habitats, but most dogs look very different from their wolf ancestors and could not live in the same habitat comfortably anymore. Their natural habitat is our homes and hearths. This is also true of Canaries, of which many breeds have been developed and domesticated by humans that bear little resemblance to the sparrowlike wild singing finch from the Canary Islands that is their ancestor.

Parrot owners, however, do have species native to a variety of habitats throughout the world. If we continue to keep companion parrots, we are likely to see some changes that point toward domestication, and in fact, we do see that in the color mutations of the more well-established Cockatiels, Budgies and Ring-necked Parakeets. New color mutations are beginning to appear in some pet parrot species already, such as Parrotlets, Grass Parakeets and Conures. But for now, our companions are very, very close to their wild cousins—and in many cases, are still being taken out of the wild.

The wild bird cousins of some of our species are endangered or live in habitats that are fast disappearing. It's possible to make a contribution to wild parrots through habitat conservation and research into the natural history or behavior of wild parrots. You'll find some parrot conservation organizations listed in Appendix B.

POINTS TO REMEMBER

- There are aviaries and bird parks in the United States and abroad that you can visit on vacations.
- Zoos and theme parks often feature bird shows where you can watch professional bird trainers work and pick up tips.
- Many companion pet owners have become local celebrities by putting on shows with their birds. It's possible to see their shows and learn from their seminars. It's also possible to do the same thing yourself.
- If you want to give back to birds because of all you get out of your relationship with your companion birds, there are numerous local, national and international organizations with which you can volunteer or to which you can contribute financially.

Chapter 17

The Future

There are many kinds of progress that can be made in teaching birds to talk and in understanding the nature of talking birds. We will review some of the areas in which we think progress is possible and how this progress might apply to humans.

ECOLOGICAL AND EVOLUTIONARY IMPLICATIONS

Understanding animal communication can help us better understand our environment. There are many populations of birds living within boundaries that are not apparent to humans when we look at geographic features and other kinds of limitations. These populations can be identified by their songs and calls. There are also regional accents that identify groups existing along borders that do not seem to change with time. There are even birds who live along these borders who speak both their own dialect and that of the neighboring population. Do they serve as a bridge population, or are they isolated in yet a different way by being multilingual?

This isolation can create genetic drift between groups, which will eventually lead to an identifiable subspecies and finally a species. (Genetic drift is evolution that occurs as gene frequencies change randomly from generation to generation. The larger the number of reproducing individuals in a population, the smaller the effects of genetic drift.) The average bird species lasts about 10,000 years before the genetic drift within the species renders it incapable of breeding with its ancient ancestors—were any still available. If two populations are separated for long enough, they may evolve into separate but related species. Understanding the language and the language differences of two neighboring groups of birds may tell us a lot about how these separations occur and how they are maintained. This could lead to understanding one of the basic forces of evolution.

DIANE GRINDOL

Could studies of bird communication and language give us insight into the evolution of a species?

THE HUMAN-ANIMAL BOND

The human-animal bond has been a much-talked-about but imperfectly understood concept for many years. It's clear that many human beings benefit from the presence of an animal in their lives, but the nature of that benefit is only partly understood. The need to care for a dependent animal, which includes getting up and going out regularly, is clearly one aspect of that benefit for the aged or homebound, but there is a lot more here than simple physical activity. There is an emotional bond that also provides physical benefits. Pets can reduce stress and give meaning to lives devoid of other sources of meaning. The way a pet interacts with a person is a primary part of the emotional content of the relationship. The presence of a bird who can actually communicate his needs in the relationship has the potential to deepen that meaning and add further enrichment to those who need these benefits.

The study of the emotional content of the human-animal bond is not limited to the homebound or the aged. There are many animals, including birds, who are used in hospitals and other institutions to enhance the environment, particularly for children. Proper training of animals for these visits is essential for the safety of both the animals and the patients. When our understanding of the requirements of both the people and the animals is deepened, we will be able to train animals to be better visitors and have a more pronounced effect on the patients.

Part of this work may be to teach the people who benefit from the animals to train the animals. Spending an hour being a model/rival might be just the thing to add some meaning and excitement to the day of a long-term hospital patient. Focusing our attention on an external challenge often keeps us from dwelling on our own problems. This reduces stress and stimulates healing.

BREEDING FOR TALKING

One of the things that happens to a species of animal kept in captivity long enough is that selective breeding occurs. This isn't always intended, but in captivity the selection of which animals will breed to produce the next generation has different results than breeding in a wild situation does. Since this is the case, we need to have a conscious breeding plan rather than a default position with no plan at all. Not many companion bird species now could be considered domesticated animals. But that looms on the horizon.

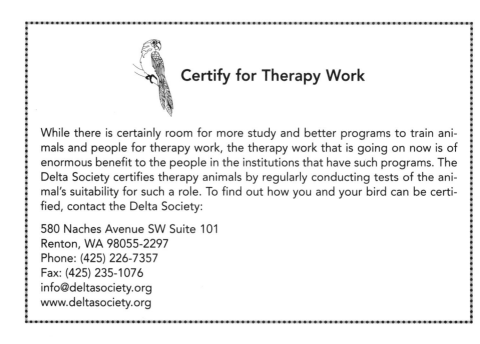

Certify for Therapy Work

While there is certainly room for more study and better programs to train animals and people for therapy work, the therapy work that is going on now is of enormous benefit to the people in the institutions that have such programs. The Delta Society certifies therapy animals by regularly conducting tests of the animal's suitability for such a role. To find out how you and your bird can be certified, contact the Delta Society:

580 Naches Avenue SW Suite 101
Renton, WA 98055-2297
Phone: (425) 226-7357
Fax: (425) 235-1076
info@deltasociety.org
www.deltasociety.org

We know from our little friend Puck, who holds the record for the bird with the largest vocabulary, that some birds learn more words than others. So why not selectively breed for learning to talk? After all, Canaries were successfully bred for singing ability long ago, when many of the genetic techniques we can apply today were unknown. We clearly have a lot of birds to choose from with a lot of variation in the population.

Selection might actually consist of talking contests. In our technological age, entrants from all over the world could participate by recording, CD, DVD or satellite television. The world record would be challenged regularly, and breeders would have a reason to breed for talking ability.

Another aspect of selective breeding should be defining and refining the bird's disposition. A domesticated bird would then be more like our dogs. We want to

We're just finding out how powerful and how healing the presence of a bird or other animal is in the life of a human being. Watch for more developments in this area.

reduce the amount of biting and screaming that goes on, while maintaining birds' sense of fun and unpredictability. What fun would a totally docile parrot be, anyway?

Ideally, we will be breeding our best pets. Currently, the really good pet parrots are in pet homes, and are not procreating. Their owners are often too attached to them to give them up for breeding. Some people who breed birds end up with plucking and nervous birds, or aggressive birds who come to them for free or a good price. The price we pay is perpetuating these traits and creating a cycle of rejected human companion parrots. A reasonable step in this process might be when an aviculturist can afford to say, "Is breeding this bird benefiting my future customers and the development of domesticated parrots?" If there were locations for the neurotic and aggressive birds to live out their lives happily without breeding, great progress would be made as well. Sanctuaries throughout the United States have begun to take on this task.

While we're breeding for talking and disposition, we shouldn't ignore the need to maintain healthy, vigorous birds. Many breeding programs for other pets have resulted in a desired physical or temperament trait being maintained while other traits related to health were lost or diminished. Properly managed breeding programs can account for all of these traits, and a great many more.

DIANE GRINDOL

More companion bird species will probably become "domesticated" like the Budgie, which is well adapted to life in captivity, comes in a rainbow of colors and associates well with people.

THE BIRD SUPPORT SYSTEM

If we are going to improve the bird and our relationship with him, we need to improve the bird's support system. This means doing enough research to find out what a bird really needs and how humans can provide it.

Nutrition

One area in which more work needs to be done with birds is nutrition. For most species of birds, there isn't a single nutrient requirement that is definitively known. That doesn't mean we can't feed a diet in which we have some confidence, but it does mean there is a lot of ground to cover to get some of the fine points nailed down. While in human nutrition we worry about the effect of the diet on our hearts and other specific organs, in birds we seek simply to avoid obvious nutritional disease.

There is still a lot to be learned about the nutrient requirements of companion birds. What does the future hold for these pet supply store shelves?

One of the areas of avian nutritional research that might be useful directly to humans is longevity. There are a great many diseases that affect humans only after the middle of their lives. These are being studied in a variety of ways, but we currently have no animals that live as long as we do that we can compare to ourselves in long-term research. There could be such animals, though. Many parrots live long lives and show specific signs of aging. These birds could be offered controlled diets that are intended to reduce the onset of aging diseases or to reduce the rate of aging. We could then measure the results. Such a study would require the long-term commitment of an institution to supply the ongoing needs of the experiment over the long lives of the birds, but this is not unheard-of.

Space Needs

An area where there is much debate in the world of biology, farming and companion animal medicine is the size of enclosure with which an animal should be provided. While we have already made a recommendation that birds be given enough space in their cages to allow them to stretch their wings easily, this is not a research finding, but a reasoned approach. We believe birds need to have enough space to walk and climb around without physical limitations. With that recommendation, however, we have not made provisions for the bird to fly. There just isn't enough room in most homes for a cage large enough for a bird to fly. What do we do about this?

For now, we hope that your bird will come out of his cage often enough that he will have some flying time. We don't know that this is essential, but it seems like a good idea. Companion parrot behavioral consultants promote wing-flapping exercise for captive parrots. This can easily become a more widespread practice and create healthier parrots in ensuing generations.

For busy people (the norm in developed countries), the idea of dog play areas, horse parks and pet day care has become popular. Play and socialization are great exercise for companion animals. With the increasing popularity of parrots, services to maintain their health and well-being could well be created. Could this include safe free-flight areas? Model-rival nursery schools or day care? Locations where older parrot mentors can teach the next generations how to preen, bathe and raise good human companions? Locations where older humans can volunteer their time to instruct young parrots in social skills? We could go several ways in parrot breeding and ownership in this new millennium. We could make a real difference in the lives of the parrots for whom we are stewards and companions.

What is required in the future is that we eliminate the need to guess about these things. We need to develop empirical criteria that will enable us to tell you why we suggest the cage size we suggest, rather than making an educated guess. Supporting avian research efforts is critical.

Our world is getting smaller. More people are traveling to other countries than ever before, or at least visiting them via the Internet or global communication systems. One of the most astounding things you can experience is seeing your favorite species of bird flying free in the wild. As they fly out of sight, it makes you pause and wonder why we've ever thought of keeping these animals in cages.

As enrichment has added to the variety and stimulation available to zoo animals, we are entering a new era of being able to provide enrichment to our companion parrot's environment through outdoor play areas, stimulating environments, travels with us in our daily routine and, of course, what we say to them.

Social Interactions

Most of the birds we keep as pets are social animals. We know they live in flocks for at least part of the year, and they learn a code of calls that is unique to their population. They must have enough social contact to learn that code, and must also have a need to use it, or else it would not have evolved. This brings up the question of how much and what kinds of social interactions are needed to maintain the health of the birds we keep. This may not seem to be a question that is easily answered, but it's an area where behaviorists are beginning to make progress.

As we learn the habits of animals in the wild, we learn what behaviors serve to allow them to survive and reproduce. As you have seen throughout this book, many of the behaviors we see as an essential part of the quality of a bird as a pet relate to the bird's reproductive effort in the wild. As we learn more about these birds in the wild, we will learn more about what we need to provide them in captivity.

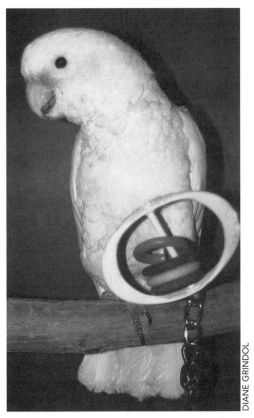

DIANE GRINDOL

Providing enlarged environments, flying time, fun toys and educational opportunities for our companion birds, like this Goffin's Cockatoo, should be a trend of the future.

THE HUMAN SUPPORT SYSTEM

Although birds are intelligent, they are dependent on their human companions to make decisions that benefit their well-being, their wild habitat and their level of care and instruction in captivity. There are model programs that teach dog owners how they and their dogs can be better members of their community. Classes are available to teach owners how to train their dogs to learn commands that make them wonderful household companions. Latchkey dogs from families who work outside the home have doggy day care. Dog parks in many areas allow exercise and socialization for our furry friends.

But the general principles of bird care have never reached the general public. Bird owners need access to a network of classes, seminars and educational materials that teach them most of the principals that are widely known by aviculturists and longtime bird owners. We don't know a bird requires frequent showers the way we know that we should take a new puppy outside frequently to piddle until he learns to ask. We don't know a bird can be taught to step up on command the way a dog can be taught to sit.

Our culture doesn't yet recognize the difference between dogs, who love to please others, and birds, who please themselves. Different training techniques are required, and our inclination to punish an undesired behavior doesn't work.

What if it becomes widespread knowledge that we should talk to our companion parrots the way we do to young children? What strides will be made for birds (and other animals) as we push the limits of interspecies communication? What level of respect will develop, and what models will exist for interpersonal, intercultural and international communication?

HUMAN RESPONSIBILITY

Finally, we have taken birds into captivity and created markets for breeding them. In the future we must take full responsibility for providing for the lives of our companion birds. We can ensure qualified homes for birds when they must change homes, and provide care for these long-lived animals even when they are not able to be companion animals. We already have adoption and placement organizations for birds, a network of foster care and sanctuaries where birds can live out their lives if their breeding careers are over or they have unacceptable behaviors. We can ensure that these ideas grow and prosper through our support and actions in the coming years.

There is some concern that we could have too large a population of companion birds, as we do with dogs and cats. But we cannot assume this will be the case, even as pet birds increase in popularity. When it comes to issues of overpopulation in birds, as compared to mammals kept as pets, birds have several advantages. Mammalian reproduction is regulated primarily by the female requiring input from the male at the time the female is receptive. This enables stray dogs and cats to reproduce without regulation, except when the availability of food and space is limited. Most pet bird species, on the other hand, must form pair bonds and have specific environmental conditions available before they breed. This means that producing more birds requires significant input from bird breeders, while producing more dogs and cats happens pretty much on its own unless we intervene to stop it. Given that bird breeders need to make a profit to continue in business, they only breed the birds they can sell. Should the availability of birds exceed the demand, prices will fall and bird breeders will limit the number of birds they breed. With the exception of keeping genetic records and making judgments about the proper pairings of birds within a species, there appear to be few unresolved issues related to bird populations at the present time.

There are, however, unwanted birds. Some of these birds have physical or behavioral problems that limit their acceptance as pets. With the increase in

DIANE GRINDOL

We are still creating organizations that take responsibility for the care of a parrot, like this Dusky Conure, through-out his whole life; through owner life transitions and life stages of the bird.

domestic breeding of birds as pets, there are fewer problems associated with importation of birds. Wild-caught birds suffer from a variety of deficiencies in handling and nutrition that result in physical defects, and traumas that result in behavioral problems. Since wild-caught birds are rare today, the problems associated with importation are declining. But there are also domestically bred birds with problems—although far fewer.

Another area in which progress is being made is in teaching pet owners to handle their birds in ways that reduce behavioral and physical problems. Much of this information is available in a spate of recent books dealing expressly with these subjects. As we learn more about these subjects, the quality of the information available will improve.

DIANE GRINDOL

We're making progress in understanding behavior modification and health in our companion birds. Take advantage of the many resources available and watch for further developments in our knowledge. (This is a Scarlet Macaw.)

Veterinary services available for birds are also improving. With the establishment of the Association of Avian Veterinarians and the board-certified specialty in avian medicine, there is a focus for further improving the tools and training that veterinarians need to treat birds. Coupled with this are programs at a number of universities that study health issues in birds. All of these advances combine to improve the treatment your bird can receive when he needs veterinary care.

Birds in transition are another topic that has received recent attention, and is likely to receive more. Birds in transition are birds who are being placed in new environments. Some birds frequently move from one home to another because of circumstances in the lives of their owners. This ranges from death and illness to divorce or a major move. Some birds are unwanted and need new homes for that reason. This usually involves a change in ownership of the bird and results in a complete change in the bird's surroundings, the people he sees and reacts to, and possibly his diet. Birds make these kinds of transitions poorly, but recent information shows that birds more easily accept changes to their environment if they are regularly exposed to new objects and circumstances. It appears that this conditions the bird to accept changes with greater ease than he might otherwise. This does not mean it is necessary to make major changes to your bird's cage or the space in which he lives every day, but rather that your bird needs to be exposed to new things occasionally. A new toy once a month or being handled regularly by a new person every few months will help pave the way for your bird to make the transition to a new home, should the need arise.

We anticipate the work that led to these insights will continue, and will lead to better understanding between our birds and us. When we look at our companion birds, it's obvious we have teamed up with incredible beings. The future promises to be more incredible—and less predictable!

POINTS TO REMEMBER

- Bird calls can help us define and understand avian territories and evolution.
- The human-animal bond has proven to benefit the health and socialization of both parties. It can grow to become an accepted method of therapy and training.
- We could make progress toward domesticating parrots through selective breeding.
- Research is incomplete in many areas of bird nutrition and space requirements, as well as other areas of a bird's environment in captivity.
- There is a growing system to support humans in learning about bird care and training, as well as to provide good homes for all birds throughout their long lives.

Appendix A

A Glossary of Bird Words

avian veterinarian A veterinarian who has bird clients. If you can get a referral from another veterinarian, a bird club member or a bird breeder, that is the wisest way to choose a local avian veterinarian.

behaviorist A "bird psychologist" who facilitates understanding between a companion parrot and his owner in a home environment. Also known as a *parrot behaviorist* or *behavioral consultant.*

bioacoustics A relatively new field of scientific inquiry. It is the study of sounds produced by or affecting living beings, especially the sounds that are forms of communication. The word comes from *bio,* meaning life, and *acoustics,* meaning sound. The science has only been possible since the 1960s, when sophisticated recording devices made capturing and isolating natural sounds feasible. Developments in this field, and in the field of acoustic ecology, could influence habitat preservation—the key to the future of many parrot species in the wild.

birdsongs Songs limited to a specific group of birds called songbirds, because scientists have defined things that way. Most of the talking birds you see are not singing, even if they learn some of our "songs."

bridge In trick training, a bridge is the sound a parrot hears when he is doing a correct behavior. The sound means "this is what is right, now you will get a reward." It takes a while to fish a food treat out of a pocket and get it to your parrot, but a bridge can happen just as the correct behavior is happening. The bridge can be a clicker sound or any other sound, including a word.

call One of the kinds of verbal communication between birds. Calls are briefer than songs, and they often serve a function related to the life and well-being of the birds uttering the calls, or to maintaining their social relationships.

certified avian veterinarian   A veterinarian who has obtained certification from the American Board of Veterinary Practitioners (ABVP). These veterinarians are officially called Board-Certified Avian Practice Specialists by the American Board of Veterinary Practitioners. They have passed a rigorous test on avian health. There are only a few certified avian veterinarians, compared to the number of veterinarians who treat birds. There certainly are competent and talented avian veterinarians who are not, or not yet, certified avian veterinarians.

clicker training   A method of training animals that uses operant conditioning with an emphasis on positive reinforcement. A clicker or clicking sound is used for communication purposes, and food and non-food rewards are used as motivation. This type of training has been used to train animals for war duties and for film work for some time, and recently became popular with dog, horse and llama trainers. Many bird owners find that it's appropriate for training birds.

clipping wings   For a companion bird, clipping the wings means cutting some of the long primary flight feathers on each wing to a shorter length. This slows a bird's flight, making it safer for the bird to be free in a house and impeding his ability to gain altitude and fly away when out of doors. Birds replace their feathers at least once a year, so the wings usually need to be clipped at least that often. The number of feathers clipped and the amount cut from each feather clipped varies by species and individual. Your avian veterinarian can perform this service, as can a bird groomer. You can learn to do it yourself, as well. Birds with clipped wings have slowed flight, making it safer for them to move about in homes with windows and mirrors, and also making them more dependent on people. Of course, birds with clipped wings also get less flight exercise. It is up to the individual parrot companion whether to clip their bird's wings or leave a bird "flighted."

cognitive behavior   A behavior in which the subject is asked to come to a decision based on rules he has learned previously.

conditioned response   The behavior an animal learns as the result of *operant conditioning,* a training method using a cue and a reward.

conjunctive task   A task in which the subject is asked to identify an object based on more than one aspect of the object. For example, he might be asked to identify an object that is both blue and wood instead of just identifying objects that are blue.

cue   The hand signal or word used to elicit a conditioned response in a trained bird.

duet   A call performed by two members of a mated pair of parrots. The notes produced by each member of the pair are sex-specific and are combined by the male and female calling alternately. The frequency and length of the notes change over the course of the call in an orderly progression.

ethologist   A scientist who studies animal behavior.

exceptional learning   Learning that may occur under some circumstances, but that is not normal learning. It's normal learning, for example, for a child to learn to speak English but exceptional learning for an African Grey Parrot to do so.

expectation cueing   A situation in which a research subject has some idea of what question is going to be asked from the kinds of questions he has been asked so far during a training or testing session. This increases the chance he will get the correct answer, even if he doesn't really know the answer. To avoid expectation cueing, many different kinds of questions are asked in a single training or testing session.

field biologist   A researcher who studies animals in the their natural habitat.

generic error   In parrot cognition studies, it is an error of identification in which the subject names the material of which a set of objects is made, but does not say the number of objects.

mimicry   A bird species copying or imitating the natural call of another, or several other species of birds and incorporating them into their own songs. Starlings and Mockingbirds are examples of species with this skill. Sometimes mimicry extends to mechanical noises or human speech. There is probably a difference among species in this ability.

operant conditioning   The technical term for training an animal to perform an action by offering it a reward. The behavior the animal then learns is called the *conditioned response*. In the vernacular, we refer to this method as trick training.

ornithologist   A scientist who studies birds, in general.

parrot behaviorist   Someone with abundant life experience handling parrots who will counsel you about your parrot's behavior problems. He or she suggests changes you can make in your own attitudes and behavior, and/or different methods of handling your problem parrot. The result is often a parrot and a family who adapt better to living with each other. As this book goes to press, there are no certification programs a parrot behaviorist must pass; they are self-taught because of their dedication to parrots living with human companions.

recursive task   A task in which the subject is presented with several objects and a question or command composed of a number of parts, and is asked to take some action on a specific object in response to the question. The recursive part is the successive analysis of each part of the question or command to choose the proper object and action.

referential input   The relationship between a label and an object to which it refers.

roost   A location where a group of birds flock to spend the night together. Pairs, singles and flocks of juvenile parrots join together and share a tree or a grove of trees overnight. They disperse again at dawn to feed and play.

social interaction   A way to show a bird which parts of the environment should be noted and what is similar between this experience and other experiences.

songs   Both songs and calls of songbirds are differentiated solely on the length of time the bird makes the sound. Songs are longer than calls.

syrinx   The organ in birds that produces sound, just as the larynx produces sound in mammals. The syrinx has two vibrating membranes that allow complex sound production in "two voices."

T-stand   A simple piece of speech-training equipment that consists of a flat base and an upright pole with a perch fastened to it perpendicular to the pole. This forms a T shape.

Appendix B

These Resources Are for the Birds

BOOKS

Athan, Mattie Sue, *Guide to a Well-Behaved Parrot*, Barron's, 1999.

Athan, Mattie Sue, *Guide to Companion Parrot Behavior*, Barron's, 1999.

Bird, Bonnie, *Training Guide Booklet*, ParrotsandProps.com, 1998.

Blanchard, Sally, *Companion Parrot Handbook*, Pet Bird Information Council, 1999.

Blanchard, Sally, *The Beak Book: Understanding, Preventing, and Solving Aggression and Biting Behaviors in Companion Parrots*, Pet Bird Information Council, 2002.

Catchpole, C. K. and P. J. B. Slater, *Bird Song: Biological Themes and Variations*, Cambridge University Press, 1995.

D'Arezzo, Carol S., *Parrot-Toys and Play Areas: How to Put Some Fun Into Your Parrot's Life*, CrowFire Publishing, 2000.

Dough, Whitney J., *Andy: 24 Years of Foul Play with a Talking Crow*, Providence House, 1997.

Grindol, Diane; Lachman, Larry PsyD; Kocher, Frank DVM, *Birds Off the Perch: Therapy and Training for Your Pet Bird*, Simon & Schuster, 2003.

Heinrich, Bernd, *Mind of the Raven: Adventures and Investigations With Wolf-Birds,* HarperCollins, 1999.

Hinshaw Patent, Dorothy, *Alex and Friends: Animal Talk, Animal Thinking,* Lerner Publications Company, 1998.

Hubbard, Jennifer, *The Parrot Training Handbook,* Parrot Press, 1997.

Kilham, Lawrence, *The American Crow and the Common Raven,* Texas A&M University Press, 1991.

Pepperberg, Irene M., *The Alex Studies: Cognitive and Communicative Abilities of Grey Parrots,* Harvard University Press, 1999.

Savage, Candace, *Bird Brains: The Intelligence of Crows, Ravens, Magpies, and Jays,* Sierra Club Books, 1995.

Short, Lester L., *The Lives of Birds: Birds of the World and Their Behavior,* Henry Holt and Company, 1993.

Skutch, Alexander F., *The Minds of Birds,* Texas A&M University Press, 1996.

Sparks, John and Soper, Tony, *Parrots: A Natural History,* Facts on File, 1990.

MAGAZINES

Companion Parrot Quarterly
P.O. Box 2428
Alameda, CA 94501
(510) 523-5303
www.companionparrot.com

Bird Talk
P.O. Box 6050
Mission Viejo, CA 92690
(949) 855-8822
animalnetwork.com/birds/default.asp

Bird Times
Pet Business Inc
7-L Dundas Circle
Greensboro, NC 27407
(336) 292-4047
www.birdtimes.com/default.htm
PetBus@nr.infi.net

WEB SITES

Alex Web Page, Communication with Parrots, Dr. Irene Pepperberg
www.alexfoundation.org

American Society of Crows and Ravens
www.ascaronline.org/

Animal Behavior Society
www.animalbehavior.org

Animal Bioacoustics
asa.aip.org/ani_bioac/

Association of Avian Veterinarians
www.aav.org

Avian veterinary links
www.birdsnways.com/birds/vets.htm

Basic Trick Training
www.parrottricktraining.com/article.htm

Bioacoustics Research Program at Cornell Lab of Ornithology
birds.cornell.edu/BRP/

Clicker Training for Birds
www.geocities.com/Heartland/Acres/9154/

Clicker Training for Free-Flying Birds
nce.aaris.net/trick.htm

National Science Foundation
www.nsf.gov

Nebraska Behavioral Biology Group
cricket.unl.edu/NBBG.html

Parrots and Props
www.parrotsandprops.com

Softbill Birds (Mynahs, Starlings, Crows, Jays)
www.softbills.com

Steve Martin's Training Videos and Frequently Asked Questions (FAQs)
www.naturalencounters.com/home.html

Tani Robar's Training Videos
www.parrottricktraining.com

INTERNET MAILING LISTS

Here are some of the locations on the Internet where you can sign up to join a list. Use an Internet search engine to look for others.

Parrot Species

www.onelist.com/ (then search for "parrot" or type of bird)

www.companionparrot.com/

Crows

groups.yahoo.com/group/crows/join

Training Resources

Exotic Animal Training and Management Course
America's Teaching Zoo
Moorpark College
7075 Campus Rd.
Moorpark, CA 93021
(805) 378-1441
eatm@vcccd.net

The International Association of Avian Trainers and Educators
350 St. Andrews Fairway
Memphis, TN 38111
(901) 685-9122
secretary@iaate.org
www.iaate.org

ORGANIZATIONS THAT SPONSOR SEMINARS

American Federation of Aviculture
(816) 421-BIRD
afa.birds.org
www.afa.birds.org

Midwest Avian Research Expo
(Locations change each year)
www.mare-expo.org

Bird Clubs of Virginia
www.birdclubsva.org

Canadian Parrot Symposium, East
108 Meadowvale Road
Toronto, Ontario
Canada, M1C 1S1
(416) 282-7375
cps@silvio-co.com
www.silvio-co.com/cps/index.htm

Canadian Parrot Symposium, West
P.O. Box 35065
Hillside Postal Outlet
Victoria, British Columbia
Canada, V8T 5G2
(250) 478-5101
www.parrotsymposium.com

International Aviculturists Society
P.O. Box 341852
Memphis, TN 38184
www.funnyfarmexotics.com/IAS/

International Parrot Convention
The Secretary
Loro Parque
SA 38400 Puerto de la Cruz
Tenerife, Spain
loroparque@jet.es

Companion Parrot Quarterly
P.O. Box 2428
Alameda, CA 94501
(510) 523-5303
www.companionparrot.com

VIDEOS

Tani Robar and Her Fantastic Performing Parrots
3767 S. 194th
Seattle, WA 98188
(206) 878-3010
www.parrottricktraining.com
tani@parrottricktraining.com

Steve Martin's Training Videos
Natural Encounters Inc.
9014 Thompson Nursery Rd.
Lake Wales, FL 33859
www.naturalencounters.com/home.html

BIRD TRAINERS AND SHOWS

Chris Biro
P.O. Box 364
Amboy, WA 98601
(206) 618-2610
www.thepiratesparrot.com

Bob Bartley and Gypsy Parrot Shows
64920 Big Sandy Rd.
San Miguel, CA 93451
(805) 239-7060
www.fowltales.com
bob@fowltales.com

Nancy Kobert's Amazing World of Birds Show
P.O. Box 1321, Dept. IG
Ramona, CA 92065
(760) 788-0531
www.birdshow.com
info@birdshow.com

Joe Tyler and Buckwheat
www.africangreys.com/contributors.html

Joanie Doss and The Amazing Amazons
www.parrothouse.com/jdoss.html

Natural Encounters Bird Shows
www.naturalencounters.com/shows.html

AVIARIES AND BIRD PARKS IN THE UNITED STATES

The National Aviary
Allegheney Commons West
Pittsburgh, PA 15212
(412) 323-7235
www.aviary.org

Parrot Jungle and Gardens
1111 Parrot Jungle Trail
Miami, FL 33132
(305) 2-JUNGLE
parrotjungle.com

Tracy Aviary
589 East 1300 South
Salt Lake City, UT 84105
801-322-BIRD
info@tracyaviary.org
www.tracyaviary.org

INTERNATIONAL AVIARIES AND BIRD PARKS

Jurong Bird Park
2 Jurong Hill
Singapore 628925
6265-0022
birdpark@singnet.com.sg
www.birdpark.com.sg/servlet/index
Southeast Asia's largest bird park, home to more than 8,000 birds of 600 species
from all over the world.

Loro Parque Fundacion
Avda. Loro Parque
38400 Puerto de la Cruz
Tenerife
Canary Islands, Spain
+34 922 373841
comercial@loroparque.com
www.loroparque.com

Paradise Park
Home of the World Parrot Trust
Hayle, Cornwall
TR27 4HY, United Kingdom
011-44-01736-753365
www.chycor.co.uk/paradise-park/index.htm

Vogelpark Walsrode
Am Rieselbach
29664 Walsrode
Germany
05161-60440
office@vogelpark-walsrode.de
www.vogelpark-walsrode.de/

PARROT CONSERVATION ORGANIZATIONS

RARE Center for Tropical Conservation
1840 Wilson Blvd., Suite 402
Arlington, VA 22201-3000
(703) 522-5070
www.rarecenter.org

World Parrot Trust
Glanmor House, Hayle, Cornwall
TR27 4HY, United Kingdom
011-44-01736-753365
www.worldparrottrust.org

World Parrot Trust USA
P.O. Box 353
Stillwater, MN 55082
(651) 275-1877
usa@worldparrottrust.org

Appendix **C**

Words and Phrases Birds Say

NAMES

Parrot's own name

Family dog

People's names

OBJECTS AND PEOPLE

Baby bird

Breakfast

Daddy

Mommy

Shoulder

Shower

Squirrel

Strawberry

Taco

Turkey

Water

QUESTIONS

Are ya hungry?

Are ya ready?

Do you want a cookie?

I can talk, can you fly?

Is it good?

Want to go out?

Whaaaa cha got cookin'?

Watcha' doin', huh?

What are you doing?

What?

Where ya goin'?

Where's (name of parrot, dog or person)?

Where's the pussycat?

INSTRUCTIONS

Be good

Be quiet

C'mere

Come here (name)

Come on

Come on step up

Come on wanna go upstairs

Come on wanna grape

Don't bite

Gimme kiss, gimme kiss, wanna grape

Gimme kisses

Here kitty kitty kitty

Hey

I gotta go shower, right back

Kiss

Kiss my beak

Knock it off

Meggie wanna shower

No

No, don't bite

(Parrot name) go bye-bye

Piece of paper, please

Quiet

Right now

Shut the door

Step up

Stop

Stop crying

Stop it

Tickle tickle tickle

Time for bed

Up

Wanna come out

Wanna go upstairs

Want a peanut, come on

Want a shower

Want go ride

Want some

Want to eat breakfast

Want water

You want some birdie bread, want some water

You want some water, want some water

Yum yum, some birdie bread, want some water

SELF-REFERENCE

(Parrot name)'s a good boy

Bad boy

Birds don't talk

Eeeek a bird

Good bird

Good boy

I can count 1, 2, 3 . . .

I love me

I'm a crybaby

It's superbird

Meg bad

Mommy's a good birdie

Pop's girl

Pretty bird

Pretty boy

Such a good boy

That's preposterous, birds don't talk!

Wheee, I'm a kid

You are a bad bird

GREETINGS

Bye-bye

Good morning

Hello

Hello, my name is (parrot's name)

Hi

Hi, guy

Hi, sweetie pie

How are you

Night, night

See you later

SOUNDS

Barking dog

Chicken

Cough

Crow

Cuckoo bird

Exercise machine

Garbage truck backing up

Laugh

Meow

Microwave oven

Mockingbird

Modem sound

Opera

Rooster

Sneeze

Telephone

Timer alarm

Wild bird calls

Wolf whistle

GENERAL

Alright bye

Awright

Dinner's ready

Friends don't let friends fly drunk

Gimme five

Go Broncos

Go poop

Goddammit

Gootchie goo

Hello, Coldwell Banker, Diane Winer 6116

Hey

Hungry

I appreciate it, bye

I hope you're not a Republican

I love you

I love you more

I love you pretty wing

I'm gonna kiss your stinky feet. . . . Peeee Uuuuu!

I'm okay

It's okay

Just fine

Kitchee-kitchee-coo

Oh oh, poopie

Oh, shit, bad word

Oh, boy!

Okay

Peekaboo

So big

Sshhhh!

Thank you

Trick or treat

Uh oh

You are my sunshine

You're so pretty

You're so sweet

You're a shit

Yum yum

Yum yum good

Flocks of Bird Lovers: National and International Societies

The African Love Bird Society
P.O. Box 142
San Marcos, CA 92079-0142
www.africanlovebirdsociety.com

African Parrot Society
P.O. Box 204
Clarinda, IA 51632-2731
www.wingscc.com/aps/

The American Budgerigar Society
A.B.S. Secretary, Linda Denny
1600 W. Meadow Lane
Visalia, CA 93277
www.upatsix.com/abs/

American Cockatiel Society Inc.
9527 60th Lane N.
Pinellas Park, FL 33782
www.acstiels.com

American Federation of Aviculture
(816) 421-BIRD
www.afa.birds.org

American Singers Club
A.S.C. Secretary, Clay Beegle
Rt. #1 Box 186-B
Ridgeley, WV 26753
www.upatsix.com/asc/

Animal Behavior Society
2611 East 10th St.
Indiana University
Bloomington, IN 47408-2603
(812) 856-5541
www.animalbehavior.org

Asiatic Parrot Association International
4542 E. Tropicana Ave., Room 330
Las Vegas, NV 89121
www.asiatic.parrots.com

The Grey Play Round Table
P.O. Box 190
Old Chatham, NY 12136-0190
www.africangreys.com

International Aviculturist's Society
P.O. Box 341852
Memphis, TN 38184
www.funnyfarmexotics.com/IAS/

International Conure Association
P.O. Box 70123
Las Vegas, NV 89170
(702) 732-1281
www.upatsix.com/ica/

International Parrotlet Society
P.O. Box 2428
Santa Cruz, CA 95063-2428
www.internationalparrotletsociety.org

National Cockatiel Society
11655 Emerald Dr.
Hayden Lake, ID 83835
www.cockatiels.org

National Finch and Softbill Society
P.O. Box 2459
Goldenrod, FL 32733-2459
www.nfss.org

North American Cockatiel Society
P.O. Box 1363
Avon, CT 06001-1363
www.cockatiels.org

Pionus Breeders Association
c/o Barb Avery, Secretary/Treasurer
6580 Providence Hill Rd.
Garden Valley, CA 95633
www.pionusbreedersassociation.com

Society of Parrot Breeders and Exhibitors
P.O. Box 777
Plymouth, MA 02362
www.spbe.org

World Parrot Trust
Glanmor House
Hayle, Cornwall
TR27 4HY, United Kingdom
011-44-01736-753365
www.worldparrottrust.org

World Parrot Trust USA
P.O. Box 353
Stillwater, MN 55082
(651) 275-1877
usa@worldparrottrust.org

About the Authors

JUDY MURPHY

Diane Grindol writes a column for *Bird Talk* magazine and lectures at seminars and bird clubs. She is the author of *The Complete Book of Cockatiels* (Howell Book House, 1998), *The Canary: An Owner's Guide to a Happy Healthy Pet* (Howell Book House, 2000) *Cockatiels For Dummies* (Wiley, 2001), and co-author of *Birds Off the Perch* (Simon & Schuster, 2003), which is about companion bird behavior. Ms. Grindol is the human companion of a small flock of Cockatiels, including her first bird, a gray hen named Dacey, who has been in her life since 1982. A Blue-headed Pionus Parrot and guinea pigs complete her family, who all live on California's Central Coast. Ms. Grindol's birds do not use English to communicate. After reading this book, you'll understand why. They live in a quiet household with a writer and plenty of bird friends who speak their own language. Her Pionus is an extraordinary communicator even without language, and is treasured as a companion. You may contact Diane via e-mail at tiels@redshift.com.

DIANE GRINDOL

Thomas Roudybush, MS, is the president of Roudybush Inc., a bird feed company. Mr. Roudybush did pioneering research on the nutrient requirements of psittacine birds as a student and employee of the Avian Sciences Department at the University of California–Davis. He was a co-founder of the Psittacine Research Project at UC–Davis and editor of its publication, the *Exotic Bird Report,* for several years. He lectures on avian nutrition to both veterinary and pet-owning audiences. Mr. Roudybush has published articles in scientific journals and consumer publications, and contributed chapters to four veterinary texts.

Index